WHERE THERE IS GOOD FOOD, PEOPLE GATHER

At the heart of all special celebrations you'll find great tasting food. Whether you're planning a traditional holiday gathering, an impromptu cocktail party or casual evening with friends, this year's *Taste of Home Holiday & Celebrations* cookbook is the place to find all the ingredients you'll need for a truly epic soirée. This unique collection features 253 recipes and 23 events to inspire any special occasion any time of year. More than just a collection of recipes, this must-have book is packed with hundreds of gorgeous photos, time-saving tips, do-it-yourself table toppers and handy timelines to make easy work of entertaining. Let the festivities begin!

WOULD YOU LIKE TO SEE ONE OF YOUR FAMILY RECIPES FEATURED IN A *TASTE OF HOME* COLLECTION?

Visit **tasteofhome.com/submit** to share your story and recipes.

PAGE 6

PAGE 136

PAGE 224

PAGE 146

PAGE 107

PAGE 116

Taste of Home
Holiday
& CELEBRATIONS

EDITORIAL
Editor-in-Chief **Catherine Cassidy**

Creative Director **Howard Greenberg**
Editorial Operations Director **Kerri Balliet**

Managing Editor/Print & Digital Books **Mark Hagen**
Associate Creative Director **Edwin Robles Jr.**

Editor **Amy Glander**
Associate Editors **Molly Jasinski, Sharon Selz**
Art Directors **Raeann Sundholm, Maggie Conners**
Layout Designer **Courtney Lovetere**
Editorial Production Manager **Dena Ahlers**
Copy Chief **Deb Warlaumont Mulvey**
Copy Editor **Mary-Liz Shaw**
Editorial Intern **Michael Welch**

Food Editor **Peggy Woodward, RD**
Recipe Editors **Mary King; Jenni Sharp, RD; Irene Yeh**
Business Analyst, Content Tools **Amanda Harmatys**
Content Operations Assistant **Shannon Stroud**
Editorial Services Administrator **Marie Brannon**

Test Kitchen & Food Styling Manager **Sarah Thompson**
Test Cooks **Nicholas Iverson (Lead), Matthew Hass, Lauren Knoelke**
Food Stylists **Kathryn Conrad (Lead), Shannon Roum, Leah Rekau**
Prep Cooks **Bethany Van Jacobson (Lead), Megumi Garcia, Melissa Hansen**

Photography Director **Stephanie Marchese**
Photographers **Dan Roberts, Jim Wieland**
Photographer/Set Stylist **Grace Natoli Sheldon**
Set Stylists **Melissa Franco, Stacey Genaw, Dee Dee Jacq**
Photo Studio Assistant **Ester Robards**
Creative Contributors **Mark Derse (Photographer); Pamela Stasney (Set Stylist); Diane Armstrong (Food Stylist)**

Editorial Business Manager **Kristy Martin**
Editorial Business Associate **Samantha Lea Stoeger**

Editor, *Taste of Home* **Jeanne Ambrose**
Associate Creative Director, *Taste of Home* **Erin Burns**
Art Director, *Taste of Home* **Kristin Bowker**

BUSINESS
Vice President, Group Publisher **Kirsten Marchioli**
Publisher, *Taste of Home* **Donna Lindskog**
General Manager, Taste of Home Cooking School **Erin Puariea**
Executive Producer, Taste of Home Online Cooking School **Karen Berner**

THE READER'S DIGEST ASSOCIATION, INC.
President & Chief Executive Officer **Bonnie Kintzer**

Chief Financial Officer **Tom Callahan**
Vice President, Chief Operating Officer, North America **Howard Halligan**
Chief Revenue Officer **Richard Sutton**
Chief Marketing Officer **Leslie Dukker Doty**
Senior Vice President, Global HR & Communications **Phyllis E. Gebhardt, SPHR**
Vice President, Content Marketing & Operations **Diane Dragan**
Vice President, Brand Marketing **Beth Gorry**
Vice President, Financial Planning & Analysis **William Houston**
Publishing Director, Books **Debra Polansky**
Chief Technology Officer **Aneel Tejwaney**
Vice President, Consumer Marketing Planning **Jim Woods**

FRONT COVER PHOTOGRAPHY
Photographer **Grace Natoli Sheldon**
Set Stylist **Melissa Franco**
Food Stylist **Kathryn Conrad**

© 2015 RDA Enthusiast Brands, LLC
1610 N. 2nd St., Suite 102, Milwaukee WI 53212-3906

International Standard Book Number: 978-1-61765-449-7
International Standard Serial Number: 1535-2781
Component Number: 118000041H

TABLE OF **CONTENTS**

'tis the season

giving thanks

easter gatherings

special celebrations

'tis the season

With the tree lit bright and the snow falling outside, Christmas is the perfect time to share a warm meal with those we love most. In this section, you'll find dozens of delightful recipes that will fill the air with enticing aromas and bring satisfied smiles to the faces of holiday guests.

Christmas is coming... and so is the family! It's time to dust off the good dishes and polish the silver. Make a bounty of magical memories this holiday season with a menu that warms the heart and pleases the palate.

Your guests won't forget the stunning Roast Pork Loin with Thyme-Honey Mustard Sauce. And rich Chipotle Shredded Sweet Potatoes with Bacon is a truly impressive Yuletide side.

With these mouthwatering dishes, a few glowing candles and Bing Crosby crooning "I'll Be Home for Christmas" in the background, you'll have everything you need for a memorable family feast.

Roast Pork Loin with Thyme-Honey Mustard Sauce (p. 10)
Roasted Beet Salad with Orange Vinaigrette (p. 9)
Asiago Dinner Rolls (p. 14)
Chipotle Shredded Sweet Potatoes with Bacon (p. 10)

HOME FOR **THE HOLIDAYS**

'tis *the* season | **HOME FOR THE HOLIDAYS** TIMELINE

A FEW WEEKS BEFORE

- Set the menu and organize recipes. Write two grocery lists: one of nonperishables to buy now and one for perishable items to buy a few days before Christmas Day.

- Make the Hearty Ragu Bolognese, except the pasta; freeze cooled sauce.

TWO DAYS BEFORE

- Buy remaining grocery items. Wash flatware and serving dishes.

- Prepare the Asian Pear and Dried Cherry Chutney; cover and chill.

CHRISTMAS EVE

- Bake the layers for the Caramel-Pecan Mocha Layer Cake, but do not assemble. Cover layers and store.

- Remove the ragu from the freezer to thaw.

- Make vinaigrette and roast beets for Roasted Beet Salad with Orange Vinaigrette; cover and chill separately.

- Make vinaigrette and cut broccoli into florets for the Warm Broccoli with Vinaigrette; cover and chill separately.

- Set the table and arrange the flowers or centerpieces.

CHRISTMAS DAY

- Mix the Cranberry White Sangria; cover and chill until serving.

- Bake the Asiago Dinner Rolls and make apple mixture for Apple-Pecan Baked Brie.

- Prepare the Chipotle Shredded Sweet Potatoes with Bacon; place in the slow cooker.

- Three hours before dinner, marinate the Roast Pork Loin with Thyme-Honey Mustard Sauce.

- One hour before dinner, assemble the cake; refrigerate until serving.

- Just before guests arrive, warm the prepped apple mixture; assemble and bake brie. Warm the ragu on the stovetop.

- Thirty minutes before serving, cook the broccoli and dress with vinaigrette; cook pasta for the ragu.

- Just before serving, dress beet salad with vinaigrette. Place dinner rolls in warm oven for 2-3 minutes to re-heat.

Roasted Beet Salad with Orange Vinaigrette

Beets, oranges and spinach sprinkled with goat cheese make a scrumptious new blend for a mixed green salad. The combination may seem unlikely, but I guarantee it will become a favorite.

—**NANCY HEISHMAN** LAS VEGAS, NV

PREP: 25 MIN. • **BAKE:** 50 MIN. + COOLING • **MAKES:** 12 SERVINGS (1 CUP EACH)

- 3 medium fresh beets (about 1 pound)
- 3 tablespoons olive oil
- 1 teaspoon grated orange peel
- 2 tablespoons orange juice
- 1 tablespoon white wine vinegar
- 2 teaspoons honey
- 1 teaspoon Dijon mustard
- ½ teaspoon salt
- ¼ teaspoon pepper
- 3 tablespoons minced fresh tarragon, divided
- 1 package (6 ounces) fresh baby spinach
- 4 cups torn mixed salad greens
- 2 medium navel oranges, peeled and sectioned
- 4 ounces crumbled goat cheese
- ½ cup chopped walnuts, toasted

1. Preheat oven to 425°. Scrub beets and trim tops to 1 in. Wrap in foil; place on a baking sheet. Bake 50-60 minutes or until tender. Remove foil; cool completely. Peel beets and cut into wedges.

2. In a small bowl, whisk oil, orange peel, orange juice, vinegar, honey, mustard, salt and pepper until blended; stir in 1 tablespoon tarragon. In a large bowl, combine spinach, salad greens and remaining tarragon. Drizzle with vinaigrette and toss gently to coat.

3. Transfer to a platter or divide among 12 salad plates. Top with orange sections and beets; sprinkle with cheese and walnuts. Serve immediately.

NOTE *To toast nuts, bake in a shallow pan in a 350° oven for 5-10 minutes or cook in a skillet over low heat until lightly browned, stirring occasionally.*

Asian Pear and Dried Cherry Chutney

My wife and I serve this with roast pork or grilled pork chops. The fruits lend a natural sweetness. This spiced chutney also makes a great appetizer with cream cheese and crackers.

—**MICHAEL WATZ** NORMAL, IL

PREP: 15 MIN. • **COOK:** 40 MIN. • **MAKES:** 12 SERVINGS (¼ CUP EACH)

- 4 cups coarsely chopped Asian or Bosc pears
- 1½ cups packed brown sugar
- 1 cup dried cherries
- 1 cup cider vinegar
- 2 tablespoons minced fresh gingerroot
- 4 garlic cloves, minced
- 1 teaspoon curry powder
- ½ teaspoon salt
- ½ teaspoon ground cinnamon
- ¼ to ½ teaspoon cayenne pepper
- ⅛ teaspoon ground cloves

In a large saucepan, combine all ingredients. Bring to a boil. Reduce heat; simmer, uncovered, 35-40 minutes or until slightly thickened and pears are tender, stirring occasionally. Serve at room temperature or chilled.

Roast Pork Loin with Thyme-Honey Mustard Sauce

A thyme, honey and mustard marinade lends special flair to this tender pork loin. My family looks forward to this roast for Christmas dinner. I even had a chef compliment me on it.

—KELLY WILLIAMS FORKED RIVER, NJ

PREP: 25 MIN. + MARINATING • **BAKE:** 1 HOUR + STANDING • **MAKES:** 6 SERVINGS

- 1 boneless pork loin roast (2 to 3 pounds)
- 1 cup chicken stock
- ½ cup honey
- ¼ cup unsweetened pineapple juice
- ¼ cup canola oil
- 1 teaspoon dried thyme
- ½ teaspoon spicy brown mustard
- ½ teaspoon salt
- ½ teaspoon coarsely ground pepper
  Coarse sea salt

1. Place roast in a large resealable plastic bag. In a small bowl, whisk stock, honey, pineapple juice, oil, thyme and mustard until blended; add to pork. Seal bag and turn to coat; refrigerate 1-2 hours.

2. Preheat oven to 375°. Transfer roast to a greased 13x9-in. baking dish; pour remaining marinade over top. Sprinkle roast with ½ teaspoon each salt and pepper.

3. Bake 60-70 minutes or until a thermometer reads 145°. Remove roast from baking dish; tent with foil. Let stand 10 minutes before slicing.

4. Meanwhile, transfer juices from baking dish to a small saucepan. Bring to a boil; cook 8-10 minutes or until liquid is reduced by half, stirring occasionally. Spoon sauce over roast; sprinkle with sea salt.

Chipotle Shredded Sweet Potatoes with Bacon

I crave a little heat with my sweet spuds, so I mix in chipotle peppers. The smoky flavor blends perfectly with this creamy, cheesy side dish.

—KATHI JONES-DELMONTE ROCHESTER, NY

PREP: 30 MIN. • **COOK:** 4 HOURS • **MAKES:** 10 SERVINGS

- 2 tablespoons olive oil
- 1 large sweet onion, finely chopped
- 2 shallots, finely chopped
- ¼ cup minced fresh parsley
- 2 teaspoons ground chipotle pepper
- 1 teaspoon coarsely ground pepper
- ½ teaspoon kosher salt
- 3 pounds large sweet potatoes (about 4 large), peeled and shredded
- 1 package (8 ounces) cream cheese, softened

- 2 cups (8 ounces) shredded Manchego or Monterey Jack cheese
- 2 cups (8 ounces) shredded Muenster cheese
- 1 package (16 ounces) applewood smoked bacon, cooked and chopped
- ½ teaspoon paprika

TOPPING
- 1 cup sour cream
- 2 tablespoons maple syrup
- ¼ teaspoon ground chipotle pepper

1. In a large skillet, heat oil over medium heat. Add onion and shallots; cook and stir 4-6 minutes or until softened.

2. Transfer onion mixture to a large bowl; stir in parsley and seasonings. Add sweet potatoes and cheeses, mixing well. Fold in chopped bacon.

3. Transfer mixture to a greased 5- or 6-qt. slow cooker. Sprinkle with paprika. Cook, covered, on low 4-5 hours or until potatoes are tender.

4. In a small bowl, mix topping ingredients. Serve with sweet potatoes.

Apple-Pecan Baked Brie

I make sure this fruity and savory Brie is in the oven as our relatives arrive so the aromas of cinnamon and apples fill the house.
—**ALICIA GOWER** AUBURN, NY

START TO FINISH: 30 MIN.
MAKES: 10 SERVINGS

- 1 tablespoon butter
- 1 small tart apple, peeled and sliced
- ⅓ cup dried cranberries
- ¼ cup chopped pecans
- 1 tablespoon brown sugar
- ¼ teaspoon ground cinnamon
  Dash ground nutmeg
- 1 round (8 ounces) Brie cheese
  Assorted crackers

1. Preheat oven to 375°. In a saucepan, heat butter over medium heat. Add apple, cranberries, pecans, brown sugar, cinnamon and nutmeg; cook and stir 5-7 minutes or until apple is tender.
2. Cut Brie horizontally in half; place bottom half in a 9-in. pie plate. Top with half of the apple mixture; replace top. Top with remaining apple mixture.
3. Bake, uncovered, 10-12 minutes or until cheese begins to melt. Serve warm with crackers.

Warm Broccoli with Vinaigrette

A sweet vinaigrette dresses up these tender broccoli spears. I drizzle it over other sides such as asparagus or green beans. It's the only way I can get my kids to eat their veggies!
—**RENEE SMITH** SPARKS, NV

PREP: 15 MIN. • **COOK:** 15 MIN. • **MAKES:** 12 SERVINGS (¾ CUP EACH)

- ½ cup olive oil
- ¼ cup white wine vinegar
- ¾ teaspoon salt
- ½ teaspoon sugar
- ¼ teaspoon pepper
- 12 cups fresh broccoli florets (about 1¾ pounds)
- ½ pound cheddar cheese, cut into ½-inch cubes
- 1 jar (2 ounces) diced pimientos, drained
- 2 green onions, chopped

1. In a small bowl, whisk the first five ingredients until blended. In a 6-qt. stockpot, bring 10 cups water to a boil. Add half of the broccoli; cook, uncovered, 3-5 minutes or until tender. Remove with a slotted spoon; drain well. Repeat with remaining broccoli.
2. Place broccoli in a large bowl; add cheese, pimientos and green onions. Drizzle with vinaigrette and toss to combine. Serve immediately.

Hearty Ragu Bolognese

My robust ragu combines ground beef, sausage and chicken. Serve it over any type of pasta or baked or fried polenta. It's even good on its own with a slice of hot, buttered garlic bread.
—CAROLINE BRODY FOREST HILLS, NY

PREP: 20 MIN. • **COOK:** 3¾ HOURS • **MAKES:** 2½ QUARTS

- 2 **medium onions, coarsely chopped**
- 2 **celery ribs, coarsely chopped**
- 1 **medium carrot, coarsely chopped**
- 4 **garlic cloves, peeled**
- 2 **tablespoons olive oil**
- 1 **tablespoon butter**
- ¼ **teaspoon ground nutmeg**
- 1 **pound ground beef**
- ¾ **teaspoon salt**
- ½ **teaspoon pepper**
- 1½ **pounds bulk Italian sausage**
- 1 **cup dry white wine**
- 1 **can (14½ ounces) beef broth**
- ½ **pound boneless skinless chicken breasts**
- 2 **cups heavy whipping cream**
- 3 **cans (6 ounces each) tomato paste**
  Hot cooked spaghetti or pasta of your choice

1. Place onions, celery, carrot and garlic in a food processor; pulse until finely chopped. In a Dutch oven, heat oil and butter over medium heat. Add vegetable mixture and nutmeg; cook and stir 6-8 minutes or until vegetables are softened.

2. Add beef; cook 6-8 minutes longer or until beef is no longer pink, breaking up beef into crumbles. Stir in salt and pepper. Remove with a slotted spoon; discard drippings from pan.

3. In same pan, cook sausage over medium heat 6-8 minutes or until no longer pink, breaking into crumbles; drain. Return beef mixture to pan. Stir in wine. Bring to a boil; cook and stir until wine is evaporated. Add broth and chicken breasts; return to a boil. Reduce heat; simmer, covered, 12-15 minutes or until a thermometer inserted in chicken reads 165°. Remove chicken; cool slightly. Finely chop chicken.

4. Add cream and tomato paste; bring to a boil, stirring occasionally. Return chicken to pot; reduce heat and simmer, covered, 3-4 hours or until flavors are blended, stirring occasionally. Serve with spaghetti.

FREEZE OPTION *Freeze cooled sauce in freezer containers. To use, partially thaw in refrigerator overnight. Heat through in a saucepan, stirring occasionally and adding a little broth if necessary.*

HOW TO COOK SPAGHETTI

- To cook spaghetti—or any type of pasta—more evenly, prevent it from sticking together and avoid boil-overs, always use a large kettle or Dutch oven. Unless you have a very large kettle, don't cook more than 2 pounds of pasta at one time.
- For 8 ounces of pasta, bring 3 quarts water to a full rolling boil. To flavor, add 1 tablespoon salt if desired. Keep noodles from sticking by adding 1 tablespoon olive or vegetable oil if desired.
- Carefully ease noodles into the water, pushing them down and swirling them around as they soften. When they are fully immersed, stir noodles to separate the strands.
- Return water to a boil. Boil noodles, uncovered, stirring occasionally until done.

Asiago Dinner Rolls

I first tasted these rolls when my boyfriend made them from a family recipe that called for Parmesan. I substitued Asiago for the Parmesan with equally good results.
—**BETHANY SHAW** MOKENA, IL

PREP: 45 MIN. + RISING • **BAKE:** 20 MIN. • **MAKES:** 1½ DOZEN

- 2 tablespoons sugar
- 2 packages (¼ ounce each) active dry yeast
- 2 teaspoons garlic salt
- 1 teaspoon Italian seasoning
- 3¾ to 4¼ cups all-purpose flour
- 1 cup 2% milk
- ½ cup water
- 4 tablespoons butter, divided
- 1 large egg
- ¾ cup shredded Asiago cheese, divided

1. In a large bowl, mix sugar, yeast, garlic salt, Italian seasoning and 2 cups flour. In a small saucepan, heat milk, water and 2 tablespoons butter to 120°-130°. Add to dry ingredients; beat on medium speed 2 minutes. Add egg; beat 2 minutes longer. Stir in ½ cup cheese and enough remaining flour to form a soft dough (dough will be sticky).

2. Turn dough onto a floured surface; knead until smooth and elastic, about 6-8 minutes. Place in a greased bowl, turning once to grease the top. Cover with plastic wrap and let rise in a warm place until doubled, about 30 minutes.

3. Punch down dough. Turn onto a lightly floured surface; divide and shape into 18 balls. Roll each ball into a 12-in. rope; tie into a loose knot. Tuck ends under. Place 3 in. apart on greased baking sheets. Melt remaining butter; brush over rolls. Sprinkle with remaining cheese.

4. Let rise in a warm place until almost doubled, about 15 minutes. Preheat oven to 375°.

5. Bake 20-25 minutes or until golden brown, rotating pans halfway through baking. Remove the rolls from pans to wire racks; serve warm.

Cranberry White Sangria

I tinkered with the ingredients in this sangria until it was perfect. It's also good with peach, apple or cherry wine and vodka.
—**PATTI LEAKE** COLUMBIA, MO

PREP: 15 MIN. + CHILLING • **MAKES:** 24 SERVINGS (¾ CUP EACH)

- 1 large Granny Smith apple, halved and thinly sliced
- ½ cup fresh or frozen cranberries
- ½ cup whiskey
- ¼ cup sugar
- ¼ cup lemon juice
- ¼ cup lime juice
- 2 bottles (750 milliliters each) sweet white wine
- 1 bottle (750 milliliters) cranberry wine or 3¾ cups cranberry juice
- Ice cubes
- 6 cups cold pineapple soda

1. In a large pitcher, combine the first six ingredients; let stand 30 minutes. Stir in wines. Refrigerate, covered, at least 30 minutes or until cold.

2. To serve, fill each glass halfway with ice; add ½ cup wine mixture. Top each with ¼ cup pineapple soda.

CRANBERRY CUES

Fresh cranberries are in season from early fall through December. Look for packages with shiny, bright red (light or dark) berries. Avoid those that are bruised, shriveled or have brown spots. Refrigerate fresh unwashed cranberries for about 1 month. Just before using, quicky rinse berries and pluck off any stems.

Caramel-Pecan Mocha Layer Cake

My version of a prize-winning chocolate cake is irresistible, especially when the rich caramel sauce oozes down the sides.
—JUDY CASTRANOVA NEW BERN, NC

PREP: 45 MIN.
BAKE: 30 MIN. + COOLING
MAKES: 12 SERVINGS

- 2 tablespoons instant coffee granules
- ⅓ cup hot water
- 1 cup unsalted butter, softened
- 2 cups packed brown sugar
- 3 large eggs
- 1½ teaspoons vanilla extract
- 2 cups cake flour
- ¾ cup baking cocoa
- 1½ teaspoons baking soda
- ¼ teaspoon salt
- 1 cup buttermilk

FILLING AND TOPPING

- 1½ cups heavy whipping cream
- ¼ cup confectioners' sugar
- ½ teaspoon vanilla extract
- ⅔ cup hot caramel or butterscotch-caramel ice cream topping, room temperature, divided
- ⅔ cup toasted chopped pecans, divided
- Bittersweet chocolate curls

1. Preheat oven to 350°. Line the bottoms of two greased 9-in. round baking pans with parchment paper; grease paper. In a small bowl, dissolve coffee granules in hot water; cool completely.
2. In a large bowl, cream butter and brown sugar until light and fluffy. Add eggs, one at a time, beating well after each addition. Beat in vanilla, then cooled coffee. In another bowl, whisk flour, cocoa, baking soda and salt; add to creamed mixture alternately with buttermilk, beating well after each addition.
3. Transfer batter to prepared pans. Bake 30-35 minutes or until a toothpick inserted in center comes out clean. Cool in pans 10 minutes before removing to wire racks; remove paper. Cool completely.
4. In a bowl, beat cream until it begins to thicken. Add confectioners' sugar and vanilla; beat until stiff peaks form.

5. Place one cake layer on a serving plate. Spread with ⅓ cup caramel topping; sprinkle with ⅓ cup pecans. Spread with half of the whipped cream. Top with remaining cake layer. Spread with the remaining caramel topping and whipped cream. Sprinkle with remaining pecans; top with chocolate curls.

NOTE *To toast nuts, bake in a shallow pan in a 350° oven for 5-10 minutes or cook in a skillet over low heat until lightly browned, stirring occasionally.*

emperatures have
fallen, days are getting
shorter and once again
we turn to crackling
fires, fuzzy slippers and home-
cooked meals to warm us from
head to toe.

After weeks of hectic holiday
preparations, it's time to draw
hearthside and enjoy a delicious
meal with those we love most.

Stovetop Root Vegetable Beef
Stew is pure comfort in a bowl. Try
it with a tender slice of fresh-baked
Sesame Herb Pull-Apart Bread for
a meal everyone will love. And
don't forget to end on a sweet note
with Classic Apple Cranberry Crisp.

If you're looking for a fun family
activity to try on your cozy night in,
create salt dough ornaments (p. 24)
to accent a homemade Christmas
tree Advent calendar (p. 25).

So settle back, throw another log
on the fire, and savor a casual
homespun dinner—it's a gift
everyone will cherish.

**Stovetop Root
Vegetable Beef Stew** (p. 18)
Sesame Herb Pull-Apart Bread (p. 20)

COZY **NIGHT IN**

Stovetop Root Vegetable Beef Stew

To me, the definition of "cozy" is a pot of tender beef simmering with sweet potatoes and parsnips. It doesn't get better than that.
—BETH ROSSOS ESTACADA, OR

PREP: 30 MIN. • **COOK:** 1¾ HOURS • **MAKES:** 8 SERVINGS (2 QUARTS)

⅔ cup all-purpose flour
1½ teaspoons salt, divided
1¼ teaspoons pepper, divided
2 pounds beef stew meat
4 tablespoons olive oil
⅔ cup Burgundy wine
3 cups water
1 can (14½ ounces) stewed tomatoes
2 garlic cloves, minced
2 teaspoons beef base
¼ teaspoon dried thyme
¼ teaspoon ground cinnamon
¼ teaspoon crushed red pepper flakes
1 large sweet potato (about 1 pound), peeled and coarsely chopped
2 medium carrots, coarsely chopped
1 medium onion, chopped
1 medium parsnip, peeled and coarsely chopped
Sliced green onions, optional

1. In a shallow bowl, mix flour and 1 teaspoon each salt and pepper. Add beef, a few pieces at a time, and toss to coat; shake off excess.

2. In a Dutch oven, heat 2 tablespoons oil over medium heat. Brown beef in batches, adding additional oil as necessary.

Remove beef with a slotted spoon. Add wine, stirring to loosen browned bits from pan.

3. Return beef to pan. Add water, tomatoes, garlic, beef base, thyme, cinnamon, pepper flakes and remaining salt and pepper; bring to a boil. Reduce heat; simmer, covered, 1¼ hours, stirring halfway through cooking.

4. Stir in sweet potato, carrots, onion and parsnip. Cook, covered, 30-45 minutes longer or until beef and vegetables are tender. If desired, sprinkle with green onions.

Oven-Roasted Green Beans

Your family will love this versatile side dish. Toss in wax beans with the green beans for variety. Or add yellow or orange peppers for an extra burst of color.
—DONNA WILKINSON MONROVIA, MD

START TO FINISH: 30 MIN. • **MAKES:** 6 SERVINGS

1 pound fresh green beans, trimmed
1 large sweet red pepper, julienned
½ large sweet onion, chopped
6 garlic cloves, minced
3 tablespoons olive oil
½ teaspoon salt
¼ teaspoon coarsely ground pepper

1. Preheat oven to 425°. In a large bowl, combine beans, red pepper, onion and garlic. Drizzle with oil; sprinkle with salt and pepper. Transfer to a greased 15x10x1-in. baking pan.

2. Roast 20-25 minutes or until tender, stirring once.

TRIMMING GREEN BEANS

To trim fresh green beans quickly, simply line up the ends of the beans; then, using a chef's knife, slice several at a time.

Risotto with Chicken and Mushrooms

Portobello mushrooms add an earthy flavor to this creamy classic, while shredded rotisserie chicken makes it a snap to prepare. You'll savor every bite.

—CHARLENE CHAMBERS ORMOND BEACH, FL

PREP: 15 MIN. • **COOK:** 50 MIN.
MAKES: 4 SERVINGS

- 1 carton (32 ounces) chicken broth
- 1 to 1½ cups water
- 4 tablespoons unsalted butter, divided
- 2 tablespoons olive oil
- ½ pound sliced baby portobello mushrooms
- 1 small onion, finely chopped
- 1½ cups uncooked arborio rice
- ½ cup dry white wine or chicken broth
- 1 tablespoon lemon juice
- 2 cups shredded rotisserie chicken
- 3 tablespoons grated Parmesan cheese
- 2 tablespoons minced fresh parsley
- ½ teaspoon salt
- ¼ teaspoon pepper

1. In a large saucepan, bring broth and water to a simmer; keep hot. In another large saucepan, heat 2 tablespoons butter and oil over medium heat. Add mushrooms and onion; cook and stir 6-8 minutes or until tender. Add rice; cook and stir 2-3 minutes or until rice is coated.

2. Stir in wine and lemon juice. Reduce heat to maintain a simmer; cook and stir until wine mixture is absorbed. Add hot broth mixture, ½ cup at a time, cooking and stirring until broth has been absorbed after each addition, until rice is tender but firm to the bite and risotto is creamy.

3. Stir in chicken, cheese, parsley, salt, pepper and remaining butter; heat through. Serve immediately.

Sesame Herb Pull-Apart Bread

The beauty of this bread is that all of the prep work is done a day ahead. The savory herbs make it irresistible.
—**MARY SHIVERS** ADA, OK

PREP: 15 MIN. + CHILLING
BAKE: 30 MIN. + COOLING
MAKES: 24 SERVINGS

- 3 **tablespoons minced fresh chives**
- 3 **tablespoons minced fresh parsley**
- 1 **teaspoon each dried basil, oregano and thyme**
- 3 **tablespoons sesame seeds**
- 24 **frozen bread dough dinner rolls**
- ¼ **cup butter, melted**

1. In a small bowl, mix chives and parsley. In another bowl, mix basil, oregano and thyme. In a greased 10-in. fluted tube pan, sprinkle 1 tablespoon sesame seeds, 2 tablespoons fresh herbs and 1 teaspoon dried herbs.
2. Arrange eight dinner rolls over herbs. Sprinkle with 1 tablespoon sesame seeds, 2 tablespoons of the fresh herbs and 1 teaspoon of the dried herbs. Drizzle with one-third of the butter. Repeat layers. Arrange remaining rolls over top; drizzle with remaining butter. Refrigerate, covered, 12-24 hours.
3. Remove from refrigerator 30 minutes before baking. Preheat oven to 350°. Bake rolls, uncovered, 20 minutes. Cover loosely with foil; bake 10-15 minutes longer or until golden brown. Cool in pan 10 minutes before inverting onto a serving plate. Serve warm.

Holiday Crab Dip

This velvety crab dip is comfort food at its finest. I add it to my holiday appetizer platter along with crackers, pita bread, English cucumber slices or celery stalks.
—**ANNE L. HALEY** BEAR, DE

PREP: 15 MIN. + CHILLING • **MAKES:** 2½ CUPS

- 1 **cup reduced-fat mayonnaise**
- 1 **green onion, thinly sliced**
- 1 **tablespoon minced fresh parsley**
- 1 **tablespoon lemon juice**
- 1 **teaspoon freshly ground black pepper**
- 1 **teaspoon Worcestershire sauce**
- ¾ **teaspoon seafood seasoning**
- 1 **pound lump crabmeat**
  Cucumber slices, water crackers or pita bread wedges

In a small bowl, combine the first seven ingredients. Gently fold in crab. Refrigerate, covered, at least 2 hours to allow flavors to blend. Serve with cucumber slices.

Lemon Shrimp Fettuccine

Pasta lovers, rejoice! You'll be amazed at how quick and easy it is to toss together this impressive seafood entree that boasts a classic white sauce with a hint of lemon.
—KATHLEEN SPECHT CLINTON, MT

START TO FINISH: 25 MIN. • **MAKES:** 6 SERVINGS

- 12 **ounces uncooked fettuccine**
- ⅓ **cup butter, cubed**
- 1⅔ **cups heavy whipping cream**
- ¾ **cup grated Parmesan cheese**
- 1½ **pounds peeled and deveined cooked shrimp (31-40 per pound)**
- ¾ **cup seeded chopped tomatoes**
- ½ **cup finely chopped roasted sweet red pepper**
- 1½ **teaspoons grated lemon peel**
- ⅓ **cup lemon juice**
- ¼ **cup slivered almonds, toasted**

1. Cook fettuccine according to package directions. Meanwhile, in a large skillet, melt butter over medium heat. Stir in cream. Bring to a gentle boil. Reduce heat; simmer, uncovered, 3-4 minutes or until slightly thickened, stirring constantly. Reduce heat to low. Whisk in cheese until smooth. Add shrimp, tomato and red pepper; heat through. Stir in lemon peel and juice.

2. Drain fettuccine; transfer to a large bowl. Add shrimp mixture; toss to combine. Sprinkle with almonds.

NOTE *To toast nuts, bake in a shallow pan in a 350° oven for 5-10 minutes or cook in a skillet over low heat until lightly browned, stirring occasionally.*

Cranberry Romaine Salad with Raspberry Vinaigrette

Dried cranberries and feta add intense flavor to this simple salad that balances perfectly with the refreshing homemade dressing.
—ELIZABETH SEIDA EDMONTON, AB

START TO FINISH: 15 MIN. • **MAKES:** 8 SERVINGS

- 8 **cups torn romaine**
- 1½ **cups crumbled feta cheese**
- 1 **cup pecan halves, toasted**
- 1 **cup dried cranberries or fresh pomegranate seeds**
- ½ **small red onion, thinly sliced**

DRESSING
- ⅓ **cup olive oil**
- 3 **tablespoons sugar**
- 2 **tablespoons raspberry vinegar**
- 1 **tablespoon sour cream**
- 1½ **teaspoons Dijon mustard**

In a large bowl, combine the first five ingredients. In a small bowl, whisk dressing ingredients. Just before serving, drizzle ¼ cup dressing over salad; toss to coat. Serve with remaining dressing.

NOTE *To toast nuts, bake in a shallow pan in a 350° oven for 5-10 minutes or cook in a skillet over low heat until lightly browned, stirring occasionally.*

FETA FACTS

Feta is a white, salty, semi-firm cheese. Traditionally it was made from sheep's or goat's milk but is now also made with cow's milk. After feta is formed in a special mold, it's sliced into large pieces, salted and soaked in brine. Although feta cheese is mostly associated with Greek cooking, "feta" comes from the Italian word "fette," meaning slice.

Classic Apple Cranberry Crisp

For a little old-fashioned goodness, treat your clan to this divine dish that bakes
up warm and bubbly. It's great on its own or served with a scoop of ice cream.
—BILLIE MOSS WALNUT CREEK, CA

PREP: 10 MIN. • **BAKE:** 25 MIN. • **MAKES:** 4 SERVINGS

- 3 cups chopped peeled tart apples
- 1½ cups fresh or frozen cranberries, thawed
- ¾ cup packed brown sugar, divided
- 1 tablespoon lemon juice
- ½ teaspoon ground cinnamon
- ½ cup all-purpose flour
- ⅓ cup cold butter, cubed
  Vanilla ice cream, optional

1. Preheat oven to 375°. In a large bowl, combine apples, cranberries, ¼ cup brown sugar, lemon juice and cinnamon. Pour into a greased 8-in.-square baking dish. In a small bowl, mix flour and remaining brown sugar. Cut in butter until crumbly. Sprinkle over fruit.

2. Bake, uncovered, 25-30 minutes or until topping is golden brown and filling is bubbly. If desired, serve with ice cream.

....

Frosted Triple Peanut Bars

Everyone loves my famous peanut bars crowned with a luscious chocolate frosting.
These goodies are rich, moist and dense—perfect with a glass of cold milk.
—LAUREN REIFF EAST EARL, PA

PREP: 25 MIN. • **BAKE:** 20 MIN. + COOLING • **MAKES:** 16 SERVINGS

- ⅔ cup peanut butter chips
- ½ cup butter, cubed
- ¼ cup creamy peanut butter
- 2 large eggs
- ¾ cup sugar
- 1 teaspoon vanilla extract
- ⅔ cup all-purpose flour
- ¼ teaspoon salt
- ½ cup chopped dry roasted peanuts

FROSTING
- 2 cups confectioners' sugar
- ½ cup baking cocoa
- ¼ cup butter, softened
- ¼ cup sour cream
- 2 teaspoons 2% milk

1. Preheat oven to 350°. In a microwave-safe bowl, melt peanut butter chips, butter and peanut butter; stir until smooth.

2. In a large bowl, beat eggs, sugar and vanilla until blended. In another bowl, whisk flour and salt; gradually beat into sugar mixture. Stir in peanut butter mixture and peanuts.

3. Transfer to a greased 9-in.-square baking pan. Bake 20-25 minutes or until a toothpick inserted in center comes out clean. Cool completely in pan on a wire rack.

4. In a small bowl, combine frosting ingredients; beat until smooth. Spread over top. Cut into bars. Store in an airtight container.

Peppermint White Hot Chocolate

My soothing white hot chocolate is a great warm-up after a wintry day spent sledding or ice skating. Or include it as a festive addition to brunch or an afternoon tea party.
—**DARLENE BRENDEN** SALEM, OR

START TO FINISH: 15 MIN. • **MAKES:** 6 SERVINGS

5½ cups 2% milk
⅓ cup heavy whipping cream
4 teaspoons crushed peppermint candies, divided
12 ounces white baking chocolate, chopped
¾ teaspoon peppermint extract
Mini marshmallows

1. In a large saucepan, heat milk over medium heat until bubbles form around sides of pan. Meanwhile, in a small bowl, beat cream until stiff peaks form. Fold in 1 teaspoon crushed candy.
2. Whisk chocolate into milk until smooth. Remove from the heat; stir in extract. Pour into mugs; top with whipped cream. Sprinkle with the remaining candy and mini marshmallows. Serve hot chocolate immediately.

Salt Dough Ornaments

PICTURED ON OPPOSITE PAGE

Kids and adults alike will enjoy creating these simple tree accents.
This recipe makes about 30 ornaments.

MATERIALS

8 cups all-purpose flour
2 cups salt
3 cups warm water
Rolling pin
Assorted 1-3-in. Christmas-themed cookie cutters
Drinking straw
Numeral stamps
Black stamping ink
Two-tone burlap twine

DIRECTIONS

1. Preheat oven to 325°. In a large bowl, mix flour and salt. Gradually add water, stirring until dough is thick. When dough becomes too thick to stir, finish mixing with hands. Knead dough until it is soft and pliable.
2. Turn the dough onto a floured surface and roll to an ⅛-in. thickness. Cut into shapes using cookie cutters. Transfer cutouts to ungreased baking sheets.
3. Using a straw, make a hole in the top of each ornament. Remove the center circle of dough. Bake the ornaments at 325° for about 1 hour or until hard.
4. Transfer the ornaments to wire racks to cool completely.
5. Stamp ornaments 1 through 25, for the 24 days leading up to Christmas, plus the holiday. Let ink dry.
6. Weave twine through the top of each ornament and tie into a loop.
7. For each day, beginning Dec. 1, hang the corresponding ornament on a tabletop Advent tree like the one on the next page, or hang on a traditional Christmas tree.

TIP: *We love the natural look of these ornaments, but if you prefer a glossy shine, brush a thin layer of non-toxic acrylic varnish after the stamping ink has thoroughly dried. The varnish will also help prevent breakage.*

Christmas Tree Advent Calendar

Take the fun of Advent calendars to new heights with this homemade tabletop tree.

MATERIALS

- 24x12-in. piece of Christmas-themed fabric
- 7-in. terra cotta pot
- 4-in. foam ball
- Artificial or dried moss
- 7 twigs, one in each of these lengths: 28 in.; 16 in.; 14 in.; 12 in.; 10 in.; 8 in.; 6 in.
- Natural burlap 2-ply twine (jute)
- Salt dough ornaments (see recipe opposite)
- Fabric stiffener
- Glue gun
- Screwdriver, optional

DIRECTIONS

1. Apply fabric stiffener to the backside of fabric. Carefully mold the fabric around the outside of the terra cotta pot, pressing firmly. Fold the edges of fabric over the lip and under the bottom of the pot. Press out any air pockets. Let dry.

2. To make tree, center the 6 shorter twigs horizontally across the 28-in. twig, with the shortest twig at the top, and leaving about 4 in. between each twig and 7 in. at the base. Wrap twine around each intersection several times. Hot-glue the back of wrapped intersections to secure.

3. Press the foam ball into the pot. Insert the tree into the ball at the base, using a screwdriver to drill a hole into the foam if necessary. Be sure the tree is stable; dab some hot glue around the tree base if necessary.

4. Arrange moss around the foam ball and across the top of the pot to cover the foam ball completely. Mound moss slightly around the base of the tree, making sure it does not overflow.

5. Beginning on Dec. 1, hang the corresponding ornament to the tree to count down the calendar days until Christmas.

P reparing for the annual office holiday potluck doesn't have to be a chore. Think festive finger food, fuss-free munchies and crowd-pleasing sweets that will wow your co-workers without eating up too much of your time.

For instance, Greek Deviled Eggs are easy to put together and require little effort once you start. Just store them in the office fridge until party time. Don't be surprised if the line for your Black Forest Ham Roll-Ups winds past the copy machine. And everyone from interns to the CEO will be negotiating for an extra turn at your Sweet & Savory Pineapple Cheese Ball.

If you're willing to put in a little kitchen overtime, sign up to bring a beautiful Baklava Cheesecake. One bite, and the team is liable to name you Employee of the Year!

HOLIDAY **OFFICE PARTY**

Pretzel Bark Candy

I usually make this pretzel candy as a gift, but it also shines at office parties. The recipe makes a big batch and stores well.
—**BETTY CLAYCOMB** ALVERTON, PA

PREP: 10 MIN. + CHILLING
MAKES: ABOUT 2 POUNDS

- **1 pound milk chocolate candy coating, chopped**
- **1 pound white candy coating, chopped**
- **2 tablespoons creamy peanut butter**
- **2 cups coarsely chopped pretzel sticks**

1. Line a 15x10x1-in. pan with foil. In a large microwave-safe bowl, melt candy coatings and peanut butter; stir till smooth. Stir in pretzels.

2. Spread into prepared pan. Refrigerate until firm. Break into pieces.

HOW TO MELT CHOCOLATE

To melt chocolate in the microwave, place it in a microwave-safe bowl. Melt semisweet chocolate on high (100% power) for 1 minute; stir. Microwave at additional 10- to 20-second intervals, stirring until smooth. Melt milk chocolate and vanilla or white chocolate at 70% power. Stir frequently until the chocolate is melted; do not overheat.

Black Forest Ham Roll-Ups

We love to entertain at home and the office. Ham and cheese rolled in tortillas make a quick and easy appetizer that's easy to transport.
—SUSAN ZUGEHOER HEBRON, KY

PREP: 25 MIN. + CHILLING • **MAKES:** ABOUT 6½ DOZEN

- 1 package (8 ounces) cream cheese, softened
- 2 teaspoons minced fresh parsley
- 2 teaspoons dried celery flakes
- 2 teaspoons Dijon mustard
- 1 teaspoon lemon juice
- ⅛ teaspoon salt
- ⅛ teaspoon pepper
- ½ cup dried cranberries, chopped
- 2 green onions, chopped
- 5 flour tortillas (10 inches), room temperature
- ½ pound thinly sliced Black Forest deli ham
- ½ pound thinly sliced Swiss cheese

1. In a small bowl, mix the first seven ingredients until blended. Stir in cranberries and green onions; spread over tortillas. Layer with ham and cheese. Roll up tightly; wrap in plastic wrap. Refrigerate at least 1 hour.
2. Just before serving, unwrap and cut each tortilla crosswise into 16 slices.

Toffee Coffee Cookies

My favorite ice cream flavor features coffee and toffee flavors, so I thought, why not pack that same great taste into a cookie? The toffee bits are a happy surprise.
—JOANNE WRIGHT NILES, MI

PREP: 30 MIN. • **BAKE:** 20 MIN./BATCH • **MAKES:** 4 DOZEN

- 3 tablespoons instant coffee granules
- 1 tablespoon hot water
- ½ cup butter, softened
- ½ cup shortening
- ¾ cup sugar
- ¾ cup packed brown sugar
- 2 large eggs
- 2 ounces semisweet chocolate, melted
- 1 teaspoon vanilla extract
- 3¼ cups all-purpose flour
- 1 teaspoon baking soda
- ½ teaspoon salt
- 1 cup milk chocolate English toffee bits
- 1 cup (6 ounces) 60% cacao bittersweet chocolate baking chips

1. Preheat oven to 350°. In a small bowl, dissolve coffee granules in hot water.
2. In a large bowl, cream butter, shortening and sugars until light and fluffy. Beat in eggs, melted chocolate, vanilla and coffee mixture. In another bowl, whisk flour, baking soda and salt; gradually beat into creamed mixture. Stir in toffee bits and baking chips.
3. Drop dough by rounded tablespoonfuls 2 in. apart onto greased baking sheets. Bake 16-18 minutes or until edges are lightly browned. Cool on pans 2 minutes. Remove cookies to wire racks to cool.

Sweet & Savory Pineapple Cheese Ball

One of my favorite dishes in childhood was my mom's pineapple and green pepper cheese ball. Now I make it, and it's always a hit.
—SUSAN HARRISON LAUREL, MD

PREP: 15 MIN. + CHILLING • **MAKES:** 2 CHEESE BALLS (2 CUPS EACH)

- 2 **packages (8 ounces each) reduced-fat cream cheese**
- 1 **can (20 ounces) crushed pineapple, well drained**
- 3 **cups finely chopped pecans, divided**
- ¼ **cup finely chopped green pepper**
- 1 **tablespoon finely chopped onion**
- 1 **teaspoon seasoned salt Assorted crackers**

1. In a large bowl, beat cream cheese until smooth. Stir in pineapple, 1½ cups pecans, green pepper, onion and seasoned salt. Shape into two balls. Wrap in plastic wrap; refrigerate at least 30 minutes.
2. Place remaining pecans in a small shallow bowl; roll cheese balls in pecans to coat evenly. Serve with crackers.

Sausage Jalapeno Dip

I make this creamy, savory dip in my slow cooker. The dip tastes great with crunchy tortilla chips or raw vegetables.
—GINA FENSLER CINCINNATI, OH

PREP: 15 MIN. • **COOK:** 5½ HOURS • **MAKES:** 6 CUPS

- 1 **pound bulk Italian sausage**
- 2 **large sweet red peppers, finely chopped**
- 3 **jalapeno peppers, finely chopped**
- 1 **cup whole milk**
- 2 **packages (8 ounces each) cream cheese, softened**
- 1 **cup (4 ounces) shredded part-skim mozzarella cheese Tortilla chips**

1. In a large skillet, cook sausage over medium heat 6-8 minutes or until no longer pink, breaking into crumbles; drain.
2. Place red peppers, jalapenos and sausage in a 3-qt. slow cooker; add milk. Cook, covered, on low 5-6 hours or until peppers are tender.
3. Stir in cheeses. Cook, covered, on low 30 minutes longer or until cheese is melted. Serve with tortilla chips.
NOTE *Wear disposable gloves when cutting hot peppers; the oils can burn skin. Avoid touching your face.*

Greek Deviled Eggs

Want a zippy update on the classic deviled egg? Tomatoes, olives and a dash of yogurt turn this Greek version into a party favorite.
—*TASTE OF HOME* TEST KITCHEN

START TO FINISH: 20 MIN.
MAKES: 1 DOZEN

- 6 **hard-cooked large eggs**
- 2 **tablespoons crumbled feta cheese**
- 1 **tablespoon plain Greek yogurt**
- 1 **tablespoon mayonnaise**
- 1 **tablespoon finely chopped oil-packed sun-dried tomato**
- 2 **Greek olives, pitted and chopped**
  Dash each salt and pepper
  Additional Greek olives, halved and thinly sliced sun-dried tomatoes, optional

Cut eggs lengthwise in half. Remove yolks, reserving whites. In a small bowl, mash yolks. Stir in cheese, yogurt, mayonnaise, chopped tomato, chopped olives, salt and pepper. Spoon or pipe into egg whites. If desired, top with olive halves and tomato strips. Refrigerate, covered, until serving.

Peppermint Punch

Try this for a new twist on punch. Pineapple and orange juices mixed with a hint of peppermint make a zingy beverage that's delicious with cake and other party foods.
—**GAY NELL NICHOLAS** HENDERSON, TX

PREP: 10 MIN. + FREEZING • **MAKES:** 20 SERVINGS (¾ CUP EACH)

ICE CUBES
Lemon-lime soda
Maraschino cherries, well drained

PUNCH
1 **can (46 ounces) pineapple juice, chilled**
2 **cups lemon-lime soda, chilled**
1 **can (12 ounces) frozen orange juice concentrate, thawed**
1 **teaspoon peppermint extract**

Fill two ice cube trays with lemon-lime soda; place a cherry in each compartment. Freeze until solid. Just before serving, combine punch ingredients in a punch bowl. Add ice cubes.

Chocolate Pecan Pie Snack Mix

My crowd-pleasing party mix is buttery, chocolaty and nutty. The recipe yields a party-size portion, but I recommend keeping it covered so it doesn't disappear before the event.
—**ANNETTE NIEMIEC** SCOTTSDALE, AZ

START TO FINISH: 30 MIN. • **MAKES:** 4 QUARTS

4 **cups Rice Chex**
4 **cups Chocolate Chex**
4 **cups Honey Nut Chex**
2 **cups coarsely chopped pecans, toasted**
1 **cup packed brown sugar**
½ **cup butter, cubed**
⅓ **cup light corn syrup**
½ **teaspoon baking soda**
2 **cups (12 ounces) semisweet chocolate chips**
2 **tablespoons shortening**

1. In a large bowl, combine cereals and pecans. In a small microwave-safe bowl, combine brown sugar, butter and corn syrup. Microwave, uncovered, on high for 2 minutes, stirring once. Whisk in baking soda. Pour over cereal mixture; toss to coat.
2. Cook in batches on high in a microwave-safe bowl for 3 minutes, stirring every minute. Spread onto waxed paper-lined baking sheets to cool completely.

In a microwave, melt chocolate chips and shortening; stir until smooth. Drizzle over cereal mixture; refrigerate until set.
3. Break into pieces. Store in an airtight container at room temperature.
NOTE *This recipe was tested in a 1,100-watt microwave.*

Baklava Cheesecake

With sugared cranberries and rosemary sprigs, my unique cheesecake makes a grand display for office parties and other special events.
—ARYANNA GAMBLE
NEW ORLEANS, LA

PREP: 1¼ HOURS
BAKE: 50 MIN. + CHILLING
MAKES: 16 SERVINGS

- 12 **sheets phyllo dough (14x9 in.)**
- ⅓ **cup butter, melted**
- 1 **cup finely chopped walnuts**
- ¼ **cup sugar**
- ½ **teaspoon ground cinnamon**
- ¼ **teaspoon ground nutmeg**
- ⅛ **teaspoon ground allspice**
- 2 **packages (8 ounces each) cream cheese, softened**
- 1 **carton (8 ounces) mascarpone cheese**
- ⅔ **cup honey**
- ¼ **cup 2% milk**
- 3 **tablespoons all-purpose flour**
- 3 **large eggs, lightly beaten**

GARNISH
- 3 **tablespoons light corn syrup**
- 3 **fresh rosemary sprigs**
- ¼ **cup sugar, divided**
- ½ **cup fresh or frozen cranberries, thawed and patted dry**

1. Preheat oven to 425°. Place one sheet of phyllo dough in a greased 9-in. springform pan, pressing phyllo onto bottom and up sides of pan; brush with butter. Layer with remaining phyllo sheets, brushing each layer and rotating sheets slightly to stagger the corners. (While working, keep unused phyllo covered with plastic wrap and a damp towel to prevent it from drying out.) Place springform pan on a 15x10x1-in. baking pan.

2. In a small bowl, mix walnuts, sugar and spices; sprinkle over bottom of phyllo. Bake 5-7 minutes or until edges are lightly browned (sides will puff). Cool on a wire rack. Reduce oven setting to 325°.

3. In a large bowl, beat cream cheese and mascarpone cheese on low speed until smooth. Beat in honey, milk and flour. Add eggs; beat on low speed just until blended. Pour into crust. Return pan to baking pan.

4. Bake 50-60 minutes or until center is almost set. Cool on a wire rack 1 hour longer. Refrigerate overnight, covering when completely cooled. Remove rim from pan.

5. For garnish, place corn syrup in a small microwave-safe bowl. Microwave, uncovered, 10 seconds or until warm. Brush corn syrup lightly over both sides of rosemary. Place on waxed paper; sprinkle with 1 tablespoon sugar.

6. If needed, reheat remaining corn syrup until warm; gently toss cranberries in syrup. Place remaining sugar in a small bowl; add cranberries and toss to coat. Place on waxed paper and let stand until set, about 1 hour.

7. Just before serving, garnish cheesecake with sugared rosemary and cranberries.

S preading holiday cheer is a jolly job—and a labor of love—for those who make Christmas cookies. After all, it wouldn't be Christmas without platters piled high with an assortment of merry morsels.

We've gathered a delicious parade of can't-miss, high-yield holiday treasures, all guaranteed to satisfy the deepest cookie craving.

Need an adorable goodie to tuck inside an equally adorable tin? You'll love Holiday Cutout Cookies (right) and Coffee Maple Spritz.

If it's your turn to plan the annual cookie swap or church bake sale, big-batch favorites like Cinnamon Gingersnaps or Stained Glass Cherry Macaroons are sure to put everyone in a festive frame of mind.

Holiday Cutout Cookies (p. 36)

BIG-BATCH **COOKIES**

Holiday Cutout Cookies

The only limit to these fun cutouts is your cookie cutter collection and your imagination! If you prefer crisp cookies, sprinkle with colored sugar before baking and skip the frosting.
—**ANNE GRISHAM** HENDERSON, NV

PREP: 20 MIN. • **BAKE:** 5 MIN./BATCH • **MAKES:** ABOUT 10 DOZEN

- 1 **cup butter, softened**
- 1 **cup shortening**
- 3 **cups sugar**
- 4 **large eggs**
- 6 **tablespoons evaporated milk**
- 2 **teaspoons vanilla extract**
- 2 **teaspoons almond extract**
- 6 **cups all-purpose flour**
- 1 **teaspoon baking soda**
- ½ **teaspoon salt**

FROSTING
- 3 **cups confectioners' sugar**
- 1 **teaspoon vanilla extract**
- 4 **to 6 tablespoons half-and-half cream**
   Food coloring of your choice, optional
   Assorted sprinkles

1. In a large bowl, cream butter, shortening and sugar until light and fluffy. Beat in eggs, milk and extracts. In another bowl, whisk flour, baking soda and salt; gradually beat into creamed mixture. Divide dough into four portions. Shape each into a disk; wrap in plastic wrap. Refrigerate, covered, overnight or until firm enough to roll.

2. Preheat oven to 400°. On a lightly floured surface, roll each portion of dough to ⅛-in. thickness. Cut with floured 3-in. holiday cookie cutters. Place 1 in. apart on ungreased baking sheets.

3. Bake 5-7 minutes or until edges are lightly brown. Remove from pans to wire racks to cool completely.

4. In a large bowl, beat confectioners' sugar, vanilla and enough cream to reach a spreading consistency. If desired, beat in food coloring. Frost and decorate cookies as desired.

FREEZE OPTION *Freeze undecorated cookies in freezer containers. To use, thaw in covered containers and decorate as desired.*

Coconut Cherry Sandies

Guests won't be able to stop at just one of these tender almond shortbread cookies studded with cherries, coconut and pistachio nuts.
—**CAROLE HOLT** MENDOTA HEIGHTS, MN

PREP: 30 MIN. • **BAKE:** 10 MIN./BATCH + STANDING • **MAKES:** ABOUT 7 DOZEN

- 1 **cup butter, softened**
- 1⅓ **cups sugar**
- ½ **cup packed brown sugar**
- 1 **cup plus 4 teaspoons canola oil, divided**
- 2 **large eggs**
- 1 **teaspoon almond extract**
- 4½ **cups all-purpose flour**
- 1 **teaspoon salt**
- 1 **teaspoon baking soda**
- 1⅓ **cups flaked coconut, toasted**
- 1⅓ **cups chopped pistachios**
- 1⅓ **cups chopped dried cherries**
- 1⅓ **cups white baking chips**

1. Preheat oven to 350°. In a large bowl, cream butter and sugars until light and fluffy. Beat in 1 cup oil, eggs and extract. In another bowl, whisk flour, salt and baking soda; gradually beat into creamed mixture. Stir in coconut, pistachios and cherries.

2. Drop by tablespoonfuls 2 in. apart on ungreased baking sheets.

Flatten slightly with a glass dipped in sugar. Bake 8-10 minutes or until set. Remove to wire racks to cool completely.

3. In a microwave, melt baking chips and remaining oil; stir until smooth. Drizzle over cookies. Let stand until set.

FREEZE OPTION *Freeze undrizzled cookies in freezer containers. To use, thaw in covered containers. Drizzle cookies as directed.*

Mint-Chocolate Dipped Shortbread Cookies

Festive buttery shortbreads are even better when dipped in chocolate and sprinkled with crushed candy.
—**DAHLIA ABRAMS** DETROIT, MI

PREP: 40 MIN. + CHILLING
BAKE: 15 MIN./BATCH + COOLING
MAKES: ABOUT 6 DOZEN

- 2 **cups butter, softened**
- 1 **cup confectioners' sugar**
- ½ **cup sugar**
- 4 **teaspoons vanilla extract**
- 4 **cups all-purpose flour**
- 1 **teaspoon salt**
- 4 **cups (24 ounces) semisweet chocolate chips**
- 2 **tablespoons shortening**
- 2 **teaspoons peppermint extract**
- ½ **cup crushed candy canes (about 5 regular size) Coarse sugar, optional**

1. In a large bowl, cream butter and sugars until light and fluffy. Beat in vanilla. In another bowl, whisk flour and salt; gradually beat into creamed mixture. Divide dough in half. Shape each into a disk; wrap in plastic wrap. Refrigerate 30 minutes or until firm enough to roll.

2. Preheat oven to 350°. On a lightly floured surface, roll each portion of dough to ¼-in. thickness. Cut with a floured 2-in. round cookie cutter. Place 2 in. apart on ungreased baking sheets.

3. Bake 12-15 minutes or until edges begin to brown. Remove cookies from pans to wire racks to cool completely.

4. In top of a double boiler or a metal bowl over barely simmering water, melt chocolate chips and shortening; stir until smooth. Stir in extract. Dip each cookie halfway into chocolate mixture; shake off excess. Place on waxed paper; sprinkle with candies and coarse sugar. Place on waxed paper-lined baking sheets; refrigerate until set.

FREEZE OPTION *Freeze decorated cookies, layered between waxed paper, in freezer containers. To use, thaw in covered containers.*

Marzipan Cups with Currant Jelly

These bite-size beauties look and taste gourmet, but they're easy to make and boast a delicate almond flavor. The hidden jelly surprise and pretty nut accent make them a nice addition to any treats tray. You can make them in advance and freeze them for up to three months, if you like.

—LORRAINE CALAND SHUNIAH, ON

PREP: 1 HOUR + CHILLING
BAKE: 15 MIN./BATCH + COOLING
MAKES: ABOUT 7 DOZEN

- 2 **cups butter, softened**
- 1 **cup sugar**
- 2 **large eggs**
- 2 **teaspoons vanilla extract**
- 4 **cups all-purpose flour**
- ½ **teaspoon salt**

FILLING
- 1 **can (8 ounces) almond paste**
- ½ **cup sugar**
- 2 **large eggs**
- ½ **teaspoon almond extract**
- 1 **cup red currant jelly**
- 84 **whole almonds**

1. In a large bowl, cream butter and sugar until light and fluffy. Beat in eggs and vanilla. In another bowl, whisk flour and salt; gradually beat into creamed mixture. Refrigerate 1 hour or until firm.

2. Preheat oven to 350°. Using well-floured hands, press tablespoonfuls of dough onto bottoms and up the sides of greased mini-muffin cups.

3. For filling, in a small bowl, mix almond paste and sugar until blended. Add eggs and extract. Place ½ teaspoon jelly in each cup; top with 1 teaspoon almond mixture. Place one almond on top of each cup. Bake 15-18 minutes or until golden brown. Cool in pans 5 minutes. Remove to wire racks to cool completely.

FREEZE OPTION *Freeze cookies, layered between waxed paper, in freezer containers. To use, thaw in covered containers overnight.*

Pumpkin Cookies with Browned Butter Frosting

The recipe for these pleasantly spiced pumpkin cookies won a champion ribbon at our local county fair. These are a family favorite, and everyone enjoys the soft, cake-like texture.
—**ROBIN NAGEL** WHITEHALL, MT

PREP: 25 MIN. • **BAKE:** 10 MIN./BATCH + COOLING • **MAKES:** ABOUT 9 DOZEN

1½ cups butter, softened
2 cups packed brown sugar
1 cup canned pumpkin
2 large eggs
½ cup crystallized ginger, finely chopped
5 cups all-purpose flour
2 teaspoons baking soda
2 teaspoons ground cinnamon
2 teaspoons ground ginger
½ teaspoon salt
FROSTING
⅔ cup butter, cubed
4 cups confectioners' sugar
1 teaspoon vanilla extract
4 to 5 tablespoons 2% milk

1. Preheat oven to 375°. In a large bowl, cream butter and brown sugar until light and fluffy. Beat in pumpkin, egg and crystallized ginger. In another bowl, whisk flour, baking soda, cinnamon, ginger and salt; gradually beat into creamed mixture.
2. Drop dough by tablespoonfuls 2 in. apart onto ungreased baking sheets. Bake 6-8 minutes or until golden brown. Remove to wire racks to cool completely.
3. In a small heavy saucepan, melt butter over medium heat.

Heat 5-7 minutes or until golden brown, stirring constantly. Transfer to a large bowl. Gradually beat in confectioners' sugar, vanilla and enough milk to achieve desired spreading consistency. Spread over cookies.
FREEZE OPTION *Freeze unfrosted cookies in freezer containers. To use, thaw in covered containers and frost as directed.*

....

Fig-Filled Walnut Cookies

My fig-filled cookies are delightful with a cup of tea after dinner or with a glass of cold milk for a snack. A hint of orange and honey adds a touch of sweetness.
—**YMI TON** SAN DIEGO, CA

PREP: 30 MIN. • **BAKE:** 10 MIN./BATCH • **MAKES:** ABOUT 7 DOZEN

1 pound dried figs
⅔ cup orange juice
¼ cup honey
2 teaspoons sugar
1 teaspoon ground cinnamon
COOKIES
1 cup butter, softened
2⅔ cups sugar
4 large eggs
2 teaspoons vanilla extract
5½ cups all-purpose flour
2 teaspoons cream of tartar
1 teaspoon baking soda
½ teaspoon salt
2 cups finely ground walnuts

1. Place first five ingredients in a food processor; process until paste consistency. Refrigerate while preparing dough.
2. Preheat oven to 350°. Meanwhile, in a large bowl, cream butter and sugar until light and fluffy. Beat in eggs and vanilla. In another bowl, whisk flour, cream of tartar, baking soda and salt; gradually beat into creamed mixture.
3. Shape dough into 1¼-in. balls. Coat bottom of a glass with cooking spray. Press cookie with

bottom of glass to flatten. Place a teaspoon of filling in the center; wrap dough around filling to cover completely. Roll in walnuts. Repeat with remaining dough, filling and walnuts.
4. Place 2 in. apart on greased baking sheets. Bake 10-12 minutes or until bottoms are golden brown. Cool on pans 1 minute. Remove to wire racks to cool.
FREEZE OPTION *Freeze cookies in freezer containers. To use, thaw in covered containers.*

Coffee Maple Spritz

PICTURED AT RIGHT

I like spritz cookies because they're easier to make than rolled cutouts but I can still be creative with different shapes and sizes. Feel free to substitute vanilla or rum extract for the maple flavoring.

—DEIRDRE COX KANSAS CITY, MO

PREP: 25 MIN. • **BAKE:** 10 MIN./BATCH • **MAKES:** ABOUT 5½ DOZEN

½ cup butter, softened
¼ cup shortening
¾ cup sugar
1 large egg
1 tablespoon instant espresso powder
2 teaspoons maple flavoring
2¼ cups all-purpose flour
¼ teaspoon baking powder
¼ teaspoon salt
Coarse white sugar

1. Preheat oven to 375°. In a large bowl, cream butter, shortening and sugar until light and fluffy. Combine egg, espresso powder and maple flavoring; beat into creamed mixture. In another bowl, whisk flour, baking powder and salt; gradually beat into creamed mixture.

2. Using a cookie press fitted with a disk of your choice, press dough 1 in. apart onto ungreased baking sheets. Bake 7-8 minutes or until bottoms are light brown. Remove from pans to wire racks to cool. Sprinkle with coarse white sugar.

FREEZE OPTION *Freeze cookies in freezer containers. To use, thaw in covered containers.*

Double Chocolate Cranberry Biscotti

I'm Italian, and this biscotti is a holiday tradition at our house. It's a low calorie treat that is heavenly dunked in coffee or tea.

—PATRICIA STIEHR EUREKA, MO

PREP: 15 MIN. • **BAKE:** 35 MIN. + COOLING • **MAKES:** ABOUT 6 DOZEN

½ cup butter, softened
1½ cups sugar
3 large eggs
3 cups all-purpose flour
¾ cup baking cocoa
1 teaspoon baking soda
¾ teaspoon baking powder
¾ teaspoon salt
1 cup dried cranberries
1 cup (6 ounces) miniature semisweet chocolate chips

1. In a large bowl, cream butter and sugar until light and fluffy. Beat in eggs. In another bowl, whisk flour, cocoa, baking soda, baking powder and salt; gradually beat into creamed mixture. Fold in cranberries and chocolate chips.

2. Preheat oven to 350°. Divide dough into four portions. On ungreased baking sheets, shape each into a 12x3-in. rectangle. Bake 25-30 minutes or until a toothpick inserted in center comes out clean. Cool on pans on wire racks 20-25 minutes or until firm.

3. Transfer baked rectangles to a cutting board. Using a serrated knife, cut crosswise into ¾-in. slices. Place on baking sheets, cut side down.

4. Bake 7-8 minutes on each side or until firm. Remove from pans to wire racks to cool. Store in airtight containers.

FREEZE OPTION *Freeze cookies in freezer containers. To use, thaw in covered containers.*

Stained Glass Cherry Macaroons

PICTURED AT RIGHT

Macaroons are a timeless treat and a family favorite in our house. These merry morsels are always the first to disappear from the cookie tray.

—JAMIE JONES MADISON, GA

PREP: 45 MIN. • **BAKE:** 15 MIN./BATCH • **MAKES:** ABOUT 7 DOZEN

- 6 **large egg whites**
- ¾ **teaspoon vanilla extract**
- ½ **teaspoon salt**
- ¾ **cup sugar**
- 8 **cups flaked coconut (22 ounces)**
- ¾ **cup finely chopped green candied cherries**
- ¾ **cup finely chopped red candied cherries**
- ⅓ **cup all-purpose flour**

1. Place egg whites in a large bowl; let stand at room temperature 30 minutes. Preheat oven to 325°. Add vanilla and salt to egg whites; beat on medium speed until foamy. Gradually add sugar, 1 tablespoon at a time, beating on high after each addition until sugar is dissolved. Continue beating until stiff glossy peaks form. In another bowl, combine coconut, cherries and flour; stir into egg white mixture.

2. Drop by tablespoonfuls 1 in. apart onto parchment paper-lined baking sheets. Bake 14-16 minutes or until edges are golden. Cool on pans 2 minutes. Remove to wire racks to cool. Store in an airtight container.

FREEZE OPTION *Freeze cookies, layered between waxed paper, in freezer containers. To use, thaw in covered containers.*

SECRETS FOR SUCCESSFUL COOKIES

- Measure ingredients accurately.
- Use heavy-gauge dull aluminum baking sheets with one or two low sides. When a recipe calls for greased baking sheets, use shortening or nonstick cooking spray. Dark finishes may cause cookies to become overly browned.
- For even baking, make cookies the same size and thickness.
- Check the cookies when the minimum baking time has been reached, baking longer if needed. Follow doneness tests given in individual recipes.
- Unless otherwise directed, let cookies cool for 1 minute on the baking sheet before removing to a wire rack. Cool completely before storing.
- Let baking sheets cool before dropping the next batch of dough on them. Otherwise, the heat from the baking sheet will soften the dough, causing it to spread.

Cinnamon Gingersnaps

Gingersnaps embody the tastes and smells of the season. Enjoy cloves, cinnamon and ginger blended into one delicious cookie.
—PAMELA BODLEY
STEVENSVILLE, MI

PREP: 15 MIN. + CHILLING
BAKE: 10 MIN./BATCH
MAKES: ABOUT 6 DOZEN

1½ cups butter, softened
2 cups sugar
2 large eggs
½ cup molasses
4 cups all-purpose flour
2 teaspoons baking powder
2 teaspoons ground cinnamon
1 teaspoon baking soda
1 teaspoon ground ginger
1 teaspoon ground cloves
½ teaspoon salt
1 package (10 ounces) cinnamon baking chips

1. In a large bowl, cream butter and sugar until light and fluffy. Beat in eggs and molasses. In another bowl, whisk flour, baking powder, cinnamon, baking soda, ginger, cloves and salt; gradually beat into creamed mixture. Stir in chips. Refrigerate 1 hour or until firm.

2. Preheat oven to 375°. Shape dough into 1¼-in. balls; place 2 in. apart on ungreased baking sheets. Bake 10-12 minutes or until edges begin to brown. Cool on pans 2 minutes. Remove to wire racks to cool.

FREEZE OPTION *Freeze cookies in freezer containers. To use, thaw in covered containers.*

Butterscotch Sandwich Cookies

Butterscotch lovers will go crazy for these cookie-jar classics.
The brickle toffee bits in the filling are a deliciously fun surprise.
—TASTE OF HOME TEST KITCHEN

PREP: 45 MIN. + CHILLING • **BAKE:** 5 MIN./BATCH + COOLING • **MAKES:** ABOUT 6 DOZEN

3 cups butter, softened
1½ cups packed brown sugar
6 cups all-purpose flour
   Granulated sugar

FILLING

3 cups packed brown sugar
1 cup 2% milk
⅓ cup butter, cubed
¼ teaspoon salt
1½ cups confectioners' sugar
3 tablespoons heavy whipping cream
3 teaspoons vanilla extract
¾ cup brickle toffee bits

1. In a large bowl, cream butter and brown sugar until light and fluffy. Gradually beat in flour. Refrigerate at least 1 hour.

2. Preheat oven to 375°. Shape dough into 1-in. balls; place 2 in. apart on ungreased baking sheets. Flatten cookies with the bottom of a glass dipped in sugar. Bake 5-7 minutes or until set. Remove from pans to wire racks to cool completely.

3. For filling, in a large saucepan, combine brown sugar, milk, butter and salt. Bring to a boil over medium heat, stirring constantly. Cook and stir until a candy thermometer reads 234° (soft-ball stage). Remove from heat; cool to room temperature.

4. Transfer mixture to a large bowl; beat in confectioners' sugar, cream and vanilla until

mixture reaches spreading consistency. Stir in toffee bits. Carefully spread on bottoms of half of the cookies; cover with remaining cookies.

FREEZE OPTION *Freeze cookies before filling in freezer containers. To use, thaw cookies in covered containers. Fill as directed.*

NOTE *We recommend that you test your candy thermometer before each use by bringing water to a boil; the thermometer should read 212°. Adjust your recipe temperature up or down based on your test.*

No-Bake Peanut Butter Snowballs

This is an easy treat to add to your Christmas cookie lineup. The snowballs freeze well in an airtight container so you can pull them out whenever you have company or just crave something sweet.
—JEAN BEVILACQUA RHODODENDRON, OR

PREP: 45 MIN. + CHILLING • **MAKES:** ABOUT 8½ DOZEN

2 cups chunky peanut butter
1½ cups heavy whipping cream
2 packages (11 ounces each) vanilla wafers, finely crushed
1½ cups chopped salted peanuts
2 cups confectioners' sugar

1. In a large bowl, beat peanut butter and cream until blended. Gradually stir in the wafers and peanuts.

2. Shape dough into 1-in. balls; roll in confectioners' sugar. Place on waxed paper-lined baking

sheets. Reroll the balls in confectioners' sugar; refrigerate 2 hours. Store between pieces of waxed paper in airtight containers in the refrigerator. If desired, reroll in confectioners' sugar before serving.

FREEZE OPTION *Freeze cookies, layered between waxed paper, in freezer containers. To use, thaw in covered containers. Reroll in confectioners' sugar before serving.*

MEASURING PEANUT BUTTER

Before putting peanut butter in a measuring cup, lightly coat the inside with water or oil. The peanut butter will easily slide out without the need to scrape with a spatula.

Apricot-Pecan Thumbprint Cookies

I enjoy experimenting with cake mixes to make new cookie recipes. I love apricot, but feel free to fill the thumbprint in the center of these goodies with any fruit preserve you like.

—NANCY JOHNSON LAVERNE, OK

PREP: 30 MIN.
BAKE: 15 MIN./BATCH + COOLING
MAKES: ABOUT 7 DOZEN

- 2 packages yellow cake mix (regular size)
- ½ cup all-purpose flour
- 1 cup canola oil
- 6 large eggs
- 1 teaspoon ground cinnamon
- ½ teaspoon ground ginger
- 3 tablespoons water
- 4 cups finely chopped pecans, divided
- ⅔ cup apricot preserves

ICING
- 2 cups confectioners' sugar
- 3 to 5 tablespoons water

1. Preheat oven to 350°. In a large bowl, beat cake mix, flour, oil, 4 eggs, cinnamon and ginger until well blended.

2. In a shallow bowl, whisk water and remaining eggs. Place half of the pecans in another shallow bowl. Shape dough into 1-in. balls. Dip in egg mixture, then coat with pecans, adding remaining pecans to bowl as needed. Place cookies 2 in. apart on greased baking sheets.

3. Press a deep indentation in center of each cookie with the end of a wooden spoon handle. Fill each with preserves. Bake 12-14 minutes. Remove to wire racks to cool.

4. In a small bowl, combine confectioners' sugar and enough water to achieve a drizzling consistency. Drizzle over cookies. Let stand until set.

FREEZE OPTION *Freeze drizzled cookies, layered between waxed paper, in freezer containers. To use, thaw in covered containers.*

ried and true dishes have earned their place at the holiday table. But just as family traditions evolve, so can menus. Liven things up this season with these tasty twists on your favorite main dishes.

Citrus-Mustard Roasted Chicken and Beef Tenderloin with Pomegranate Chutney are familiar enough to feel friendly but adventurous enough to impress.

Pecan-Smoked Turkey adds a little flair while keeping a classic vibe. And Butternut Lasagna and Seared Scallops with Cheddar-Onion Grits will please the traditionalist and the culinary rebel alike.

Butternut Lasagna (p. 52)

HOLIDAY ENTREES
WITH A TWIST

Beef Tenderloin with Pomegranate Chutney

When I want to show family and friends some culinary love, I roast a tenderloin and serve it with a sweet-tart pomegranate and apple chutney.

—DEVON DELANEY WESTPORT, CT

PREP: 20 MIN.
BAKE: 40 MIN. + STANDING
MAKES: 8 SERVINGS

- 2 **tablespoons minced fresh thyme**
- 1 **tablespoon minced fresh rosemary**
- 1 **tablespoon brown sugar**
- 1 **teaspoon sea salt**
- 1 **teaspoon freshly ground pepper**
- 1 **beef tenderloin roast (3 pounds)**
- 2 **tablespoons Dijon mustard**

CHUTNEY
- 1 **pomegranate**
- 2 **tablespoons olive oil**
- 1 **medium tart apple, peeled and chopped**
- 4 **shallots, coarsely chopped**
- 2 **tablespoons minced fresh gingerroot**
- 1 **garlic clove, minced**
- ¼ **cup sugar**
- ¼ **cup brandy**
- ¼ **cup cider vinegar**
- ¼ **teaspoon sea salt**
- ¼ **teaspoon coarsely ground pepper**

1. Preheat oven to 425°. In a small bowl, mix thyme, rosemary, brown sugar, salt and pepper. Place tenderloin on a rack in a shallow roasting pan. Brush mustard over roast; sprinkle with herb mixture. Roast 40-45 minutes or until meat reaches desired doneness (for medium-rare, a thermometer should read 145°; medium, 160°; well-done, 170°). Remove roast from oven; tent with foil. Let stand 10 minutes before slicing.

2. Meanwhile, for chutney, cut pomegranate in half. Working over a small bowl and using a small spoon, separate pomegranate seeds from membranes, placing seeds in bowl and discarding membranes. In a large skillet, heat oil over medium heat. Add apple and shallots; cook and stir 8-10 minutes or until tender. Add ginger and garlic; cook 1 minute longer. Remove from heat. Add sugar, brandy, vinegar, salt and pepper. Bring to a boil. Reduce heat; simmer, uncovered, until slightly thickened. Stir in pomegranate seeds; heat through. Serve with roast.

Pecan-Smoked Turkey

I love the sweet, nutty flavor that pecan wood chips give to a brined turkey.
Use the grill or a smoker to bring out this marvelous flavor.
—**WENDY GALES** JACKSONVILLE, FL

PREP: 30 MIN. + MARINATING • **GRILL:** 2½ HOURS + STANDING • **MAKES:** 14 SERVINGS

- 2 **cartons (32 ounces each) vegetable broth**
- 1 **cup kosher salt**
- 6 **bay leaves**
- 1 **tablespoon each dried sage, thyme, savory and rosemary, crushed**
- 2 **quarts cold water**
- 1 **turkey (14 to 16 pounds)**
- 2 **turkey-size oven roasting bags**
- 4 **cups soaked pecan wood chips**
- 1 **small onion, finely chopped**
- ½ **cup minced fresh parsley**
- 4 **tablespoons butter, melted, divided**
- 3 **tablespoons olive oil, divided**
- 2 **tablespoons lemon juice**
- 12 **fresh sage leaves, minced**
- 1 **teaspoon pepper**

1. In a 6-qt. stockpot, combine broth, salt, bay leaves and dried herbs. Bring to a boil; cook and stir until salt is dissolved. Remove from heat. Add cold water to cool the brine to room temperature.

2. Place one oven roasting bag inside the other. Place turkey inside both bags; pour in cooled brine. Seal the bags, pressing out as much air as possible; turn to coat the turkey. Place in a shallow roasting pan. Refrigerate 18-24 hours, turning occasionally.

3. Prepare the grill for indirect heat, using a drip pan. Add the wood chips to the grill according to the manufacturer's directions. In a small bowl, mix the onion, parsley, 2 tablespoons butter, 1 tablespoon oil, lemon juice, sage and pepper.

4. Remove turkey from brine; rinse and pat dry. Discard brine. With fingers, carefully loosen skin from turkey breast; rub herb mixture under the skin. In another bowl, mix remaining butter and oil; rub over outside of turkey. Tuck wings under turkey; tie drumsticks together.

5. Place turkey over drip pan, breast side up. Grill, covered, over indirect medium heat 1 hour. Tent turkey with foil; grill 1½ to 2 hours longer or until a thermometer inserted in thickest part of thigh reads 170°-175°. Cover and let stand 20 minutes before carving.

Citrus-Mustard Roasted Chicken

Tender roast chicken is an elegant dish that's easy to make. We love the
tang of orange and lemon slices and the subtle heat from mustard.
—**DEBRA KEIL** OWASSO, OK

PREP: 20 MIN. + CHILLING • **BAKE:** 1¼ HOURS + STANDING • **MAKES:** 4 SERVINGS

- 3 **tablespoons mustard seed**
- ¼ **cup olive oil**
- 1 **tablespoon minced fresh chervil or 1 teaspoon dried chervil**
- 1 **tablespoon champagne vinegar**
- 1 **tablespoon Worcestershire sauce**
- ½ **teaspoon pepper**
- 1 **broiler/fryer chicken (3 to 4 pounds)**
- 2 **orange slices**
- 2 **lemon slices**
- 2 **onion slices**
- 3 **sprigs fresh parsley, stems removed**

1. In a spice grinder or with a mortar and pestle, grind mustard seed to a powder; transfer to a small bowl. Stir in oil, chervil, vinegar, Worcestershire sauce and pepper. Rub over the outside and inside of chicken; place on a large plate. Refrigerate chicken, covered, overnight.

2. Preheat oven to 350°. Place chicken in a shallow roasting pan, breast side up. Loosely stuff chicken with orange, lemon, onion and parsley. Tuck wings under chicken; tie drumsticks together.

3. Roast 1¼ to 1¾ hours or until a thermometer inserted in thickest part of thigh reads 170°-175°. (Cover loosely with foil if chicken browns too quickly.) Remove chicken from oven; tent with foil. Let stand 15 minutes before carving.

Roasted Pork Tenderloin with Fennel and Cranberries

PICTURED AT RIGHT

Fennel, rosemary and a touch of heat from cayenne pepper add wonderful flavor to pork tenderloin. Any leftovers are delicious grilled into paninis with brie.

—JUDY ARMSTRONG PRAIRIEVILLE, LA

PREP: 25 MIN. • **BAKE:** 20 MIN. • **MAKES:** 8 SERVINGS

- 1 teaspoon kosher salt
- 1 teaspoon fennel seeds, crushed
- 1 teaspoon paprika
- ¼ teaspoon cayenne pepper
- 2 pork tenderloins (1 pound each)
- 2 tablespoons olive oil, divided
- 2 medium fennel bulbs, halved and thinly sliced
- 2 shallots, thinly sliced
- 3 garlic cloves, minced
- 1½ cups dry white wine or chicken broth
- 1 cup dried cranberries
- 2 tablespoons minced fresh rosemary or 2 teaspoons dried rosemary, crushed
  Fennel fronds, optional

1. Preheat oven to 425°. In a small bowl, mix salt, fennel seeds, paprika and cayenne. Rub over pork.
2. In a large skillet, heat 1 tablespoon oil over medium-high heat. Brown pork on all sides. Transfer to a rack in a shallow roasting pan. Roast 20-25 minutes or until a thermometer reads 145°. Remove tenderloins from oven; tent with foil. Let stand 5 minutes before slicing.
3. Meanwhile, in same skillet, heat remaining oil over medium-high heat. Add fennel and shallots; cook and stir 4-6 minutes or until tender. Add garlic; cook 1 minute longer.
4. Stir in wine, cranberries and rosemary. Bring to a boil. Reduce heat; simmer, covered, 10 minutes.
5. To serve, spoon fennel mixture onto a serving platter. Top with tenderloin slices and, if desired, fennel fronds.

Seared Scallops with Cheddar-Onion Grits

My holiday guests love shrimp and grits, but I wanted to shake things up one year. These pan scallops are crisp and tender and contrast well with the creamy cheddar grits.

—JANICE ELDER CHARLOTTE, NC

PREP: 20 MIN. • **COOK:** 35 MIN. • **MAKES:** 4 SERVINGS

- 2 tablespoons butter
- 3 medium onions, chopped
- ½ teaspoon salt
- 1 garlic clove, minced
- 2 cans (14½ ounces each) reduced-sodium chicken broth
- ¾ cup quick-cooking grits
- 1 cup (4 ounces) shredded sharp cheddar cheese
- ½ cup sour cream
- 12 sea scallops (about 1½ pounds)
- ½ teaspoon Cajun seasoning
- ¼ cup yellow cornmeal
- 2 tablespoons canola oil
  Minced fresh parsley

1. In a large saucepan, heat butter over medium heat. Add onions and salt; cook and stir 8-10 minutes or until softened. Reduce heat to medium-low; cook 15-20 minutes or until golden brown, stirring occasionally. Add garlic; cook 1 minute longer.
2. Add broth to onion mixture; bring to a boil. Slowly stir in grits. Reduce heat to medium-low; cook, covered, about 5 minutes or until thickened, stirring occasionally. Stir in cheese and sour cream until cheese is melted. Remove from heat; keep warm.
3. Meanwhile, pat scallops dry with paper towels. Sprinkle with Cajun seasoning. Press flat sides into cornmeal. In a large skillet, heat oil over medium-high heat. Add scallops; cook 2-3 minutes on each side or until golden brown and firm.
4. Serve with grits; sprinkle with parsley.

Butternut Lasagna

I love butternut squash, a comfort food with gourmet possibilities. This squash lasagna offers a fresh, updated flavor profile that will rival even the mightiest roasted bird.
—SHANNON CORNELIUS SALT LAKE CITY, UT

PREP: 45 MIN. • **COOK:** 55 MIN. • **MAKES:** 12 SERVINGS

- 1 medium butternut squash (about 4 pounds), peeled and cubed
- 3 tablespoons olive oil
- 1 teaspoon salt, divided
- ½ teaspoon ground nutmeg
- ¼ teaspoon pepper
- 12 lasagna noodles
- ½ cup butter, cubed
- ¼ cup all-purpose flour
- 3 cups 2% milk
- 1 cup heavy whipping cream
- 1½ cups (6 ounces) shredded Swiss or Gruyere cheese, divided
- 2 teaspoons grated lemon peel
- 3 cups fresh baby spinach

1. Preheat oven to 400°. In a large bowl, combine squash, oil, ½ teaspoon salt, nutmeg and pepper. Transfer to two greased 15x10x1-in. baking pans.

2. Roast 30-35 minutes or until tender, stirring occasionally; cool slightly. Process in batches in a food processor until pureed.

Meanwhile, cook lasagna noodles according to package directions; drain.

3. Reduce oven setting to 375°. For sauce, in a small saucepan, melt butter. Stir in flour and remaining salt until smooth; gradually add milk and cream. Bring to a boil; cook and stir 1-2 minutes or until slightly thickened. Stir in 1 cup cheese and lemon peel until the cheese is melted.

4. Spread 1 cup sauce into a greased 13x9-in. baking dish. Layer with four noodles, half of the squash mixture, 1½ cups spinach and 1½ cups sauce. Repeat layers. Top with remaining noodles and sauce.

5. Bake, covered, 45 minutes. Sprinkle with remaining cheese. Bake, uncovered, 10-15 minutes longer or until bubbly and cheese is melted. Let stand 10 minutes before serving.

PREPARING BUTTERNUT SQUASH

To prepare butternut squash for use in recipes, place it on a cutting board and carefully cut with a heavy butcher knife. Or, for easiest cutting, partially cook the squash first. Pierce a whole squash several times and microwave on high for 2-3 minutes or bake at 375° for 10-15 minutes. Cut squash in half; remove and discard the seeds. Use as halves or lay each half flat side down and cut slices ½ inch thick, discarding the ends. If desired, remove the outer shell from the strips with a sharp paring knife, then cube or mash the flesh as needed.

Pork Roast with Zesty Tomato Sauce

All eight of my sisters agree: Our mom's cooking was her best gift to us. We love filling the house with the tantalizing aroma of this roast, which was one of her specialties.
—**NELLA PARKER** HERSEY, MI

PREP: 15 MIN.
BAKE: 1¼ HOURS + STANDING
MAKES: 10 SERVINGS

- 1 **boneless rolled pork loin roast (4 to 5 pounds)**
- ¼ **cup packed brown sugar**
- 1 **tablespoon cornstarch**
- ½ **teaspoon salt**
- ⅛ **teaspoon pepper**
- ¼ **cup water**
- 1 **can (8 ounces) tomato sauce**
- ¼ **cup cider vinegar**
- ¼ **cup dark corn syrup**

1. Preheat oven to 350°. Place roast on a rack in a shallow roasting pan, fat side up. Roast 1 hour.

2. Meanwhile, in a large saucepan, combine brown sugar, cornstarch, salt and pepper. Gradually whisk in water until smooth. Stir in tomato sauce, vinegar and corn syrup. Bring to a boil over medium-high heat. Cook and stir 2 minutes or until thickened and bubbly.

3. Brush roast with some of the sauce. Roast 15-30 minutes longer or until a thermometer reads 145°, brushing occasionally with more sauce. Remove roast from oven; tent with foil. Let stand 15 minutes before slicing. Serve with the remaining sauce.

Cod with Lime Butter

It may seem easy to dismiss fish for a holiday meal, but once you taste the buttery goodness in this moist and flaky lime-infused cod, you'll want it year after year.
—**BARBARA BURGE** LOS GATOS, CA

START TO FINISH: 30 MIN.
MAKES: 6 SERVINGS

- 4 **medium limes**
- ½ **cup dry vermouth**
- ¼ **teaspoon salt**
- 6 **cod fillets (5 ounces each)**
- ¼ **cup butter, softened**
- ¼ **cup heavy whipping cream**
- ¼ **teaspoon pepper**
- ¼ **cup sliced almonds, toasted**

1. Preheat oven to 350°. Finely grate peel from one lime. Squeeze juice from all limes to measure ½ cup. Reserve 2 tablespoons juice for lime butter. In a small bowl, mix vermouth, salt and remaining lime juice.

2. Place cod fillets in an ungreased 13x9-in. baking dish; pour vermouth mixture over cod. Bake, uncovered, 20-25 minutes or until fish just begins to flake easily with a fork.

3. For lime butter, in a small bowl, beat butter and cream until fluffy. Gradually add reserved juice; stir in lime peel and pepper. Serve with fish; sprinkle with almonds.

NOTE *To toast nuts, bake in a shallow pan in a 350° oven for 5-10 minutes or cook in a skillet over low heat until lightly browned, stirring occasionally.*

Stout & Shiitake Pot Roast

A bit of stout beer, mushrooms and onions add excellent flavor to my pot roast. This one-dish wonder may taste even better the next day.
—**MADELEINE BESSETTE** COEUR D' ALENE, ID

PREP: 30 MIN. • **COOK:** 1¾ HOURS • **MAKES:** 6 SERVINGS

- 3 **tablespoons olive oil, divided**
- 1 **boneless beef chuck roast (2 to 3 pounds)**
- 2 **medium onions, sliced**
- 1 **garlic clove, minced**
- 1 **bottle (12 ounces) stout or non-alcoholic beer**
- ½ **ounce dried shiitake mushrooms (about ½ cup)**
- 1 **tablespoon brown sugar**
- 1 **teaspoon Worcestershire sauce**
- ½ **teaspoon dried savory**
- 1 **pound red potatoes (about 8 small), cut into 1-inch pieces**
- 2 **medium carrots, sliced**
- ½ **cup water**
- ½ **teaspoon salt**
- ¼ **teaspoon pepper**

1. In a Dutch oven, heat 1 tablespoon oil over medium heat. Brown roast on all sides; remove from pan.

2. In same pan, heat remaining oil. Add onions and garlic; cook and stir until tender. Add beer, stirring to loosen browned bits from pan. Stir in mushrooms, brown sugar, Worcestershire sauce and savory. Return roast to pan. Bring to a boil. Reduce heat; simmer, covered, 1½ hours.

3. Stir in remaining ingredients. Return to a boil. Reduce heat; simmer, covered, 15-25 minutes longer or until meat and vegetables are tender. If desired, skim fat and thicken cooking juices for gravy.

Spinach-Pesto Turkey Tenderloins

My husband and I love turkey tenderloin stuffed with spinach and goat cheese. This deliciously easy variation on a classic entree takes Christmas dinner to a new level.
—HAYLEY LONG OXFORD, AL

PREP: 20 MIN. • **BAKE:** 25 MIN.
MAKES: 4 SERVINGS

- 6 **cups fresh baby spinach (about 6 ounces), coarsely chopped**
- 1 **cup crumbled goat cheese**
- 2 **garlic cloves, minced**
- 2 **turkey breast tenderloins (8 ounces each)**
- ⅓ **cup prepared pesto**
- ¼ **cup shredded Parmesan cheese**

1. Preheat oven to 350°. In a large saucepan, bring ½ in. of water to a boil. Add spinach; cover and boil 3-5 minutes or until wilted. Drain well.

2. In a small bowl, combine spinach, cheese and garlic. Cut a pocket in each tenderloin by slicing horizontally to within ½ in. of opposite side. Fill with cheese mixture; secure with kitchen string if necessary.

3. Place tenderloins on a greased 15x10x1-in. baking pan; brush with pesto. Bake 20 minutes. Sprinkle with Parmesan cheese. Bake 5-10 minutes longer or until a thermometer reads 165°. Cut each tenderloin into four slices.

GOAT CHEESE

Goat cheese is a soft, easily spreadable cheese with a tangy flavor made from the milk of goats. Varieties include chevre, a very soft cheese, and feta, a semi-soft cheese.

It's the most wonderful time of the year...and the busiest. Shopping, baking, wrapping presents and a full social calendar can leave even the most jovial of merrymakers feeling a little tapped out. It's time to put the spark back in the season with an impromptu, at-home happy hour, don't you think?

Afraid you can't pull together a festive fête in flash? Fear not. Our selection of beverages and savory small bites will have you and your guests bubbling with joy.

Quench everyone's thirst while stirring up party buzz with Bourbon Slush, Butterscotch Martinis, Cranberry Pomegranate Margaritas and other fun and flavorful libations.

And a party isn't complete without tasty tidbits such as Blue Cheese-Stuffed Shrimp or Red Velvet Baby Cakes.

So raise your glass to a good time—you deserve it!

LAST-MINUTE
COCKTAIL PARTY

Festive Dip

My daughter helps me make this quick and easy recipe featuring black-eyed peas mixed with colorful peppers. It's tangy, salty and zippy—everything a dip should be.
—DONNA KOLLAR
AUSTINTOWN, OH

START TO FINISH: 10 MIN.
MAKES: 4 CUPS

- 1 can (15½ ounces) black-eyed peas, rinsed and drained
- 1 medium sweet red pepper, finely chopped
- 1 medium green pepper, finely chopped
- ⅓ cup finely chopped onion
- 1 jalapeno pepper, seeded and chopped
- ½ cup Italian salad dressing
  Corn chips

In a large bowl, combine the first five ingredients. Drizzle with salad dressing; toss to coat. Serve with corn chips.
NOTE *Wear disposable gloves when cutting hot peppers; the oils can burn skin. Avoid touching your face.*

Blue Cheese-Stuffed Shrimp

Cooked shrimp look impressive when stuffed with blue cheese and parsley. Serve them on their own or with cocktail sauce.
—AMY DOLLIMOUNT GLACE BAY, NS

PREP: 20 MIN. + CHILLING • **MAKES:** 2 DOZEN

- 1 package (3 ounces) cream cheese, softened
- ⅔ cup minced fresh parsley, divided
- ¼ cup crumbled blue cheese
- 1 teaspoon chopped shallot
- ½ teaspoon Creole mustard
- 24 cooked jumbo shrimp, peeled and deveined

1. In a small bowl, beat cream cheese until smooth. Beat in ⅓ cup parsley, blue cheese, shallot and mustard. Refrigerate at least 1 hour.
2. Starting with the tail end of each shrimp, make a deep slit along the deveining line to within ¼ to ½ in. of the bottom. Stuff with cream cheese mixture; press remaining parsley onto cream cheese mixture.

Sparkling Fruit Punch

We served this elegant punch of champagne, white wine and fruit juices at our wedding. It's become our signature drink for celebrating life's memorable events.
—ANITA GEOGHAGAN WOODSTOCK, GA

PREP: 10 MIN. + FREEZING • **MAKES:** 16 SERVINGS (¾ CUP)

3 orange slices, halved
  fresh or frozen cranberries
2½ cups unsweetened pineapple
  juice
1½ cups ginger ale
2 bottles (750 milliliters each)
  brut Champagne, chilled
1 bottle (375 milliliters) sweet
  white wine, chilled
1 can (12 ounces) frozen
  lemonade concentrate,
  thawed

1. Line bottom of a 4½-cup ring mold with orange slices and cranberries. Combine pineapple juice and ginger ale; pour over fruit. Freeze until solid.

2. Just before serving, unmold ice ring into a punch bowl. Gently stir in remaining ingredients.

Maple Jalapenos

Try my maple-flavored twist on stuffed jalapenos. One bite and you won't be able to stop!
—NICOLE LARSON AMERICAN FORK, UT

PREP: 45 MIN. • **BAKE:** 20 MIN. • **MAKES:** 50 APPETIZERS

25 jalapeno peppers
1 package (8 ounces) cream
  cheese, softened
1 cup (4 ounces) crumbled feta
  cheese
½ cup maple syrup
½ pound bacon strips, cooked
  and crumbled
¼ cup packed brown sugar

1. Cut jalapenos in half lengthwise and remove seeds. Set aside. In a small bowl, beat the cream cheese, feta cheese and syrup until smooth. Spoon into pepper halves.

2. Place in two greased 15x10x1-in. baking pans. Top with bacon and sprinkle with brown sugar. Bake at 350° for 20 minutes for spicy flavor, 30 minutes for medium and 40 minutes for mild.

NOTE *Wear disposable gloves when cutting hot peppers; the oils can burn skin. Avoid touching your face.*

Mocha Fondue

Guests rave over the hint of coffee in this smooth, luscious fondue. Set out cubes of pound cake, strawberries and bananas for dipping.

—KAREN BOEHNER GLEN ELDER, KS

START TO FINISH: 20 MIN. • **MAKES:** 10 SERVINGS

- 2 cups (12 ounces) semisweet chocolate chips
- ¼ cup butter, cubed
- 1 cup heavy whipping cream
- 3 tablespoons strong brewed coffee
- ⅛ teaspoon salt
- 2 large egg yolks, lightly beaten
  Cubed pound cake, sliced bananas and fresh strawberries and pineapple chunks

1. In a heavy saucepan, combine the first five ingredients; cook and stir over medium heat until chips are melted. Remove from heat. In a small bowl, whisk a small amount of hot mixture into egg yolks; return all to pan, whisking constantly. Cook and stir until a thermometer reads 160°.

2. Transfer to a fondue pot and keep warm. Serve with cake and fruit.

Sage & Prosciutto Pinwheels

My prosciutto pinwheels are an ideal party food because you can make them ahead of time and freeze them. Just slice and bake as needed.

—KATE DAMPIER QUAIL VALLEY, CA

START TO FINISH: 30 MIN. • **MAKES:** 3 DOZEN

- 1 package (17.3 ounces) frozen puff pastry, thawed
- ¼ cup honey mustard
- 1 cup (4 ounces) shredded Gruyere or Swiss cheese
- 8 thin slices prosciutto or deli ham, chopped
- 2 tablespoons chopped fresh sage

1. Preheat oven to 400°. Unfold one pastry sheet. Spread 2 tablespoons mustard to within ½ in. of edges. Sprinkle with ½ cup cheese; top with half each chopped prosciutto and sage. Roll up jelly-roll style. Using a serrated knife, cut roll crosswise into 18 slices.

2. Place cut side down on a greased baking sheet. Repeat with remaining ingredients. Bake 12-15 minutes or until golden brown. Serve warm.

Mulled Red Cider

Red wine gives a rosy glow to this warm spiced cider. Its pleasing aroma never fails to draw people in.
—**STEVE FOY** KIRKWOOD, MO

START TO FINISH: 20 MIN.
MAKES: 7 SERVINGS (¾ CUP EACH)

Cinnamon-sugar, optional
1¾ **cups apple cider or unsweetened apple juice**
½ **cup sugar**
3 **cinnamon sticks (3 inches)**
4 **whole cloves**
1 **bottle (750 milliliters) dry red wine**

1. If desired, moisten the rims of seven mugs with water. Sprinkle cinnamon-sugar on a plate; dip rims in cinnamon-sugar. Set mugs aside.
2. In a large saucepan, combine the cider, sugar, cinnamon sticks and cloves. Cook and stir over medium heat until sugar is dissolved.
3. Add wine and heat through. Remove from the heat. Cover and steep for 10 minutes; strain. Serve in prepared mugs.

Red Velvet Baby Cakes

My friend gave me the recipe for these sweet, petite treats. They feature pie crust on the bottom, raspberry jam in the middle and cake on top—scrumptious for any gathering!
—**DANA BECKSTROM** SALT LAKE CITY, UT

PREP: 20 MIN. • **BAKE:** 15 MIN. + COOLING • **MAKES:** 2 DOZEN

Pastry for double-crust pie
   (9 inches)
½ cup seedless raspberry jam
1 package red velvet cake mix
   (regular size)
1 can (16 ounces) vanilla
   frosting
   Assorted sprinkles

1. Roll pastry to ⅛-in. thickness. Cut twenty-four 2½-in. circles. Press onto the bottom and ½ in. up the sides of greased muffin cups. Top each with 1 teaspoon jam; set aside.
2. Prepare cake mix batter according to package directions for cupcakes. Fill prepared muffin cups three-fourths full.
3. Bake at 350° for 14-16 minutes or until a toothpick inserted near the center comes out clean. Cool for 10 minutes before removing from pans to wire racks to cool completely. Frost with vanilla frosting and decorate with sprinkles.

Pomegranate Pistachio Crostini

I wanted a way to serve pomegranate seeds beyond putting them in a bowl, so I spread them on French bread with pistachios and chocolate.
—**ELISABETH LARSEN** PLEASANT GROVE, UT

START TO FINISH: 30 MIN. • **MAKES:** 3 DOZEN

36 slices French bread baguette
   (¼ inch thick)
1 tablespoon butter, melted
4 ounces cream cheese,
   softened
2 tablespoons orange juice
1 tablespoon honey
1 cup pomegranate seeds
½ cup finely chopped pistachios
2 ounces dark chocolate candy
   bar, finely shaved

1. Preheat oven to 400°. Place bread slices on an ungreased baking sheet; brush one side with butter. Bake 5-7 minutes or until light brown. Remove from pan to a wire rack to cool.
2. Meanwhile, in a small bowl, beat cream cheese, orange juice and honey until blended; spread over toasts. Top with pomegranate seeds, pistachios and chocolate.

Bourbon Slush

An icy slush of bourbon, tea and juices is always a crowd-pleaser. I experiment with different flavored teas for variety, including black tea, green tea and orange spice.
—**DARCENE SIGLER** LOUISVILLE, OH

PREP: 10 MIN. + FREEZING • **MAKES:** 24 SERVINGS (1 CUP EACH)

- 7 **cups water**
- 1½ **cups sugar**
- 1 **can (12 ounces) frozen orange juice concentrate**
- 1 **can (12 ounces) frozen lemonade concentrate**
- 2 **cups strong brewed tea, cooled**
- 2 **cups bourbon**
- 3 **liters lemon-lime soda, chilled**

1. In a Dutch oven, combine water and sugar; bring to a boil, stirring to dissolve sugar. Remove from heat.

2. Stir in orange juice and lemonade concentrates, tea and bourbon. Transfer to freezer containers; freeze 12 hours or overnight.

3. To serve, place about ½ cup bourbon mixture in each glass; top with ½ cup soda.

Butterscotch Martinis

PICTURED ON PAGE 56

A cocktail party isn't complete without a martini on the menu. This sweet concoction is a butterscotch lover's dream. Shake away!
—**CLARA COULSON MINNEY** WASHINGTON COURT HOUSE, OH

START TO FINISH: 10 MIN. • **MAKES:** 2 SERVINGS

- **Ice cubes**
- 2 **ounces clear creme de cacao**
- 2 **ounces creme de cacao**
- 1½ **ounces vodka**
- 1½ **ounces butterscotch schnapps liqueur**
- 6 **semisweet chocolate chips**

1. Fill a shaker three-fourths full with ice. Add the creme de cacao, vodka and schnapps.

2. Cover and shake for 10-15 seconds or until condensation forms on outside of shaker. Divide chocolate chips between two chilled cocktail glasses; strain butterscotch mixture over chips.

MAD FOR MARTINIS

Here are a few tips for mixing the perfect martini. When shaking a drink, use small cubes or crushed ice to chill your drink faster. Add any garnishes before mixing or shaking. It'll add more flavor. Frost glasses in the freezer for a few minutes before pouring.

Cranberry Pomegranate Margaritas

Cranberry and pomegranate juices put a fun twist on margaritas. Dip the rims of chilled glasses into sugar crystals to make these drinks extra special.
—**MINDIE HILTON** SUSANVILLE, CA

START TO FINISH: 5 MIN.
MAKES: 12 SERVINGS (¾ CUP EACH)

- 4½ **cups diet lemon-lime soda, chilled**
- 1½ **cups tequila**
- 1½ **cups cranberry juice, chilled**
- 1½ **cups pomegranate juice, chilled**
- **Pomegranate slices and frozen cranberries, optional**

In a pitcher, combine the soda, tequila and juices. Serve in chilled glasses. Garnish drinks with pomegranate and cranberries if desired.

The stockings have been emptied and all the presents unwrapped. But wait...another gift is in the kitchen.

Christmas breakfast can be as simple or indulgent as your family traditions dictate. If you make merry on Christmas Eve and awake as sleepy as Santa, hot coffee and a Poppy Seed Mini Muffin or frosted Pumpkin Eggnog Roll are sure to hit the spot. Or maybe you need to fuel up before a marathon of holiday house calls. In that case, a hearty Italian Brunch Torte or Eggs Benedict Casserole would be in order.

Need a surefire way to lure the kids to lunch, away from their new toys? Coax them to the table with Strawberries with Chocolate Cream Filling and Egg & Sausage Roll-Ups.

Once your family samples these tasty starts to the day, they are likely to ask you to make them all year long.

Poppy Seed Mini Muffins (p. 74)
Italian Brunch Torte (p. 71)

CHRISTMAS **BREAKFAST**

Pumpkin Eggnog Rolls

I had some eggnog that I wanted to use up, so I substituted it for milk in my sweet roll recipe. Even those who usually don't care for eggnog go back for seconds of these frosted treats.

—REBECCA SOSKE DOUGLAS, WY

PREP: 40 MIN. + RISING
BAKE: 20 MIN. • **MAKES:** 1 DOZEN

- ½ cup sugar
- 1 package (¼ ounce) active dry yeast
- ½ teaspoon salt
- 4½ cups all-purpose flour
- ¾ cup eggnog
- ½ cup butter, cubed
- ¼ cup canned pumpkin
- 2 large eggs

FILLING

- ½ cup sugar
- 1 teaspoon ground cardamom
- 1 teaspoon ground allspice
- ¼ cup butter, melted

FROSTING

- 2 ounces cream cheese, softened
- 2 tablespoons eggnog
- 1 tablespoon canned pumpkin
- ¼ teaspoon ground cardamom
- 2 cups confectioners' sugar

1. In a large bowl, mix sugar, yeast, salt and 2 cups flour. In a small saucepan, heat eggnog, butter and pumpkin to 120°-130°. Add to dry ingredients; beat on medium speed 2 minutes. Add eggs; beat on high 2 minutes. Stir in enough remaining flour to form a firm dough.

2. Turn dough onto a floured surface; knead until smooth and elastic, about 6-8 minutes. Place in a greased bowl, turning once to grease the top. Cover with plastic wrap and let rise in a warm place until doubled, about 1 hour.

3. In a small bowl, mix sugar, cardamom and allspice. Punch dough down. Turn onto a lightly floured surface. Roll into an 18x12-in. rectangle. Brush with butter to within ½ in. of edges; sprinkle with sugar mixture. Roll up jelly-roll style, starting with a long side; pinch seam to seal. Cut into 12 slices.

4. Place in a greased 13x9-in. baking pan, cut side down. Cover with a kitchen towel; let rise in a warm place until doubled, about 45 minutes. Preheat oven to 350°. Bake rolls 20-25 minutes or until golden brown.

5. In a small bowl, beat cream cheese, eggnog, pumpkin and cardamom until blended. Gradually beat in confectioners' sugar; beat until smooth. Spread over warm rolls.

NOTE *This recipe was tested with commercially prepared eggnog.*

Eggs Benedict Casserole

This breakfast bake is just as special and delicious as classic Eggs Benedict but offers crowd-pleasing convenience. Assembling it the night before keeps morning food prep easy.

—SANDIE HEINDEL LIBERTY, MO

PREP: 25 MIN. + CHILLING • **BAKE:** 45 MIN. • **MAKES:** 12 SERVINGS (1⅔ CUPS SAUCE)

12 ounces Canadian bacon, chopped
6 English muffins, split and cut into 1-inch pieces
8 large eggs
2 cups 2% milk
1 teaspoon onion powder
¼ teaspoon paprika

HOLLANDAISE SAUCE
4 large egg yolks
½ cup heavy whipping cream
2 tablespoons lemon juice
1 teaspoon Dijon mustard
½ cup butter, melted

1. Place half of the Canadian bacon in a greased 3-qt. or 13x9-in. baking dish; top with English muffins and remaining bacon. In a large bowl, whisk eggs, milk and onion powder; pour over top. Refrigerate, covered, overnight.

2. Preheat oven to 375°. Remove casserole from refrigerator while oven heats. Sprinkle top with paprika. Bake, covered, 35 minutes. Uncover; bake 10-15 minutes longer or until a knife inserted near the center comes out clean.

3. In top of a double boiler or a metal bowl over simmering water, whisk egg yolks, cream, lemon juice and mustard until blended; cook until mixture is just thick enough to coat a metal spoon and temperature reaches 160°, whisking constantly. Reduce heat to very low. Very slowly drizzle in warm melted butter, whisking constantly. Serve immediately with casserole.

Pineapple Fruit Boat

Served in a pineapple shell, this fancy salad goes together surprisingly quickly with a handful of ingredients. It's an impressive way to present fresh fruit.

—NANCY REICHERT THOMASVILLE, GA

START TO FINISH: 30 MIN. • **MAKES:** 6 SERVINGS

1 fresh pineapple
1½ cups sliced fresh strawberries
1 medium navel orange, peeled and sectioned
1 medium firm banana, sliced
2 ounces cream cheese, softened

1. Stand pineapple upright and vertically cut a third from one side, leaving the leaves attached; set cut piece aside.

2. Using a paring or grapefruit knife, remove pineapple from large section in strips, leaving a ½-in. shell; discard core. Cut strips into bite-size chunks. Set aside 2 tablespoons juice from pineapple; invert shell onto paper towel to drain. Remove fruit from the small pineapple piece and cut into chunks; discard peel. Place shell in a large serving bowl or on a serving platter.

3. In a large bowl, combine pineapple chunks, strawberries, orange and banana. In a small bowl, beat cream cheese and reserved pineapple juice; spoon over fruit and stir gently. Spoon into pineapple boat.

HOW TO TELL IF A PINEAPPLE IS RIPE

Since fresh pineapples do not continue to ripen after they are harvested, it's important to know how to identify one that is ripe. Check for ripeness by lifting the pineapple by a single leaf (choose one towards the top). If the leaf comes out of the tuft, it's ripe. Avoid pineapples whose skin is easily dented, which may mean they are overripe. Also, a ripe pineapple should have only a scant light scent. A heavy scent indicates it's overripe.

Mini Spinach Frittatas

Guests can't get enough of these pop-in-your-mouth mini frittatas. They're a cinch to make, freeze well and the recipe easily doubles for a crowd.
—NANCY STATKEVICUS TUCSON, AZ

START TO FINISH: 30 MIN. • **MAKES:** 2 DOZEN

- 1 **cup whole-milk ricotta cheese**
- ¾ **cup grated Parmesan cheese**
- ⅔ **cup chopped fresh mushrooms**
- 1 **package (10 ounces) frozen chopped spinach, thawed and squeezed dry**
- 1 **large egg**
- ½ **teaspoon dried oregano**
- ¼ **teaspoon salt**
- ¼ **teaspoon pepper**
- 24 **slices pepperoni**

1. Preheat oven to 375°. In a small bowl, combine the first eight ingredients. Place a pepperoni slice in each of 24 greased mini-muffin cups; fill three-fourths full with cheese mixture.
2. Bake 20-25 minutes or until completely set. Carefully run a knife around sides of muffin cups to loosen frittatas. Serve warm.

Maple Twist Coffee Cake

If you like maple flavor, you'll want to add this recipe to your "keeper" file. The coffee cake makes a pretty addition to a Christmas morning spread.
—DEANNA RICHTER ELMORE, MN

PREP: 45 MIN. + RISING • **BAKE:** 20 MIN. • **MAKES:** 16 SERVINGS

- 1 **package (¼ ounce) active dry yeast**
- ¾ **cup warm milk (110° to 115°)**
- ¼ **cup butter, softened**
- 3 **tablespoons sugar**
- 1 **large egg**
- 1 **teaspoon maple flavoring**
- ½ **teaspoon salt**
- 2¾ to 3 **cups all-purpose flour**

FILLING
- ½ **cup sugar**
- ⅓ **cup chopped walnuts**
- 1 **teaspoon ground cinnamon**
- 1 **teaspoon maple flavoring**
- ¼ **cup butter, melted**

GLAZE
- 1 **cup confectioners' sugar**
- 2 **tablespoons butter, melted**
- 1 to 2 **tablespoons milk**
- ½ **teaspoon maple flavoring**

1. In a large bowl, dissolve yeast in warm milk. Add the butter, sugar, egg, maple flavoring, salt and 1½ cups flour. Beat until smooth. Stir in enough remaining flour to form a soft dough.
2. Turn onto a floured surface; knead until smooth and elastic, about 6-8 minutes. Place in a greased bowl, turning once to grease top. Cover and let rise in a warm place until doubled, about 1 hour. Meanwhile, in a small bowl, combine the sugar, walnuts, cinnamon and maple flavoring; set aside.
3. Punch dough down. Turn onto a lightly floured surface; divide into thirds. Roll each portion into a 12-in. circle; place one circle on a greased baking sheet or 12-in.

pizza pan. Spread with a third of the butter; sprinkle with a third of the filling. Repeat layers twice. Pinch edges of dough to seal.
4. Carefully place a glass in center of circle. With scissors, cut from outside edge just to the glass, forming 16 wedges. Remove glass; twist each wedge five to six times. Pinch ends to seal and tuck under. Cover and let rise until doubled, about 30 minutes.
5. Bake at 375° for 18-20 minutes or until golden brown. In a small bowl, combine glaze ingredients; set aside. Carefully remove coffee cake from pan by running a metal spatula under it to loosen; transfer to a wire rack. Drizzle with glaze.

Italian Brunch Torte

I serve this impressive layered breakfast bake with a salad of mixed greens and tomato wedges. It's one of my most requested dishes and can be enjoyed warm or cold.

—DANNY DIAMOND
FARMINGTON HILLS, MI

PREP: 50 MIN.
BAKE: 1 HOUR + STANDING
MAKES: 12 SERVINGS

- 2 **tubes (8 ounces each) refrigerated crescent rolls, divided**
- 1 **teaspoon olive oil**
- 1 **package (6 ounces) fresh baby spinach**
- 1 **cup sliced fresh mushrooms**
- 7 **large eggs**
- 1 **cup grated Parmesan cheese**
- 2 **teaspoons Italian seasoning**
- ⅛ **teaspoon pepper**
- ½ **pound thinly sliced deli ham**
- ½ **pound thinly sliced hard salami**
- ½ **pound sliced provolone cheese**
- 2 **jars (12 ounces each) roasted sweet red peppers, drained, sliced and patted dry**

1. Preheat oven to 350°. Place a greased 9-in. springform pan on a double thickness of heavy-duty foil (about 18 in. square). Securely wrap foil around pan. Unroll one tube of crescent dough and separate into triangles. Press onto bottom of prepared pan to form a crust, sealing seams well. Bake crust 10-15 minutes or until set.

2. Meanwhile, in a large skillet, heat oil over medium-high heat. Add spinach and mushrooms; cook and stir until mushrooms are tender. Drain on several layers of paper towels, blotting well. In a large bowl, whisk six eggs, Parmesan cheese, Italian seasoning and pepper.

3. Layer crust with half of each of the following: ham, salami, provolone cheese, red peppers and spinach mixture. Pour half of the egg mixture over top. Repeat the layers; top with the remaining egg mixture.

4. On a work surface, unroll and separate remaining crescent dough into triangles. Press together to form a circle and seal seams; place over filling. Whisk remaining egg; brush over dough.

5. Bake, uncovered, 1 to 1¼ hours or until a thermometer reads 160°, covering loosely with foil if needed to prevent overbrowning. Carefully loosen sides from pan with a knife; remove rim from pan. Let stand 20 minutes.

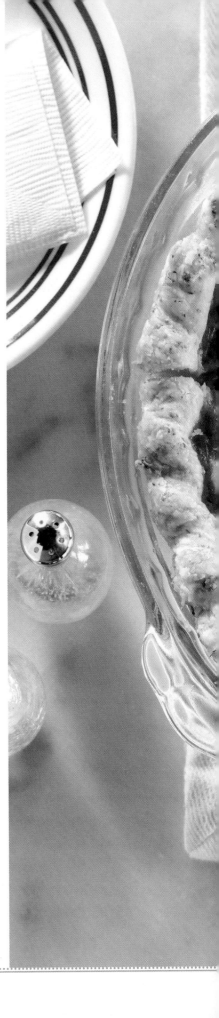

Canadian Bacon Onion Quiche

PICTURED AT RIGHT

For over 20 years, we sold our homegrown specialty onions at our local farmers market. I handed out this classic breakfast quiche recipe to our customers.

—JANICE REDFORD CAMBRIDGE, WI

PREP: 30 MIN. • **BAKE:** 40 MIN. • **MAKES:** 8 SERVINGS

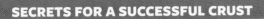

- 1 cup all-purpose flour
- ¾ teaspoon salt, divided
- ½ cup plus 3 tablespoons cold butter, divided
- ½ cup 4% small-curd cottage cheese
- 3 large sweet onions, sliced (about 6 cups)
- 4 ounces Canadian bacon, diced
- ¼ teaspoon pepper
- 3 large eggs, lightly beaten
- 1 cup (4 ounces) shredded cheddar cheese

1. Preheat oven to 350°. In a small bowl, mix flour and ¼ teaspoon salt; cut in ½ cup butter until crumbly. Gradually add cottage cheese, tossing with a fork until dough holds together when pressed. Shape into a disk.

2. On a floured surface, roll dough to a ⅛-in.-thick circle; transfer to a 9-in. pie plate. Trim pastry to ½ in. beyond rim of plate; flute edge.

3. In large skillet, heat remaining butter over medium heat. Add onions; cook and stir until golden brown. Stir in Canadian bacon, pepper and remaining salt. Remove from heat; add eggs and cheddar cheese. Pour mixture into pastry shell.

4. Bake on a lower oven rack 40-45 minutes or until a knife inserted near the center comes out clean. Let stand 10 minutes before cutting.

SECRETS FOR A SUCCESSFUL CRUST

- Measure the ingredients accurately.
- A floured surface is essential to prevent sticking when rolling out the dough. A pastry cloth and rolling pin cover are good investments—they keep the dough from sticking and minimize the amount of flour used. The less flour added while rolling, the lighter and flakier the crust.
- Because of the high fat content in the dough, do not grease the pie plate unless the recipe directs.
- Gently ease the dough into the pie plate. Stretching it will cause it to shrink during baking.
- Never prick the bottom of the crust when the filling and crust will be baked together.
- If the edge of the crust is browning too quickly during baking, shield the edge with a ring of foil.

Banana French Toast Bake

Hamburger buns and bananas unite in this whimsical, make-ahead dish the whole family will love. It's the ultimate holiday breakfast. It's great for dinner, too!

—NANCY ZIMMERMAN
CAPE MAY COURT HOUSE, NJ

PREP: 20 MIN. + CHILLING
BAKE: 55 MIN. + STANDING
MAKES: 8 SERVINGS

- 6 whole wheat hamburger buns
- 1 package (8 ounces) reduced-fat cream cheese, cut into ¾-inch cubes
- 3 medium bananas, sliced
- 6 large eggs
- 4 cups fat-free milk
- ¼ cup sugar
- ¼ cup maple syrup
- ½ teaspoon ground cinnamon

1. Preheat oven to 350°. Cut buns into 1-in. cubes; place half in a 13x9-in. baking dish coated with cooking spray. Layer with cream cheese, bananas and remaining cubed buns.

2. In a large bowl, whisk eggs, milk, sugar, syrup and cinnamon; pour over top. Refrigerate, covered, 8 hours or overnight.

3. Remove from refrigerator 30 minutes before baking. Bake, covered, 30 minutes. Bake, uncovered, 25-30 minutes longer or until a knife inserted near the center comes out clean. Let stand 10 minutes before serving.

Poppy Seed Mini Muffins

Everyone loves the combination of poppy seeds and lemon in these moist muffins. They may be small, but they're always a big hit on a breakfast buffet, as a quick snack or even packed inside a brown-bag lunch.

—KATHY ANDERSON CASPER, WY

PREP: 20 MIN. • **BAKE:** 15 MIN. • **MAKES:** 3½ DOZEN

- 2 cups all-purpose flour
- ¾ cup sugar
- 1 teaspoon baking powder
- 1 teaspoon baking soda
- ¼ teaspoon salt
- 1 cup (8 ounces) sour cream
- 2 large eggs
- ½ cup canola oil
- 2 tablespoons poppy seeds
- 2 tablespoons milk
- ½ teaspoon lemon extract
- ½ teaspoon vanilla extract

1. Preheat oven to 400°. In a large bowl, whisk the first five ingredients. In another bowl, whisk remaining ingredients until blended. Add to flour mixture; stir just until moistened.

2. Fill greased or paper-lined mini-muffin cups two-thirds full. Bake 12-15 minutes or until a toothpick inserted in center comes out clean. Cool 5 minutes before removing from pans to wire racks. Serve warm.

Egg & Sausage Roll-Ups

My tender and flaky phyllo dough roll-ups put a fun twist on traditional breakfast wraps. They make great party fare and are excellent on the go, too.

—MARY LISA SPEER PALM BEACH, FL

PREP: 50 MIN. • **BAKE:** 30 MIN. • **MAKES:** 12 SERVINGS

- 1 pound bulk pork sausage
- 1 cup chopped sweet onion
- 1 garlic clove, minced
- ½ teaspoon pepper, divided
- 8 large eggs
- 3 tablespoons whole milk
- ¼ teaspoon salt
- 1 tablespoon butter
- ¾ cup shredded sharp cheddar cheese
- 3 green onions, chopped
- 15 sheets phyllo dough (14x9 in.)
- ⅓ cup butter, melted

1. In a large skillet, cook sausage, sweet onion, garlic and ¼ teaspoon pepper over medium heat 6-8 minutes or until meat is no longer pink, breaking into crumbles; drain. Remove and keep warm.

2. In a small bowl, whisk eggs, milk, salt and remaining pepper. In same skillet, melt butter over medium-high heat. Pour in egg mixture; cook and stir until almost set. Stir in cheese, green onions and sausage mixture. Remove from heat.

3. Preheat oven to 350°. Place one sheet of phyllo dough on a work surface; brush with melted butter. Layer with four additional phyllo sheets, brushing with butter after each layer. (Keep remaining phyllo covered with plastic wrap and a damp towel to prevent it from drying out.) Repeat, making three stacks.

4. Cut each stack in half lengthwise and in half crosswise, forming four 7x4½-in. rectangles. Spoon ¼ cup egg mixture along a long side of each rectangle; roll up.

5. Place on an ungreased baking sheet, seam side down. With a sharp knife, make four shallow slashes across each roll; brush with butter. Bake 30-35 minutes or until golden brown.

Pumpkin-Pecan Baked Oatmeal

Here's a delectable wintertime treat. My husband rarely eats in the morning, but when I make my baked oatmeal around the holidays, he can't wait to dig right in.
—**ALEX MUEHL** AUSTIN, TX

PREP: 15 MIN. + CHILLING
BAKE: 30 MIN. • **MAKES:** 6 SERVINGS

- 2 **large eggs**
- 3 **cups quick-cooking oats**
- 1 **can (15 ounces) solid-pack pumpkin**
- 1 **cup 2% milk**
- ¾ **cup packed brown sugar**
- ½ **cup dried cranberries**
- ⅓ **cup butter, melted**
- 1½ **teaspoons baking powder**
- 1 **teaspoon vanilla extract**
- ½ **teaspoon ground nutmeg**
- ¼ **teaspoon salt**
- ¼ **teaspoon ground cloves**
- ¼ **cup chopped pecans**
  Additional 2% milk and brown sugar

1. In a large bowl, combine the first 12 ingredients. Transfer to a greased 11x7-in. baking dish. Refrigerate, covered, 8 hours or overnight.

2. Remove oatmeal from refrigerator 30 minutes before baking. Preheat oven to 350°. Uncover and stir oatmeal; sprinkle with pecans. Bake, uncovered, 30-35 minutes or until a thermometer reads 160°. Serve warm with additional milk and brown sugar.

Strawberries with Chocolate Cream Filling

These party-pretty bites are as easy to make as they are delicious. Try them as a refreshing fruit appetizer for a Christmas morning brunch.
—**LISA HUFF** WILTON, CT

START TO FINISH: 30 MIN. • **MAKES:** 3 DOZEN

- 1½ **ounces semisweet chocolate, grated, divided**
- 1 **package (8 ounces) cream cheese, softened**
- 1 **teaspoon vanilla extract**
- 1 **cup whipped topping**
- 18 **large fresh strawberries, halved**

1. Set aside 2 tablespoons chocolate. In a microwave, melt remaining chocolate; stir until smooth. Cool.

2. In a small bowl, beat cream cheese and vanilla until smooth. Beat in the melted chocolate. Fold in the whipped topping and 1 tablespoon grated chocolate. Cut a small hole in the tip of a pastry bag or in the corner of a food-safe plastic bag; insert #21 star pastry tip. Fill the bag with cream cheese mixture.

3. Place strawberries on a serving platter, cut side up. Pipe cream cheese mixture onto strawberries. Sprinkle with remaining grated chocolate. Refrigerate leftovers.

A re you ready for the sweetest Christmas ever? Forget the fruitcake in favor of some truly delectable confections.

There's no better way to nourish the holiday spirit than with a well-stocked goodie tray. Deck yours with Rum Raisin Truffles and Chocolate-Dipped Meringue Sandwich Cookies that look almost too pretty to eat. Need a festive centerpiece? Turn to page 87, and see how easy it is to put together an elegant treat tower to show off Cookies and Cream Banana Cupcakes.

If you're craving a simple Christmas dinner dessert, Berries & Cream Trifles are your answer. Feel like something fun and bite-size? Give Toffee Cheesecake Pops a whirl. Sweet tooths of all ages will love them!

CHRISTMAS CONFECTIONS

White Chocolate Mousse with Pomegranate Sauce

A luscious pomegranate sauce and a sprinkling of seeds add a festive touch to this elegant mousse served in a cone made of chocolate. It's lovely for romantic occasions, too.
—**JOANN MATHIAS** HOSCHTON, GA

PREP: 1 HOUR + CHILLING
COOK: 15 MIN. + CHILLING
MAKES: 8 SERVINGS

- ¾ **cup unsalted butter, cubed**
- 1 **package (12 ounces) white baking chips**
- 2 **cups heavy whipping cream, divided**
- ¾ **cup sugar**
- 5 **large egg yolks, lightly beaten**
- 1 **envelope unflavored gelatin**
- ⅓ **cup cold water**

CHOCOLATE CONES
- **Parchment paper**
- 9 **ounces bittersweet chocolate, melted**

SAUCE
- 2 **tablespoons cornstarch**
- ¼ **cup cold water**
- 1 **bottle (16 ounces) pomegranate juice**
- ½ **cup pomegranate seeds**

1. In a large saucepan, combine butter, baking chips, ¾ cup cream and sugar; cook and stir over low heat until smooth and sugar is dissolved. In a small bowl, whisk a small amount of hot mixture into egg yolks; return all to pan. Cook and stir 2 minutes or until mixture is slightly thickened. Remove from the heat.

2. In a large bowl, sprinkle gelatin over cold water; let stand 1 minute. Add a small amount of hot white chocolate mixture; stir until gelatin is dissolved. Stir in remaining white chocolate mixture. Place bowl in a pan of ice water; stir occasionally until mixture is thickened, about 30 minutes.

3. In another bowl, beat remaining 1¼ cups cream until soft peaks form. Add a third of the whipped cream to the chilled white chocolate mixture; beat on low speed just until blended. Fold in remaining whipped cream. Refrigerate, covered, at least 30 minutes or until serving.

4. For chocolate cones, make eight paper cones to coat with chocolate. Cut four 8-in. circles from parchment paper; cut each circle in half. Form each into a 3-in.-wide cone, overlapping edges and being sure the cone is closed at the pointed end.

5. Brush about half of the melted chocolate on the inside of the paper cones, beginning at the seam. Stand cones upright in champagne flutes or narrow drinking glasses; refrigerate until set, about 5 minutes. Add a second coat of chocolate; refrigerate until serving.

6. For sauce, in a small saucepan, whisk cornstarch and water until blended; stir in pomegranate juice. Bring to a boil; cook and stir 1-2 minutes or until thickened. Cool completely.

7. To serve, spoon sauce onto dessert plates. Carefully peel parchment paper from chocolate cones. Fill cones with mousse; arrange carefully over sauce. Sprinkle with pomegranate seeds.

Family-Favorite Cinnamon Candy

I have fond memories of standing at my grandmother's stove with my mom and my aunts, helping to make this cherished recipe. Now I share the tradition with my kids.
—**WENDY HAGAN** OAK GROVE, LA

PREP: 10 MIN. • **COOK:** 40 MIN. + COOLING • **MAKES:** 3½ POUNDS

- 1 **tablespoon butter**
- 3¾ **cups sugar**
- 1¼ **cups light corn syrup**
- 1 **cup water**
- 3 **packages (6 ounces each) Red Hots**
- ¼ **cup confectioners' sugar**

1. Grease two 15x10x1-in. pans with butter.

2. In a large heavy saucepan, combine sugar, corn syrup and water. Bring to a boil over medium heat, stirring constantly to dissolve sugar. Add Red Hots; return to a boil, stirring carefully until Red Hots are melted, about 10 minutes. (Mixture will be very hot; wear an oven mitt while stirring to prevent burns.) Cook, without stirring, until a candy thermometer reads 300° (hard-crack stage).

3. Remove from heat. Immediately divide mixture between prepared pans; cool completely, about 1 hour.

4. Break candy into pieces. Place confectioners' sugar in a large resealable bag. In batches, add candy and toss to coat lightly.

NOTE *We recommend that you test your candy thermometer before each use by bringing water to a boil; the thermometer should read 212°. Adjust your recipe temperature up or down based on your test.*

Cherry Cordial Creme Brulee

Dazzle your family this Christmas with the queen of all desserts—creme brulee. A chocolate-covered cherry in each ramekin is a regal surprise.
—**TERESA BILLINGS** PLAIN CITY, UT

PREP: 45 MIN. • **BAKE:** 50 MIN. + CHILLING • **MAKES:** 8 SERVINGS

- 4 **cups heavy whipping cream**
- 10 **large egg yolks**
- ½ **cup plus 2 tablespoons sugar, divided**
- 1 **teaspoon vanilla extract**
- 8 **dark chocolate-covered cherries**
- 2 **tablespoons brown sugar**

1. Preheat oven to 325°. In a large saucepan, heat cream until bubbles form around sides of pan; remove from heat. In a large bowl, whisk egg yolks and ½ cup sugar until blended but not foamy. Slowly stir in hot cream. Stir in vanilla.

2. Place eight 6-oz. broiler-safe ramekins in a baking pan large enough to hold them without touching. Place a cherry in each ramekin. Pour egg mixture over cherries. Place pan on oven rack; add very hot water to pan to within ½ in. of top of ramekins. Bake 50-60 minutes or until a knife inserted near the center comes out clean; centers will still be soft. Immediately remove ramekins from water bath to a wire rack; cool 10 minutes. Refrigerate until cold.

3. In a small bowl, mix brown sugar and remaining sugar. To caramelize topping with a kitchen torch, sprinkle custards evenly with sugar mixture. Hold torch flame about 2 in. above custard surface and rotate it slowly until sugar is evenly caramelized. Serve immediately or refrigerate up to 1 hour.

4. To caramelize topping in a broiler, place ramekins on a baking sheet; let stand at room temperature 15 minutes. Preheat broiler. Sprinkle custards evenly with sugar mixture. Broil 3-4 in. from heat 1-2 minutes or until sugar is caramelized. Serve creme brulee immediately or refrigerate up to 1 hour.

Chocolate-Dipped Meringue Sandwich Cookies

These light, airy morsels are twice as nice with two meringue cookies and velvety ganache in between.
—DONNA POCHODAY-STELMACH MORRISTOWN, NJ

PREP: 1 HOUR + CHILLING
BAKE: 40 MIN./BATCH + STANDING • **MAKES:** 7 DOZEN

4 **large egg whites**
1 **cup confectioners' sugar**
½ **cup almond flour**
⅔ **cup sugar**
GANACHE
6 **ounces semisweet chocolate, chopped**
3 **ounces unsweetened chocolate, chopped**
1¼ **cups heavy whipping cream**
1 **tablespoon light corn syrup**
TOPPINGS
¾ **cup colored sprinkles**
¾ **cup crushed peppermint candies**

1. Place egg whites in a large bowl; let stand at room temperature 30 minutes.
2. Preheat oven to 225°. In a bowl, whisk confectioners' sugar and almond flour until blended. Beat egg whites on medium speed until foamy. Gradually add ⅔ cup sugar, 1 tablespoon at a time, beating on high after each addition until sugar is dissolved. Continue beating until stiff glossy peaks form. Fold in confectioners' sugar mixture.
3. Cut a small hole in the tip of a pastry bag or in a corner of a food-safe plastic bag; insert #805 round pastry tip. Fill bag with meringue. Pipe 1-in. diameter cookies 1 in. apart onto parchment paper-lined baking sheets. Using a finger moistened with water, smooth the tops of the cookies.
4. Bake 40-45 minutes or until firm to the touch. Turn oven off

(do not open oven door); leave cookies in oven for 1 hour. Remove from oven; cool completely on baking sheets.
5. For ganache, place semisweet and unsweetened chocolate in a small bowl. In a small saucepan, combine cream and corn syrup; bring just to a boil. Pour over chocolate; stir with a whisk until smooth. Remove 1 cup ganache to another bowl; refrigerate 25-30 minutes or until mixture is thick enough to pipe, stirring occasionally. Reserve remaining ganache for dipping; let stand, covered, at room temperature, stirring occasionally.
6. Cut a small hole in the tip of a pastry bag or in a corner of a food-safe plastic bag; insert #802 round pastry tip. Fill bag with chilled ganache. Pipe onto bottoms of half of the cookies; cover with remaining cookies. (Ganache may soften as it warms. If necessary, return ganache to refrigerator until it is firm enough to pipe.)
7. Place toppings in separate shallow bowls. Dip each sandwich cookie halfway in room temperature ganache; allow excess to drip off. (If necessary, warm ganache in microwave for 10 seconds to thin slightly.) Dip in toppings as desired; place on waxed paper and let stand until set. Store in airtight containers at room temperature.

Fresh Orange Soft Custard

When sweet, juicy honeybells or tangelos are in season, it's time to make this refreshing orange custard, which brings a little sunshine to our cold winter days.
—**SUZANNE KESEL** COHOCTON, NY

PREP: 20 MIN.
COOK: 20 MIN. + CHILLING
MAKES: 10 SERVINGS

1 **cup sugar**
½ **cup cornstarch**
¼ **teaspoon salt**
3 **cups orange juice**
6 **large egg yolks**
¼ **cup butter, cubed**
2 **cups plain yogurt**
4 **teaspoons grated orange peel**
1 **cup orange sections (about 2 medium oranges)**

1. In a large saucepan, mix sugar, cornstarch and salt; gradually stir in orange juice until smooth. Cook and stir over medium heat until thickened and bubbly. Reduce heat to low; cook and stir 2 minutes longer. Remove from the heat.

2. In a small bowl, whisk a small amount of hot mixture into egg yolks; return all to pan, whisking constantly. Bring to a gentle boil; cook and stir 2 minutes. Remove from heat; stir in butter, yogurt and orange peel. Cool slightly.

3. Spoon into 10 dessert dishes. Refrigerate, covered, at least 2 hours. Top with orange sections just before serving.

Berries & Cream Trifles

Layers of cubed cake, berries and a creamy ricotta mixture make up these pretty trifles that taste as rich as cheesecake.
—**JOAN DUCKWORTH** LEE'S SUMMIT, MO

PREP: 30 MIN. • **COOK:** 10 MIN. + CHILLING • **MAKES:** 8 SERVINGS

- 2 **cups fresh or frozen cranberries**
- 1 **cup fresh or frozen blueberries**
- ½ **cup sugar**
- ½ **cup water**
- 1 **cup whole-milk ricotta cheese**
- 4 **ounces cream cheese, cubed and softened**
- ¼ **cup confectioners' sugar**
- ½ **teaspoon vanilla extract**
- 1 **loaf (10¾ ounces) frozen pound cake, thawed and cut into ½-in. cubes**

1. In a small saucepan, combine cranberries, blueberries, sugar and water; bring to a boil, stirring to dissolve sugar. Reduce heat; simmer, uncovered, 5 minutes. Transfer to a small bowl; cool completely. Refrigerate, covered, at least 1 hour or until cold.

2. Place ricotta cheese, cream cheese, confectioners' sugar and vanilla in a small food processor. Process until smooth.

3. In each of eight parfait glasses, layer 1 tablespoon berry sauce, ⅓ cup cake cubes, 2 tablespoons ricotta mixture and 2 tablespoons berry sauce. Repeat cake and cheese layers; top with 1 tablespoon berry sauce. Refrigerate, covered, until serving or up to 2 hours.

Chocolate Fudge with Hazelnut

My husband loves peanut butter fudge, and I love chocolate fudge. Hazelnut spread boasts both a cocoa and nut flavor, so now we finally have a fudge we can enjoy together.
—**AMY REASONER** OZARK, MO

PREP: 10 MIN. • **COOK:** 10 MIN. + CHILLING • **MAKES:** ABOUT 2½ POUNDS (64 PIECES)

- 1 **teaspoon butter**
- ½ **cup butter, cubed**
- 2 **cups packed brown sugar**
- ½ **cup whole milk**
- 1 **cup Nutella**
- 1 **teaspoon vanilla extract**
- 3 **cups confectioners' sugar**
- ½ **cup chopped hazelnuts, optional**

1. Line an 8-in.-square pan with foil; grease foil with 1 teaspoon butter.

2. In a large saucepan, combine cubed butter, brown sugar and milk. Bring to a full boil over medium heat, stirring constantly. Cook 2 minutes, stirring frequently. Remove from heat.

3. Stir in Nutella and vanilla; transfer to a large bowl. Add confectioners' sugar; beat on medium speed 2 minutes or until smooth. Immediately spread into prepared pan. If desired, sprinkle with hazelnuts. Refrigerate, covered, 1 hour or until firm.

FUDGE PARTY FAVORS

Cookie cutters filled with fudge make a festive party favor for guests at your holiday gathering. Wrap them in cellophane and tie with a ribbon. Don't forget to attach a copy of the recipe!

Fritters with Lemon Mousse and Strawberries

Deep-fried fritters are wonderful on their own but become over-the-top amazing with a creamy lemon mousse and sweet strawberries. Raspberries and blueberries yield equally good results.
—**SHANNON BELL** WOODSTOCK, GA

PREP: 1 HOUR + CHILLING • **COOK:** 5 MIN./BATCH • **MAKES:** 10 SERVINGS

2 large egg yolks
¼ cup sugar
¼ cup lemon juice
1½ cups heavy whipping cream
¼ cup confectioners' sugar

TOPPING
1 cup sliced fresh strawberries
1 tablespoon honey
¼ teaspoon sugar

FRITTERS
1 cup all-purpose flour
1 tablespoon sugar
1 teaspoon baking powder
½ teaspoon salt
1 large egg
½ cup 2% milk
1 tablespoon butter, melted
2 teaspoons grated orange peel
Oil for deep-fat frying

1. In a small heavy saucepan, whisk egg yolks, sugar and lemon juice until blended. Cook over medium-low heat, whisking constantly, until thickened and a thermometer reads at least 170°. Do not allow to boil. Immediately remove from heat. Transfer to a small bowl; cool 10 minutes. Refrigerate, covered, at least 30 minutes or until cold.

2. In a large bowl, beat cream until it begins to thicken. Add confectioners' sugar; beat until soft peaks form. Fold into lemon mixture. Refrigerate, covered, until serving.

3. For topping, in a small bowl, toss strawberries with honey and sugar. Let stand until juices are released from strawberries.

4. For fritters, in a large bowl, whisk flour, sugar, baking powder and salt. In another bowl, whisk egg, milk, melted butter and orange peel until blended. Add to dry ingredients, stirring just until moistened.

5. In an electric skillet or deep fryer, heat oil to 375°. Drop batter by tablespoonfuls, a few at a time, into hot oil. Fry 1-2 minutes on each side or until golden brown. Drain on paper towels.

6. To serve, spoon mousse into dessert dishes; top with strawberries. Serve with fritters.

Walnut Caramels

My grandmother was the queen of care packages. The Christmas season didn't start until the mail carrier arrived with her anticipated box of goodies. These caramels are my father's favorite.
—**ELISABETH LARSEN** PLEASANT GROVE, UT

PREP: 10 MIN. • **COOK:** 25 MIN. + STANDING • **MAKES:** 3¾ POUNDS (117 PIECES)

2 teaspoons butter
⅓ cup butter, cubed
2 cups sugar
2 cups heavy whipping cream, divided
1 cup light corn syrup
1½ cups chopped walnuts
1 teaspoon vanilla extract

1. Line a 13x9-in. pan with foil; grease foil with 2 teaspoons butter.

2. In a large heavy saucepan, combine cubed butter, sugar, 1 cup cream and corn syrup. Cook and stir over medium heat until a candy thermometer reads 238° (soft-ball stage). Stir in remaining cream very slowly so that mixture does not stop boiling.

3. Using a pastry brush dipped in water, wash down the sides of the pan to eliminate sugar crystals. Cook and stir until thermometer reads 245° (firm-ball stage).

4. Remove from heat; stir in walnuts and vanilla. Immediately pour into prepared pan (do not scrape saucepan). Let stand until firm, about 5 hours or overnight.

5. Using foil, lift candy out of pan; remove foil. Using a buttered knife, cut caramel into 1-in. squares. Wrap individually in waxed paper; twist ends.

NOTE *We recommend that you test your candy thermometer before each use by bringing water to a boil; the thermometer should read 212°. Adjust your recipe temperature up or down based on your test.*

Toffee Cheesecake Pops

PICTURED AT RIGHT

Goodbye, sticky fingers! Everyone adores food on a stick, and these cute pops combine that novelty with the fabulous flavors of cheesecake and toffee.

—LAURALEE ENGLEHART FREDERICTON, NB

PREP: 55 MIN. + FREEZING • **BAKE:** 40 MIN. + CHILLING • **MAKES:** ABOUT 6½ DOZEN

3 packages (8 ounces each)
  cream cheese, softened
¾ cup sugar
3 teaspoons vanilla extract
3 large eggs, lightly beaten
2 packages (8 ounces each)
  brickle toffee bits, divided
80 lollipop sticks (4 inches long)
1¾ pounds dark chocolate candy
  coating, melted

1. Preheat oven to 350°. Coat bottom and sides of a 9-in. springform pan with cooking spray.

2. In a large bowl, beat cream cheese and sugar until smooth. Beat in vanilla until blended. Add eggs; beat on low speed just until blended. Fold in one package of toffee bits. Pour into prepared pan; place on a baking sheet. Bake 40-45 minutes or until center is almost set. Cool on a wire rack 10 minutes. Loosen sides from pan with a knife. Cool 1 hour longer. Refrigerate overnight, covering when completely cooled.

3. Shape cheesecake mixture into eighty 1-in. balls (about 1 tablespoon each); insert a lollipop stick in each. Place on waxed paper-lined baking sheets. Freeze 1 hour or until firm.

4. Place remaining bag of toffee bits in a small bowl. Dip pops in melted candy coating; allow excess to drip off. Dip tops in toffee bits. Place on waxed paper-lined baking sheets; let stand until set. Store in airtight containers in the refrigerator.

Chocolate-Dipped Peanut Nougat

With crunchy peanuts and fluffy marshmallow creme, these sweet sensations are great to include on a holiday dessert tray or to give as gifts. I swirl in green and red food coloring for a festive touch.

—EMILY HANSON LOGAN, UT

PREP: 40 MIN. • **COOK:** 20 MIN. + STANDING • **MAKES:** ABOUT 4½ POUNDS (ABOUT 150 PIECES)

1 tablespoon butter
1 jar (16 ounces) dry roasted
  peanuts
3 jars (7 ounces each)
  marshmallow creme
2¼ cups sugar
2¼ cups corn syrup
6 tablespoons butter, cubed
1½ teaspoons vanilla extract
¼ teaspoon salt
1 to 1½ pounds dark or milk
  chocolate candy coating,
  melted

1. Line a 15x10x1-in. pan with foil, letting ends extend over sides by 1 in.; grease foil with 1 tablespoon butter. Sprinkle peanuts evenly into pan.

2. Place marshmallow creme in a large heatproof bowl. In a large heavy saucepan, combine sugar and corn syrup. Bring to a boil over medium heat, stirring constantly to dissolve sugar. Using a pastry brush dipped in water, wash down the sides of the pan to eliminate sugar crystals. Cook, without stirring, until a candy thermometer reads 280° (soft-crack stage), about 10 minutes.

3. Remove from heat; cool 2 minutes. Pour over marshmallow creme (do not scrape saucepan). Stir in cubed butter, vanilla and salt. Immediately pour mixture over peanuts in pan, spreading

evenly. Let stand at least 3 hours or until set.

4. Using foil, lift candy out of pan. Gently peel off foil. With a greased knife, cut candy into 1-in. squares.

5. Dip candy into melted candy coating; allow excess to drip off. Place on waxed paper-lined baking sheets; refrigerate until set. Store between layers of waxed paper in airtight containers.

NOTE *We recommend that you test your candy thermometer before each use by bringing water to a boil; the thermometer should read 212°. Adjust your recipe temperature up or down based on your test.*

Rum Raisin Truffles

I entered a state fair culinary challenge and earned a ribbon for these rum-flavored truffles. Now I like to treat the chocolate lovers on my list by including them on my Christmas dessert platter. The divine little bites get enthusiastic reviews.
—GERRY COFTA MILWAUKEE, WI

PREP: 40 MIN. + CHILLING • **COOK:** 5 MIN. + COOLING • **MAKES:** ABOUT 2½ DOZEN

3 tablespoons raisins, finely chopped
3 tablespoons golden raisins, finely chopped
2 tablespoons rum
12 ounces milk chocolate, very finely chopped
⅓ cup heavy whipping cream
Baking cocoa

COATING
12 ounces milk chocolate, chopped
1 tablespoon shortening

1. In a microwave-safe bowl, toss all raisins with rum. Microwave, covered, on high for 30 seconds; cool slightly.

2. Place chocolate in a shallow bowl. In a small heavy saucepan, heat cream just to a boil. Pour over chocolate; let stand 2 minutes. Stir until smooth, then stir in raisins. Press plastic wrap onto surface of chocolate mixture. Cool to room temperature or until firm enough to shape.

3. With cocoa-dusted hands, shape chocolate mixture into 1-in. balls. Place on a waxed paper-lined 15x10x1-in. baking pan. Refrigerate until very firm, about 30 minutes.

4. For coating, in top of a double boiler or a metal bowl over barely simmering water, melt chocolate and shortening; stir until smooth. Dip truffles in chocolate mixture; allow excess to drip off. Place on a waxed paper-lined 15x10x1-in. baking pan. Refrigerate until set. Store in an airtight container.

NOTE *This recipe was tested with Ghirardelli Milk Chocolate Baking Bars; results may vary when using a different product.*

Cookies and Cream Banana Cupcakes

PICTURED AT RIGHT

It's become an annual tradition that my sister and I get together to make these kid-friendly cupcakes with her son as our taster and helper.
—ALINA BANNAVONG AMARILLO, TX

PREP: 30 MIN. • **BAKE:** 20 MIN. + COOLING • **MAKES:** 2 DOZEN

1 package white cake mix (regular size)
3 medium ripe bananas, mashed
1 cup water
3 large egg whites
10 Oreo cookies, coarsely chopped

TOPPINGS
1 cup white baking chips
2 tablespoons heavy whipping cream
1 tablespoon butter
10 Oreo cookies, coarsely chopped
½ cup milk chocolate chips
2 teaspoons shortening

1. Preheat oven to 350°. Line 24 muffin cups with paper or silicone liners. In a large bowl, combine cake mix, bananas, water and egg whites; beat on low speed 30 seconds. Beat on medium 2 minutes. Fold in chopped cookies.

2. Fill prepared cups three-fourths full. Bake 20-25 minutes or until a toothpick inserted in center comes out clean. Cool in pans 10 minutes before removing to wire racks to cool completely.

3. In a microwave-safe bowl, combine baking chips, cream and butter; microwave on high for 30-60 seconds or until smooth, stirring occasionally. Dip tops of cupcakes into baking chip mixture. Top cupcakes with chopped cookies. Let stand until set.

4. In a small microwave-safe bowl, melt milk chocolate chips and shortening; stir until smooth. Drizzle over cupcakes.

Holiday Treat Tower

Add a chic pop of color to your holiday tablescape by decorating and stacking simple cake stands for a dramatic tiered effect. This tower makes it easy and fun to showcase cupcakes, candies and other confections in a festive style.

MATERIALS

- 2 porcelain or ceramic square cake stands (1 medium, 1 large)
- 4-6 strips self-adhesive 3-in.-wide decorative tape (we used Tape Works™)
- 2 long strips self-adhesive 1-in.-wide decorative tape (we used Tape Works™)
- 2 long strips self-adhesive ½-in.-wide ribbon or braided trim (we used Stick-A-Bilities)
- Craft knife
- Glue gun, optional

DIRECTIONS

1. Adhere 2-3 strips of 3-in.-wide self-adhesive decorative tape to the top of each cake stand, overlapping the strips slightly to prevent gaps. Flip stands over and trim with a craft knife for a clean edge.

2. Measure strips of 1-in. self-adhesive decorative tape to fit around the rim of each stand. Adhere.

3. Measure strips of ½-in.-wide self-adhesive ribbon or trim to fit around each stand. Adhere over 1-in.-wide tape. Hot-glue to secure if needed.

4. Stack 1 cake stand on top of the other to make a tower. Add cupcakes, cookies or confections with coordinating decorative packaging or trims.

giving thanks

When we think of Thanksgiving, the centerpiece turkey quickly comes to mind. But a memorable holiday meal is also made up of a variety of side dishes, desserts, traditions and hospitality. And while we take comfort in the familiar, it's fun to stumble on a new recipe or ritual. With delicious items like Cape Cod Corn Pudding, Spiced Sweet Potato Soup and Butterscotch Pie with Walnut-Bacon Toffee, everyone is sure to find a new favorite.

Festive gatherings should be fun for everyone, including the hostess. But pulling together a holiday dinner with all the trimmings can be daunting, even for the most experienced cook.

This year, try a menu that's simple and special. The recipes here will result in an impressive Thanksgiving dinner but they are easy enough to make that you'll have time to enjoy the day.

You can prepare some dishes ahead; others you should make the day of. Use the timeline on p. 92 to plan your menu preparation and get a jump on the big day.

Armed with the best bird, stress-free sides, kid-friendly foods, and vegetarian selections, your Turkey Day will be as easy as pie!

Cheddar Corn Biscuits (p. 102)
Southern Green Beans with Apricots (p. 98)
Fruit-Glazed Roast Turkey (p. 94)

A FAMILY-STYLE
THANKSGIVING

giving thanks
A FAMILY-STYLE THANKSGIVING TIMELINE

A FEW WEEKS BEFORE

- Set the menu and organize recipes. Write two grocery lists: one of nonperishables to buy now and one for perishable items to buy a few days before Thanksgiving Day.

- Bake the Autumn Pumpkin Cupcakes, but don't frost. Cool completely, store in an airtight container, then freeze.

ONE DAY BEFORE

- Make the dressing for the Apple & Ginger Tossed Salad; cover and chill until serving.

- Prepare the Creamy Bacon-Cheddar Spread and the cranberry mixture for the Cranberry Fluff Salad. Cover and chill separately.

- Make the Creamy Pumpkin Pie but don't garnish with whipped cream; cover and chill until serving.

- Bake the Chewy Choco-Caramel Squares; don't cut into bars; cover with foil.

- Set the table and arrange flowers or centerpieces.

THANKSGIVING DAY

- In the morning, thaw the cupcakes. Prepare the Spiced Sweet Potato Soup and place in the slow cooker. Bake the Cheddar Corn Biscuits; cool completely and cover.

- Prepare the glaze for the turkey. Place the turkey in the oven and start the Buttermilk Smashed Potatoes.

- About two hours before the turkey is done, prepare the Herbed Apple-Cranberry Bread Dressing and Lasagna-Style Spaghetti Squash.

- Just before guests arrive, mix together the Favorite Berry Punch, cut caramel squares in bars and finish the Cranberry Fluff Salad.

- Thirty minutes before serving, prepare the Southern Green Beans with Apricots.

- Just before serving, assemble the salad and add dressing. Frost the cupcakes and garnish the pumpkin pie. Place biscuits in a warm oven for 2-3 minutes to re-heat.

Buttermilk Smashed Potatoes

My family loves this decadent homestyle recipe of buttermilk, potatoes and butter.
Serve with your favorite toppings and enjoy!
—**MARLA CLARK** ALBUQUERQUE, NM

START TO FINISH: 30 MIN. • **MAKES:** 8 SERVINGS

- 4 **pounds Yukon Gold potatoes, peeled and cubed (about 8 cups)**
- ½ **cup butter, softened**
- 1¼ **teaspoons salt**
- ¼ **teaspoon pepper**
- ¾ **to 1 cup buttermilk**
  Optional toppings: crumbled cooked bacon, sour cream and thinly sliced green onions

1. Place potatoes in a 6-qt. stockpot; add water to cover. Bring to a boil. Reduce heat; cook, uncovered, 10-15 minutes or until tender.

2. Drain; return to pan. Mash potatoes, gradually adding butter, salt, pepper and enough buttermilk to reach desired consistency. Serve with toppings as desired.

PEELING POTATOES

Cut each potato in half before peeling. That way, you'll know if one has gone bad inside before going through the trouble of peeling the entire potato.

Fruit-Glazed Roast Turkey

Apple, cranberry and raspberry flavors blend with fresh herbs in a tangy glaze for the roasted turkey. It's a welcome change to a traditional entree.
—**AYSHA SCHURMAN** AMMON, ID

PREP: 20 MIN. • **BAKE:** 2½ HOURS
MAKES: 14 SERVINGS

- ¼ **cup unsweetened applesauce**
- ¼ **cup whole-berry cranberry sauce**
- ¼ **cup fresh raspberries**
- 2 **tablespoons orange juice**
- 2 **tablespoons olive oil**
- 1 **tablespoon molasses**
- 1 **tablespoon fresh parsley leaves**
- 1 **tablespoon fresh cilantro leaves**
- 1 **teaspoon pepper**
- ½ **teaspoon salt**
- 1 **turkey (14 to 16 pounds)**

1. Preheat oven to 400°. Place the first 10 ingredients in a blender; cover and process until blended. Place turkey on a rack in a shallow roasting pan, breast side up. Tuck wings under turkey; tie drumsticks together. Roast, uncovered, 1 hour.

2. Reduce oven setting to 325°. Brush turkey with half of the glaze. Roast 1½ to 2 hours longer or until a thermometer inserted in thickest part of thigh reads 170°-175°, brushing turkey with remaining glaze during the last 45 minutes. (Cover loosely with foil if turkey browns too quickly.)

3. Remove turkey from oven; tent with foil. Let stand 20 minutes before carving.

Cranberry Fluff Salad

It wasn't Thanksgiving without my grandmother's cool and tangy cranberry fluff.
With only four ingredients, it's a cinch to make. Now my siblings and I carry on her tradition.
—**LEAH NICHOLES** SAN DIEGO, CA

PREP: 10 MIN. + CHILLING • **MAKES:** 10 SERVINGS

1 package (12 ounces) fresh or frozen cranberries, thawed
2 cups sugar
1 cup chopped pecans, toasted
2 cups heavy whipping cream

1. Place cranberries in a food processor; pulse until coarsely chopped. Transfer to a large bowl; stir in sugar. Refrigerate, covered, at least 2 hours.

2. Just before serving, stir pecans into cranberry mixture. In a large bowl, beat cream until soft peaks form; fold into mixture.

Creamy Bacon-Cheddar Spread

My mom was famous for her bacon dip. It looks complicated but comes together in a snap.
Spread it on celery sticks or form it into a fancy shape and serve it with crackers on the side.
—**LYNETTE ABDERHALDEN** SALEM, OR

PREP: 15 MIN. + CHILLING • **MAKES:** 2 CUPS

1 package (8 ounces) cream cheese, softened
1 cup (4 ounces) shredded cheddar cheese
½ cup Miracle Whip
4 bacon strips, cooked and crumbled

¼ cup chopped almonds
2 tablespoons chopped fresh parsley
1 teaspoon Worcestershire sauce
½ teaspoon onion powder
Celery sticks and crackers

In a small bowl, beat the first eight ingredients. Refrigerate, covered, at least 1 hour before serving. Serve with celery and crackers.

Apple & Ginger Tossed Salad

Looking for an easy Thanksgiving salad that's full of flavor? This zippy medley combines
crisp apples and crystallized ginger with leafy greens and crunchy pecans.
—**LYNNETTE BRADLEY** RIVERBANK, CA

START TO FINISH: 15 MIN. • **MAKES:** 8 SERVINGS (⅔ CUP DRESSING)

½ cup mayonnaise
2 tablespoons apple juice
1 tablespoon sugar
1 tablespoon white balsamic vinegar
1 package (10 ounces) Italian-blend salad greens

2 medium apples, chopped
1 cup pecan halves, toasted
¼ cup chopped crystallized ginger

In a small bowl, mix mayonnaise, apple juice, sugar and vinegar until blended. In large bowl, combine salad greens, apples, pecans and ginger. Serve with dressing.

TO MAKE AHEAD *Dressing can be made a day in advance; cover and refrigerate.*

Lasagna-Style Spaghetti Squash

My lasagna-inspired spaghetti squash is a meatless alternative to the famed bird. It's great for vegetarians or anyone who craves something on the lighter side.

—JENNY LOFTHUS GOLETA, CA

PREP: 30 MIN. • **COOK:** 15 MIN. • **MAKES:** 6 SERVINGS

- 1 small spaghetti squash (about 2 pounds)
- 1 tablespoon olive oil
- ½ teaspoon salt
- ¼ teaspoon pepper
- 2 cups marinara sauce
- 2 cups (16 ounces) 2% cottage cheese
- 1 package (10 ounces) frozen chopped spinach, thawed and squeezed dry
- 2 medium tomatoes, chopped
- ¼ cup chopped fresh basil
- ¼ cup grated Parmesan cheese
  Additional grated Parmesan cheese and chopped fresh basil, optional

1. Cut squash lengthwise in half; remove and discard seeds. Place squash on a microwave-safe plate, cut side down. Microwave, uncovered, on high 16-18 minutes or until tender.

2. When squash is cool enough to handle, use a fork to separate strands; transfer to a microwave-safe dish. Drizzle with oil; sprinkle with salt and pepper and toss to coat. Stir in marinara sauce, cottage cheese, spinach, tomatoes, basil and Parmesan cheese.

3. Cook, covered, on high 14-16 minutes or until heated through. If desired, sprinkle with additional Parmesan cheese and basil.

NOTE *This recipe was tested in a 1,100-watt microwave.*

CUTTING WINTER SQUASH

Like acorn squash, butternut squash and pumpkins, spaghetti squash is a winter squash. These hardy vegetables are harvested in the fall and keep well through the cold winter months.

But the hard shells of winter squash can be difficult to cut. Try this method, using a rubber mallet and a large chef's knife: Cover the mallet with a plastic food storage bag and tie it to the handle with a rubber band or twist tie. Press the length of the knife blade into the squash at the center. Holding the knife handle with one hand, grasp the mallet in the other hand and strike the top of the blade sharply. Hit the blade a few more times until the squash splits in two.

Spiced Sweet Potato Soup

This Thanksgiving serve your spuds as soup. It makes a unique first course, and guests will love the creamy texture and flavors of ginger, cinnamon and curry.

—MARY LISA SPEER PALM BEACH, FL

PREP: 20 MIN. • **COOK:** 6 HOURS
MAKES: 12 SERVINGS (2¼ QUARTS)

- 2 pounds sweet potatoes (about 4 medium), peeled and chopped
- 1 large sweet onion, finely chopped
- 1 medium sweet red pepper, finely chopped
- 1½ teaspoons curry powder
- 1 teaspoon sea salt
- ½ teaspoon ground cinnamon
- ¼ teaspoon ground ginger
- ¼ teaspoon ground allspice
- ¼ teaspoon grated lemon peel
- ⅛ teaspoon coarsely ground pepper
- 6 cups reduced-sodium chicken broth
  Salted pumpkin seeds or pepitas, optional

1. In a 5-qt. slow cooker, combine the first 11 ingredients. Cook, covered, on low 6-8 hours or until vegetables are tender.
2. Puree soup using an immersion blender. Or, cool soup slightly and puree in batches in a blender; return to slow cooker and heat through. If desired, top servings with pumpkin seeds.

Herbed Apple-Cranberry Bread Dressing

Not all stuffings are created equal. My version of the classic side dish features
apples for a sweet crunch and cranberries for a little tartness.

—AYSHA SCHURMAN AMMON, ID

PREP: 30 MIN. • **BAKE:** 45 MIN. • **MAKES:** 16 SERVINGS (¾ CUP EACH)

- 1 cup butter, cubed
- 3 medium red onions, chopped (about 2⅔ cups)
- 2 to 3 celery ribs, chopped (about 1⅓ cups)
- 5 cups dry bread crumbs
- 3 medium tart apples, chopped (about 2⅔ cups)
- 1⅓ cups dried cranberries
- 1⅓ cups minced chives
- 1 cup chicken broth
- 1 cup unsweetened applesauce
- ⅔ cup orange juice
- ¼ cup minced fresh cilantro
- ¼ cup minced fresh parsley
- 4 teaspoons minced fresh rosemary
- 4 garlic cloves, minced
- 1½ teaspoons salt
- 1 teaspoon pepper

1. Preheat oven to 325°. In a 6-qt. stockpot, heat butter over medium-high heat. Add onions and celery; cook and stir 6-8 minutes or until onions are tender. Stir in remaining ingredients. Transfer to a greased 13x9-in. baking dish.
2. Bake, covered, 30 minutes. Uncover; bake 15-20 minutes longer or until lightly browned.

Southern Green Beans with Apricots

Green beans and apricots have become a
family tradition. Enhanced with balsamic vinegar,
the flavors will make your taste buds pop.

—ASHLEY DAVIS EASLEY, SC

PREP: 15 MIN. • **COOK:** 20 MIN. • **MAKES:** 8 SERVINGS

- 2 pounds fresh green beans, trimmed
- 1 can (14½ ounces) chicken broth
- ½ pound bacon strips, chopped
- 1 cup dried apricots, chopped
- ¼ cup balsamic vinegar
- ¾ teaspoon salt
- ¾ teaspoon garlic powder
- ¾ teaspoon pepper

1. Place beans and broth in a large saucepan. Bring to a boil. Cook, covered, 4-7 minutes or until beans are crisp-tender; drain.
2. In a large skillet, cook bacon over medium heat until crisp, stirring occasionally. Remove with a slotted spoon; drain on paper towels. Discard drippings, reserving 1 tablespoon drippings in pan.

3. Add apricots to drippings; cook and stir over medium heat until softened. Stir in vinegar, salt, garlic powder, pepper and beans; cook and stir 2-3 minutes longer or until beans are coated.

Autumn Pumpkin Cupcakes

These little cupcakes are capped with cream cheese frosting and drizzled with a homemade salted caramel sauce. They're soft and sweet.

—WENDY RUSCH TREGO, WI

PREP: 30 MIN.
BAKE: 20 MIN. + COOLING
MAKES: 2 DOZEN

- 2 **cups sugar**
- 1 **can (15 ounces) solid-pack pumpkin**
- 4 **large eggs**
- ¾ **cup canola oil**
- 1 **teaspoon vanilla extract**
- 2 **cups all-purpose flour**
- 2 **teaspoons baking soda**
- 2 **teaspoons pumpkin pie spice**
- 1 **teaspoon salt**
- 1 **teaspoon baking powder**

SAUCE
- ½ **cup packed brown sugar**
- 6 **tablespoons heavy whipping cream**
- ¼ **cup butter, cubed**
- ⅛ **teaspoon salt**
- ½ **teaspoon vanilla extract**

FROSTING
- 1 **package (8 ounces) cream cheese, softened**
- 1 **cup butter, softened**
- 1 **teaspoon vanilla extract**
- 3 **cups confectioners' sugar**

1. Preheat oven to 350°. Line 24 muffin cups with paper liners. In a large bowl, beat sugar, pumpkin, eggs, oil and vanilla until well blended. In another bowl, whisk flour, baking soda, pie spice, salt and baking powder; gradually beat the dry ingredients into pumpkin mixture.

2. Fill prepared cups two-thirds full. Bake 20-22 minutes or until a toothpick inserted in center comes out clean. Cool in pans 10 minutes before removing to wire racks to cool completely.

3. For sauce, in a small heavy saucepan, combine brown sugar, cream, butter and salt; bring to boil. Reduce heat; cook and stir 2-3 minutes or until thickened. Remove mixture from the heat; stir in the vanilla. Cool sauce to room temperature.

4. Meanwhile, in a large bowl, beat cream cheese, butter and vanilla until blended. Gradually beat in confectioners' sugar until smooth. Frost cupcakes; drizzle with sauce.

Chewy Choco-Caramel Squares

These rich, chewy bars make a quick and easy dessert for Thanksgiving. They're popular at bake sales and classroom parties, too.
—**ROD & SUE BRUSIUS** OMRO, WI

PREP: 15 MIN. • **BAKE:** 30 MIN. + COOLING • **MAKES:** 2 DOZEN

1 package butter recipe golden cake mix (regular size)
2 large eggs
⅓ cup canola oil
2 cups (12 ounces) semisweet chocolate chips
1 cup white baking chips
½ cup toffee bits
1 can (14 ounces) sweetened condensed milk
32 caramels
½ cup butter, cubed

1. Preheat oven to 350°. In a large bowl, combine cake mix, eggs and oil; beat on low speed 30 seconds. Beat on medium 2 minutes. Fold in chocolate chips, baking chips and toffee bits.

2. Press half of mixture into a greased 13x9-in. baking pan. Bake 10 minutes. Meanwhile, in a large saucepan, combine milk, caramels and butter. Cook and stir over medium heat until smooth.

3. Pour caramel mixture over crust. Crumble remaining cake mixture over top. Bake 20-25 minutes longer or until edges begin to brown and topping is set. Cool completely in pan on a wire rack. Cut into bars.

Favorite Berry Punch

A friend from church shared the recipe for this zingy strawberry-infused punch. It's great for bridal showers, anniversary parties and holiday gatherings.
—**JOAN HALLFORD** NORTH RICHLAND HILLS, TX

START TO FINISH: 10 MIN. • **MAKES:** 22 SERVINGS (¾ CUP EACH)

1 container (16 ounces) frozen sweetened sliced strawberries, thawed
2 bottles (1 liter each) club soda, chilled
1 bottle (1 liter) ginger ale, chilled
1 can (12 ounces) frozen lemonade concentrate, thawed
1 can (12 ounces) frozen cranberry juice concentrate, thawed

Place strawberries in a blender; cover and process until pureed. Pour into a punch bowl; stir in remaining ingredients.

PUNCH POINTERS

Chill all of the punch ingredients before mixing so that you don't have to dilute the punch with ice to get it cold. Or consider garnishing it with an ice ring made from punch ingredients instead of water. The ice ring will last longer than ice cubes. It also adds an attractive touch.

Cheddar Corn Biscuits

Skip standard bake-and-serve dinner rolls this year and try my fast-to-fix biscuits studded with cheddar and corn. It's almost impossible to resist eating one right from the oven!
—SUSAN BRAUN SWIFT CURRENT, SK

PREP: 20 MIN. • **BAKE:** 20 MIN. • **MAKES:** 16 BISCUITS

- 4¼ cups all-purpose flour
- 2 tablespoons baking powder
- 1 teaspoon ground mustard
- ¾ teaspoon salt
- ¾ cup cold butter, cubed
- 1 can (14¾ ounces) cream-style corn
- 1½ cups (6 ounces) shredded cheddar cheese
- 2 large eggs, lightly beaten

1. Preheat oven to 425°. In a large bowl, whisk flour, baking powder, mustard and salt. Cut in butter until mixture resembles coarse crumbs. Add the corn, cheese and eggs; stir just until moistened.

2. Turn onto a lightly floured surface; knead gently 8-10 times. Pat or roll dough to 1-in. thickness; cut with a floured 2½-in. biscuit cutter. Place 2 in. apart on ungreased baking sheets; brush with milk. Bake 18-22 minutes or until golden brown. Serve warm.

Creamy Pumpkin Pie

For make-ahead convenience, you can't beat this simple, no-bake pumpkin pie. It boasts a luscious cheesecake-style texture and a sweet touch of spice.
—VIRGINIA KRITES CRIDERSVILLE, OH

PREP: 15 MIN. + CHILLING • **MAKES:** 8 SERVINGS

- 1 package (8 ounces) cream cheese, softened
- 1 cup canned pumpkin
- ½ cup sugar
- ¾ teaspoon pumpkin pie spice
- 1 carton (8 ounces) frozen whipped topping, thawed, divided

- 1 graham cracker crust (9 inches)
  Ground cinnamon

In a large bowl, beat cream cheese, pumpkin, sugar and pie spice until smooth. Fold in 2½ cups whipped topping. Spoon into crust.

Refrigerate 2 hours or until set. Serve with remaining whipped topping; sprinkle with cinnamon.

Turkey Centerpiece

This centerpiece does double duty: It adds a whimsical accent to the kids' table, and, with the paper table covering, it encourages kids to do some creative doodling as they wait for their meal.

MATERIALS

- 12-in. white foam wreath form
- 50-ft. length natural burlap heavy twine (100% Jute)
- Red burlap fabric
- 12 multi-colored feathers (we used Zucker Turkey Flat Feathers in Rainbow)
- 12 colored pencils
- 2 large google eyes
- Orange card stock
- Brown kraft paper (36-in.x100-ft. roll for table surface)
- Scissors
- Small hacksaw or large serrated knife
- Glue gun

DIRECTIONS

1. Using hacksaw or serrated knife, cut wreath form in half. Stand one half upright on your craft table. (Save the other half for another use.)
2. Apply a dab of hot glue to the bottom right of the semicircle. Press one end of the twine onto the glue; let dry.
3. Wrap the twine carefully around the foam, beginning at the bottom and moving up the semicircle, without overlapping or twisting the twine layers. Apply dabs of hot glue as you go to keep the twine flat and secure.
4. At top, trim the twine and tuck the end to the inside. Hot-glue in place.
5. Cut a peanut shape from red burlap fabric for the wattle (neck)

and hot-glue to center front. Cut a triangle from orange cardstock (nose) and hot-glue at top of wattle. Hot-glue eyes above nose.
6. Hot-glue a feather to the dull end of each colored pencil. Poke the sharpened ends into the foam

for the tail feathers.
7. Cut kraft paper to fit tabletop. Draw place settings onto the kraft paper if desired. Set burlap turkey in the center within easy reach of the young diners.

This Thanksgiving, go beyond the bird. In addition to your family favorites, introduce one or several signature dishes from various regions of the U.S., and turn the traditional feast into a culinary road trip.

Venture to the Pacific Northwest for Dried Cherry & Sausage Dressing, then head south for fresh Collard Greens & Beans. Want a taste of New England? Go with Cape Cod Corn Pudding. Then visit the Midwest for Roasted Pumpkin and Brussels Sprouts.

If you're really looking for adventure, Cheddar, Bacon & Green Chile Grits is just the ticket—a southern classic with a southwestern accent. Thanksgiving is a time to reflect on our nation at its best and celebrate what unites us—including home cooking!

Cape Cod Corn Pudding (p. 107)
Dried Cherry & Sausage Dressing (p. 111)
Potato Salad with Kalamata-Hazelnut Vinaigrette (p. 112)

REGIONAL **SIDE DISHES**

Wild Rice, Quinoa & Cranberry Salad

This fragrant salad is a vitamin and protein powerhouse. Toss in leftover cooked turkey to make it a meal the next day.

—JERILYN KORVER
BELLFLOWER, CA

PREP: 20 MIN. • **COOK:** 1 HOUR
MAKES: 12 SERVINGS (¾ CUP EACH)

- 2 cups uncooked wild rice
- 2 cartons (32 ounces each) reduced-sodium chicken broth, divided
- 1½ cups quinoa, rinsed
- 1 medium onion, chopped
- 4 garlic cloves, minced
- 2 medium navel oranges
- 1 cup dried cranberries
- 1 cup sliced almonds
- 2 tablespoons minced fresh parsley or 2 teaspoons dried parsley flakes
- 3 tablespoons olive oil
- 2 teaspoons minced fresh thyme or ½ teaspoon dried thyme
- 2 teaspoons rice vinegar
- 1 teaspoon salt
- ½ teaspoon pepper

1. Rinse wild rice thoroughly; drain. In a large saucepan, combine rice and 5 cups broth; bring to a boil. Reduce heat; simmer, covered, 60-70 minutes or until rice is fluffy and tender. Drain if necessary.

2. Meanwhile, in a small saucepan, bring remaining broth to a boil. Add quinoa. Reduce heat; simmer, covered, 15-20 minutes or until liquid is absorbed. Remove from heat; fluff with a fork.

3. Place a large nonstick skillet coated with cooking spray over medium-high heat. Add onion; cook and stir 6-8 minutes or until tender. Add garlic; cook 1 minute longer.

4. Finely grate enough peel from oranges to measure 2 teaspoons; place in a large bowl. Cut a thin slice from the top and bottom of each orange; stand orange upright on a cutting board. With a knife, cut off peel and outer membrane from orange. Working over the same large bowl with orange peel to catch juices, cut along the membrane of each segment to remove fruit. Cut orange sections in half; stir into orange juice and peel. Add cranberries, almonds, parsley, rice, quinoa and onion mixture.

5. In a small bowl, whisk oil, thyme, vinegar, salt and pepper until blended. Pour over rice mixture; toss to coat.

Cape Cod Corn Pudding

A family member passed along this recipe for corn baked with cheddar and ricotta. Don't skip the fresh basil—it adds a hint of sweet flavor reminiscent of mint and anise.
—**MELINDA MESSER** BENSON, NC

PREP: 20 MIN. • **BAKE:** 30 MIN. + STANDING • **MAKES:** 8 SERVINGS

¼ cup butter, cubed
5 cups frozen corn (about 24 ounces)
1 medium onion, finely chopped
4 large eggs, lightly beaten
2 cups whole milk
1 cup whole-milk ricotta cheese
½ cup cornmeal
1 tablespoon sugar
1 teaspoon salt
¾ teaspoon pepper
1½ cups (6 ounces) shredded cheddar cheese, divided

2 tablespoons chopped fresh basil, optional

1. Preheat oven to 375°. In a 6-qt. stockpot, heat butter over medium-high heat. Add corn and onion; cook and stir 6-8 minutes or until corn is crisp-tender. Remove from heat.
2. In a large bowl, whisk eggs, milk, ricotta cheese, cornmeal, sugar, salt and pepper. Stir in ¾ cup cheddar cheese, corn mixture and, if desired, basil.

3. Transfer to a greased 11x7-in. baking dish. Sprinkle with remaining cheddar cheese. Bake, uncovered, 30-35 minutes or until set. Let casserole stand 10 minutes before serving.

Fresh Citrus & Seafood Salad

I get rave reviews for this seafood salad placed on a bed of arugula. Grapefruit and clementines add color and tang to the crab and shrimp.
—**LINDA HICKAM** HEALDSBURG, CA

START TO FINISH: 20 MIN. • **MAKES:** 12 SERVINGS

2 medium grapefruit
2 cups lump crabmeat (about 10 ounces), drained
2 bunches green onions, thinly sliced
6 ounces peeled and deveined cooked shrimp (61-70 per pound)
4 clementines, peeled and segmented or 1 cup mandarin oranges
1⅓ cups canola oil
½ cup red wine vinegar
2 garlic cloves, minced
1 teaspoon salt
12 cups fresh arugula

2 medium ripe avocados, chopped
½ cup sliced almonds, toasted

1. Cut a thin slice from the top and bottom of each grapefruit; stand grapefruit upright on a cutting board. With a knife, cut off peel and outer membrane from grapefruit. Working over a large bowl to catch juices, cut along the membrane of each segment to remove fruit.
2. Add crab, onions, shrimp, clementines and grapefruit sections to reserved juices. In

a small bowl, whisk oil, vinegar, garlic and salt until blended; pour over seafood mixture and toss to coat. Place arugula in a large shallow bowl. Spoon seafood mixture over arugula. Top with avocados; sprinkle with almonds.
NOTE *To toast nuts, spread in a 15x10x1-in. baking pan. Bake at 350° for 5-10 minutes or until lightly browned, stirring occasionally. Or place in a dry nonstick skillet and heat over low heat until lightly browned, stirring occasionally.*

Cranberry-Orange Chutney

We have Thanksgiving at an elementary school and play basketball before the meal. This zingy chutney of cranberries, apples, walnuts and gingerroot is a favorite among the guests.
—**VICTORIA DAVIS** WILDER, VERMONT

PREP: 25 MIN. • **COOK:** 20 MIN. • **MAKES:** 5 CUPS

- 4 small navel oranges
- 4 cups fresh or frozen cranberries (about 16 ounces)
- 1½ cups packed brown sugar
- 1 medium apple, chopped
- 1 cup raisins
- ½ cup chopped walnuts
- ½ cup orange juice
- 1 tablespoon minced fresh gingerroot
- 1 tablespoon cider vinegar
- 2 teaspoons ground cinnamon
- ½ teaspoon ground nutmeg
- ¼ teaspoon ground cloves

1. Finely grate enough peel from oranges to measure 2 tablespoons. Cut a thin slice from the top and bottom of each orange; stand orange upright on a cutting board. With a knife, cut off peel and outer membrane from orange. Cut along the membrane of each segment to remove fruit.

2. Place grated orange peel and sections in a large saucepan; add remaining ingredients. Bring to a boil. Reduce heat; simmer, uncovered, 8-10 minutes or until cranberries pop, stirring occasionally. Serve warm or cold.

Cheddar, Bacon & Green Chile Grits

In the South, grits are served plain with a little butter or loaded with extras, like my recipe with bacon, cheddar and green chilies.
—**AMANDA REED** NASHVILLE, TN

START TO FINISH: 30 MIN. • **MAKES:** 12 SERVINGS (¾ CUP EACH)

- 8 cups water
- 2 cups uncooked old-fashioned grits
- 1 teaspoon salt
- ¼ teaspoon paprika
- 2 cups (8 ounces) shredded white cheddar cheese
- 5 bacon strips, cooked and crumbled
- 1 can (4 ounces) chopped green chilies

1. In a 6-qt. stockpot, bring water to a boil. Slowly stir in grits, salt and paprika. Reduce heat; cook, covered, 15-20 minutes or until thickened, stirring occasionally.

2. Reduce heat to low. Stir in cheese, bacon and chilies until cheese is melted.

Beans, Bacon & Tomato Bake

PICTURED AT LEFT

Bacon, tomatoes and lima beans combine for a nutrient-packed side dish that makes the perfect accompaniment to turkey.

—KAREN KUMPULAINEN
FOREST CITY, NC

PREP: 10 MIN. • **BAKE:** 35 MIN.
MAKES: 12 SERVINGS (⅔ CUP EACH)

- 8 bacon strips, cut into 1-inch pieces
- 1 cup finely chopped onion
- ⅔ cup finely chopped celery
- ½ cup finely chopped green pepper
- 2 garlic cloves, minced
- 2 teaspoons all-purpose flour
- 2 teaspoons sugar
- 2 teaspoons salt
- ¼ teaspoon pepper
- 2 cans (14½ ounces each) diced tomatoes, undrained
- 8 cups frozen lima beans (about 42 ounces), thawed

1. Preheat oven to 325°. In a 6-qt. stockpot, cook bacon, onion, celery and green pepper over medium heat until bacon is crisp and vegetables are tender. Add garlic; cook 1 minute longer. Stir in flour, sugar, salt and pepper. Add tomatoes. Bring to a boil, stirring constantly; cook and stir 1-2 minutes or until thickened. Stir in beans.
2. Transfer to a greased 3-qt. baking dish. Bake, covered, 35-40 minutes or until beans are tender.

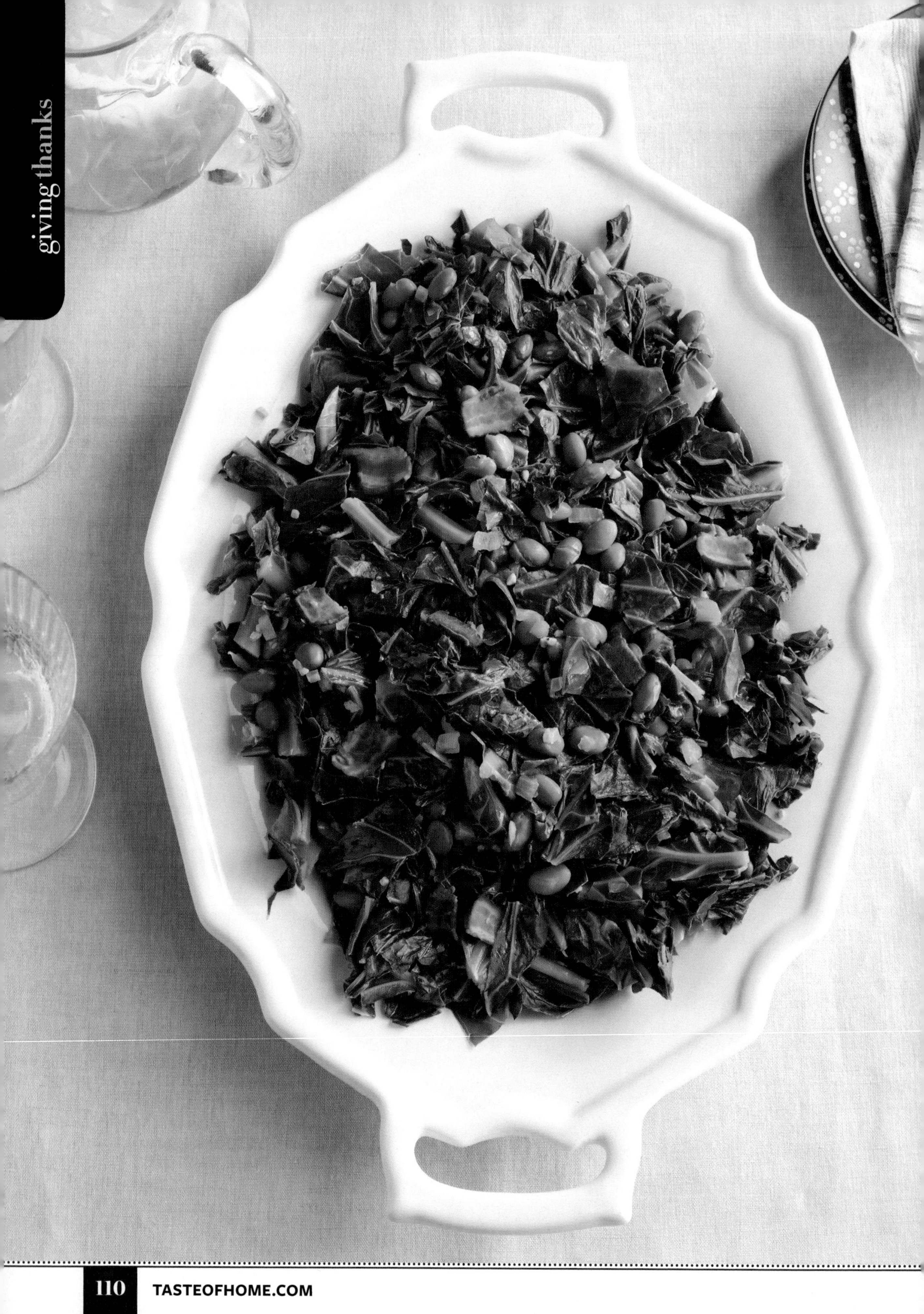

Collard Greens & Beans

PICTURED AT LEFT

I never tried collard greens until a friend gave me this recipe that calls for bacon and pinto beans. Now I look forward to serving this southern staple on Thanksgiving.
—APRIL BURROUGHS VILONIA, AR

PREP: 20 MIN. • **COOK:** 55 MIN. • **MAKES:** 8 SERVINGS

- 2 **pounds collard greens**
- 3 **bacon strips, chopped**
- 1 **small red onion, chopped**
- 2 **garlic cloves, minced**
- 2½ **cups water**
- 2 **tablespoons brown sugar**
- 1 **tablespoon cider vinegar**
- ¾ **teaspoon salt**
- ½ **teaspoon pepper**
- 1 **can (15 ounces) pinto beans, rinsed and drained**

1. Remove and discard center ribs and stems from collard greens. Cut leaves into 1-in. pieces. In a Dutch oven, cook bacon over medium heat until crisp, stirring occasionally.
2. Add onion and garlic to bacon and drippings; cook and stir 2 minutes. Add collard greens; cook and stir until they begin to wilt. Stir in water, brown sugar, vinegar, salt and pepper. Bring to a boil. Reduce heat; simmer, covered, 55-65 minutes or until greens are tender, adding beans during the last 15 minutes.

Dried Cherry & Sausage Dressing

Apples and dried cherries add a sweet-tart flavor to my homemade stuffing. It makes a holiday dinner to remember.
—CONNIE BOLL CHILTON, WI

PREP: 40 MIN. • **BAKE:** 45 MIN. • **MAKES:** 20 SERVINGS (¾ CUP EACH)

- 1 **loaf (1 pound) unsliced Italian bread**
- ¼ **cup cherry juice blend or unsweetened apple juice**
- 1 **cup dried cherries**
- 1 **pound bulk Italian sausage**
- 2 **celery ribs, chopped**
- 1 **medium onion, chopped**
- 2 **medium Granny Smith apples, chopped**
- ½ **cup chopped fresh parsley**
- ½ **cup butter, melted**
- 1 **teaspoon Italian seasoning**
- 1 **teaspoon fennel seed**
- 1 **teaspoon rubbed sage**
- ½ **teaspoon salt**
- ¼ **teaspoon pepper**
- 2 **large eggs**
- 2 **cups chicken stock**

1. Preheat oven to 375°. Cut bread into 1-in. cubes; transfer to two 15x10x1-in. baking pans. Bake 10-15 minutes or until toasted. Cool slightly. In a small saucepan, bring juice blend to a boil. Stir in cherries. Remove from the heat; let stand 10 minutes. Drain.
2. Meanwhile, in a large skillet, cook sausage, celery and onion over medium heat 8-10 minutes or until sausage is no longer pink and vegetables are tender, breaking up sausage into crumbles; drain. Transfer to a large bowl; stir in apples, parsley, butter, seasonings, bread cubes and drained cherries. In a small bowl, whisk eggs and chicken stock; pour over bread mixture and toss to coat.
3. Transfer to a greased 13x9-in. baking dish (dish will be full). Bake, covered, 30 minutes. Bake, uncovered, 15-20 minutes or until golden brown.

Potato Salad with Kalamata-Hazelnut Vinaigrette

Potato salad tossed with vinaigrette has a lighter taste than traditional mayo versions. I add velvety avocado and hazelnuts for cool texture and crunch.
—LAURIE BOCK LYNDEN, WA

PREP: 20 MIN. • **COOK:** 15 MIN. + CHILLING • **MAKES:** 10 SERVINGS

- 2 **pounds Yukon Gold potatoes (about 5 medium), cut into ¼-inch slices**
- ½ **cup chopped hazelnuts, toasted, divided**
- 5 **tablespoons rice vinegar, divided**
- ¼ **cup water**
- ¼ **cup olive oil**
- 2 **tablespoons minced fresh oregano**
- 2 **garlic cloves, minced**
- 1½ **teaspoons sugar**
- ¾ **teaspoon salt**
- ½ **teaspoon crushed red pepper flakes**
- ½ **teaspoon coarsely ground pepper**
- ¼ **cup chopped Kalamata olives**
- 2 **medium ripe avocados**
- 1 **small red onion, finely chopped**

1. In a 6-qt. stockpot, place a steamer basket over 1 in. of water. Place potatoes in basket. Bring water to a boil. Reduce heat to maintain a simmer; steam, covered, 15-18 minutes or until tender. Transfer to a large bowl; refrigerate 30 minutes.

2. Place 2 tablespoons hazelnuts in a food processor. Add 4 tablespoons rice vinegar, water, oil, oregano, garlic, sugar, salt, pepper flakes and pepper. Pulse until blended. Stir in olives and remaining hazelnuts.

3. Peel and thinly slice avocados; toss with remaining vinegar. Layer a fourth of the potatoes, avocados and onion in a large bowl; drizzle with a fourth of the vinaigrette. Repeat layers three times. Serve at room temperature.

Balsamic-Mushroom Bread Pudding

We love fresh mushrooms, especially when they're part of this rich savory bread pudding.
—CATHERINE WILKINSON DEWEY, AZ

PREP: 45 MIN. + STANDING • **BAKE:** 40 MIN. • **MAKES:** 12 SERVINGS

- 3 **tablespoons butter, divided**
- 1½ **pounds sliced fresh mushrooms**
- 1 **large onion, chopped**
- ½ **cup balsamic vinegar**
- 1 **teaspoon dried marjoram**
- ½ **teaspoon salt**
- ¼ **teaspoon pepper**
- 1 **can (10½ ounces) condensed beef consomme, undiluted**
- 1 **cup heavy whipping cream**
- 2 **large eggs**
- 2 **large egg yolks**
- 1 **tablespoon minced fresh thyme or ¼ teaspoon dried thyme**
- 6 **cups day-old cubed sourdough bread**
- 1 **package (8 ounces) cream cheese, cut into ½-inch cubes**

1. Preheat oven to 350°. In a large skillet, heat 2 tablespoons butter over medium heat. Add half of the mushrooms and onion; cook and stir 6-8 minutes or until mushrooms are tender. Remove from pan. Repeat with remaining butter and mushrooms.

2. Return mushrooms and onion to pan. Add vinegar, marjoram, salt and pepper. Cook until liquid evaporates, stirring frequently, about 5 minutes. Remove from heat; cool slightly.

3. In a large bowl, whisk consomme, cream, eggs, egg yolks and thyme until blended. Stir in bread cubes and mushroom mixture; let stand 10 minutes or until bread is softened.

4. Transfer to a greased 13x9-in. baking dish; top with cream cheese. Bake, uncovered, 40-45 minutes or until set. Serve warm.

Roasted Pumpkin and Brussels Sprouts

While traveling in Taiwan, I had the pleasure of trying a unique vegetable dish that included fresh pumpkin. It inspired me to roast pumpkin with Brussels sprouts.
—PAM CORRELL BROCKPORT, PA

PREP: 15 MIN. • **BAKE:** 35 MIN.
MAKES: 8 SERVINGS

- 1 **medium pie pumpkin (about 3 pounds), peeled and cut into ¾-inch cubes**
- 1 **pound fresh Brussels sprouts, trimmed and halved lengthwise**
- 4 **garlic cloves, thinly sliced**
- ⅓ **cup olive oil**
- 2 **tablespoons balsamic vinegar**
- 1 **teaspoon sea salt**
- ½ **teaspoon coarsely ground pepper**
- 2 **tablespoons minced fresh parsley**

1. Preheat oven to 400°. In a large bowl, combine pumpkin, Brussels sprouts and garlic. In a small bowl, whisk oil, vinegar, salt and pepper; drizzle over vegetables and toss to coat.

2. Transfer mixture to a greased 15x10x1-in. baking pan. Roast 35-40 minutes or until tender, stirring once. Sprinkle with parsley.

HOW TO PEEL A PUMPKIN

Peeling pumpkins can be tricky. To make easy work of it, cut the pumpkin into large pieces and remove the fibrous strings and seeds. Then peel the pumpkin using a small sharp knife or vegetable peeler.

A big turkey dinner with all the trimmings deserves an equally grand dessert.

Pies and tarts have long been Thanksgiving Day staples, but if plain-Jane pumpkin pie sounds a little humdrum this year, turn to this assortment of unforgettable remixed classics.

Satisfy both your chocolate and tea fix with one dish, Chai Truffle Tart. Fruit lovers will appreciate ripe-for-the-picking Cinnamon Swirl Apple Pie and Lattice-Topped Pear Slab Pie.

And because everything is better with bacon, Butterscotch Pie with Walnut-Bacon Toffee is as close to heaven as a dessert can get.

So gather your guests around the dessert table for slices of sweet, flaky perfection. Any way you cut it, you're in for a treat!

White Chocolate Cranberry Almond Tart (p. 120)

PIES & TARTS

Chai Truffle Tart

My chai-flavored tart boasts chocolate and caramel layers tucked inside a salty pretzel crust. Truffles on top make it extra indulgent.

—CHANTAL BOURBON
MONTREAL, QC

PREP: 55 MIN. + CHILLING
MAKES: 16 SERVINGS

- 2 **cups crushed pretzels**
- ¼ **cup packed brown sugar**
- ¾ **cup butter, melted**
- ½ **cup hot caramel ice cream topping**
- 16 **ounces 70% cacao dark baking chocolate, chopped**
- 1 **cup heavy whipping cream**
- 2 **tablespoons butter**
- 4 **chai tea bags**
- 2 **tablespoons baking cocoa**
- 3 **ounces milk chocolate, melted**
- 2 **tablespoons finely chopped crystallized ginger**

1. Preheat oven to 350°. In a large bowl, mix pretzels and brown sugar; stir in butter. Press crumbs onto bottom and up sides of greased 9-in. fluted tart pan with removable bottom. Bake 12-15 minutes or until golden brown. Drizzle caramel topping over crust; cool on a wire rack.

2. Place dark chocolate in a large bowl. In a small saucepan, bring cream and butter just to a boil; remove from heat. Add tea bags; let mixture stand 10 minutes. Discard tea bags.

3. Reheat cream mixture just to a boil. Pour over dark chocolate; let stand 5 minutes. Stir with a whisk until smooth. Pour 1½ cups ganache into prepared crust. Refrigerate, covered, 1 hour or until firm. Press plastic wrap onto surface of remaining ganache. Refrigerate 35-40 minutes or until firm enough to shape into balls.

4. Shape reserved ganache into sixteen 1-in. balls; roll in cocoa.

Drizzle milk chocolate over tart; sprinkle with ginger. Arrange truffles around edge of tart. Refrigerate until serving.

Mile-High Peppermint Pie

Peppermint ice cream and minty chocolate make this a divine holiday pie.
I top it with a classic "mile-high" meringue and a drizzle of rich fudge sauce.
—**NANCY LARKIN** MAITLAND, FL

PREP: 40 MIN. + FREEZING • **BAKE:** 5 MIN. • **MAKES:** 8 SERVINGS

1½ cups crushed chocolate-covered mint cookies (about 24 cookies)
2 tablespoons butter, melted
5 cups peppermint ice cream
CHOCOLATE SAUCE
1 ounce semisweet chocolate
1 tablespoon butter
½ cup sugar
3 tablespoons water
2 tablespoons light corn syrup
⅛ teaspoon salt
½ teaspoon vanilla extract
MERINGUE
5 large egg whites, room temperature
⅔ cup sugar

1. In a small bowl, mix crushed cookies and melted butter. Press onto the bottom and up sides of a 9-in. metal pie pan. Freeze, covered, 1 hour or until firm.

2. Spread ice cream into crust. Freeze, covered, until firm.

3. To serve, preheat oven to 450°. In a small saucepan, melt chocolate and butter over medium-low heat. Stir in sugar, water, corn syrup and salt. Bring to a boil. Stir to dissolve sugar. Reduce heat; simmer, uncovered, 4-5 minutes or until slightly thickened, stirring frequently. Stir in vanilla; keep warm.

4. For meringue, in a small heavy saucepan, combine egg whites and sugar. Using a hand mixer, beat on low speed 1 minute. Place saucepan over low heat; continue beating on low until a thermometer reads 160°.

5. Transfer mixture to a bowl. Beat on high until stiff glossy peaks form. Spread meringue over frozen pie. Bake 2-3 minutes or until meringue is lightly browned. Serve the pie immediately with warm chocolate sauce.

Gingersnap Sweet Potato Praline Pie

This luscious mix of sweet potatoes, spices and nuts is like serving pecan pie
and sweet potato pie together. Bake it and watch everyone devour it.
—**EMILY HOBBS** OZARK, MO

PREP: 35 MIN. • **BAKE:** 30 MIN. + CHILLING • **MAKES:** 8 SERVINGS

1½ cups crushed gingersnap cookies (about 30 cookies)
¼ cup butter, melted
FILLING
¼ cup butter, softened
1 cup plus 3 tablespoons packed brown sugar, divided
1½ cups mashed sweet potatoes
1 teaspoon ground cinnamon
½ teaspoon ground ginger
¼ teaspoon ground nutmeg
¼ teaspoon salt
3 large egg yolks
1 can (5 ounces) evaporated milk
1 teaspoon vanilla extract
1¼ cups pecan halves

TOPPING
1 cup heavy whipping cream
3 tablespoons maple syrup

1. Preheat oven to 325°. In a small bowl, mix crushed cookies and melted butter. Press onto bottom and up sides of an ungreased 9-in. pie plate. Bake 8-10 minutes or until set. Cool on a wire rack.

2. Increase oven setting to 375°. In a bowl, cream butter and 1 cup brown sugar until fluffy. Beat in sweet potatoes, spices and salt until blended. Beat in egg yolks, milk and vanilla. Pour into crust.

3. Arrange pecans over filling; sprinkle with remaining brown sugar. Bake 30-35 minutes or until a knife inserted near the center comes out clean. Cover edge loosely with foil during the last 20 minutes if needed to prevent overbrowning. Remove foil. Cool completely on a wire rack. Refrigerate at least 2 hours before serving.

4. In a small bowl, beat cream until it begins to thicken. Add maple syrup; beat until stiff peaks form. Serve with pie.

Cinnamon Swirl Apple Pie

PICTURED AT RIGHT

Apples and cinnamon go together like peanut butter and jelly. It's no wonder my kids love this scrumptious pie that uses refrigerated cinnamon rolls to make a deliciously fun crust.

—BARBARA CURRAN LEBANON, NJ

PREP: 20 MIN. • **BAKE:** 40 MIN. + COOLING • **MAKES:** 8 SERVINGS

- 1 **tube (12.4 ounces) refrigerated cinnamon rolls with icing**

FILLING

- 5 **cups thinly sliced peeled tart apples (about 5 medium)**
- 2 **tablespoons lemon juice**
- ¾ **cup sugar**
- ¼ **cup all-purpose flour**
- ¾ **teaspoon ground cinnamon**
- ¼ **teaspoon ground nutmeg**

TOPPING

- ⅓ **cup graham cracker crumbs**
- ⅓ **cup packed brown sugar**
- 3 **tablespoons all-purpose flour**
- 3 **tablespoons cold butter**

1. Preheat oven to 400°. Refrigerate icing from cinnamon rolls. Separate cinnamon rolls; press onto bottom and up the sides of an ungreased 9-in. deep-dish pie plate. Bake 7-9 minutes or until set. Cool crust on a wire rack. Reduce oven setting to 350°.

2. For filling, in a large bowl, toss apples with lemon juice. In a small bowl, mix sugar, flour, cinnamon and nutmeg. Add to apple mixture; toss to coat. Pour filling into prepared crust.

3. For topping, in a small bowl, mix cracker crumbs, brown sugar and flour; cut in butter until crumbly. Sprinkle over filling. Bake 40-45 minutes or until filling is bubbly and topping is golden brown. Cover top loosely with foil during the last 15 minutes if needed to prevent overbrowning. Remove foil. Cool on a wire rack.

4. Just before serving, place reserved icing in a microwave-safe bowl; microwave, uncovered, 10 seconds or until softened. Drizzle over pie.

TIPS FOR BUYING BAKING APPLES

- Select apples that are firm, crisp, deeply colored and have a smooth, unblemished skin.
- Store apples in an open bag in the refrigerator and don't wash until you're ready to eat them or use them in baking. Apples can be refrigerated for up to 6 weeks.
- There are many varieties of tart baking apples to choose from, including Baldwin, Cortland, Golden Russet, Granny Smith, Ida Red, Jonathan, Lady Apple, McIntosh, Macoun, Newtown Pippin, Northern Spy, Rhode Island Greening, Rome Beauty, Winesap, Wolf River or York Imperial.

Best-of-Show Citrus Pie

When I entered this pie in a baking contest, I decorated it with kiwi, orange and pineapple slices and scored top marks. The simplified version is just as delicious.
—HELEN CUNNINGHAM
HESPERIA, CA

PREP: 25 MIN. + FREEZING
MAKES: 8 SERVINGS

- 2 **cups graham cracker crumbs**
- 1 **tablespoon sugar**
- ¼ **teaspoon ground nutmeg**
- ½ **cup butter, melted**

FILLING
- 1 **cup heavy whipping cream**
- 1 **package (8 ounces) cream cheese, softened**
- 1 **can (14 ounces) sweetened condensed milk**
- ¾ **cup thawed orange juice concentrate**
  Sweetened whipped cream and orange slices

1. Preheat oven to 375°. In a small bowl, mix cracker crumbs, sugar and nutmeg; stir in butter. Press onto bottom and up sides of a greased 9-in. pie plate. Bake 8-10 minutes or until lightly browned. Cool completely on a wire rack.

2. In a small bowl, beat cream until soft peaks form. In a large bowl, beat cream cheese until smooth. Beat in milk and orange juice concentrate until blended. Fold in whipped cream. Pour into crust. Freeze, covered, at least 4 hours or overnight.

3. Serve with sweetened whipped cream and orange slices.

White Chocolate Cranberry Almond Tart

A sweet white chocolate drizzle perfectly balances the tangy cranberries in my signataure holiday dessert. I also make this tart for local coffee houses and restaurants.

—TRISHA KRUSE EAGLE, ID

PREP: 55 MIN. • **BAKE:** 20 MIN. + CHILLING • **MAKES:** 12 SERVINGS

½ cup slivered almonds, toasted
3 tablespoons sugar
1⅔ cups all-purpose flour
¼ teaspoon salt
¼ cup butter, melted
¼ cup heavy whipping cream
⅔ cup white baking chips

FILLING
2 cups fresh or frozen cranberries
1 cup sugar
½ cup dried cranberries
⅓ cup orange juice
2 tablespoons butter

TOPPING
⅔ cup white baking chips
2 teaspoons shortening
⅓ cup slivered almonds, toasted

1. Preheat oven to 375°. Place almonds and sugar in a food processor; pulse until almonds are ground. Add flour and salt; pulse until blended. Transfer mixture to a small bowl; stir in melted butter and cream. Press onto bottom and up sides of an ungreased 9-in. fluted tart pan with removable bottom.

2. Bake 15-18 minutes or until lightly browned. Remove from oven; sprinkle baking chips evenly over bottom. Cool on a wire rack.

3. In a saucepan, combine filling ingredients; bring to a boil. Reduce heat, simmer, uncovered,

10-15 minutes or until slightly thickened, stirring occasionally. Pour over baking chips.

4. Bake 20-25 minutes or until filling is bubbly and crust is golden brown. Cool tart on a wire rack. Refrigerate 2 hours or until cold.

5. In a microwave, melt baking chips and shortening; stir until smooth. Drizzle over tart. Sprinkle with almonds.

NOTE *To toast nuts, bake in a shallow pan in a 350° oven for 5-10 minutes or cook in a skillet over low heat until lightly browned, stirring occasionally.*

Cinnamon-Caramel Peanut Butter Tart

Peanut butter and cinnamon create a unique, upscale flavor combination. This rich and creamy creation is one of my daughter's favorites. Keep copies of the recipe handy—everyone wants it.

—MARY HAWKES PRESCOTT, AZ

PREP: 30 MIN. + CHILLING • **MAKES:** 12 SERVINGS

2½ cups crushed peanut butter-filled sandwich cookies (about 27 cookies)
¼ cup butter, melted

FILLING
⅔ cup peanut butter chips
½ cup creamy peanut butter
⅔ cup fat-free caramel ice cream topping
½ teaspoon ground cinnamon
1¼ cups heavy whipping cream
Sweetened whipped cream and chopped peanuts

1. Preheat oven to 325°. In a small bowl, mix crushed cookies and butter. Press mixture onto bottom and up sides of an ungreased 9-in. fluted tart pan with removable bottom. Bake 7-9 minutes or until edges are lightly browned. Cool on a wire rack.

2. In a small saucepan over medium-low heat, melt peanut butter chips and peanut butter with caramel topping and cinnamon; stir until smooth.

Transfer to a large bowl; cool to lukewarm (90°), about 25-30 minutes.

3. In a small bowl, beat cream until stiff peaks form. Fold a third of the whipped cream into peanut butter mixture, then fold in remaining whipped cream; spread over crust. Refrigerate, covered, at least 4 hours or overnight.

4. Serve with sweetened whipped cream; sprinkle with peanuts.

Butterscotch Pie with Walnut-Bacon Toffee

This recipe started as an experiment in making bacon toffee, but by the time I was done I had this sweet and savory butterscotch pie.
—**JULIANN STODDART** CHICAGO, IL

PREP: 1¾ HOURS + CHILLING
MAKES: 12 SERVINGS PLUS 1 POUND TOFFEE

1½ cups all-purpose flour
1¾ teaspoons sugar
¼ teaspoon salt
⅔ cup cold unsalted butter, cubed
5 to 6 tablespoons ice water

BACON TOFFEE
½ teaspoon unsalted butter
2 cups sugar
Dash salt
2 cups unsalted butter, cubed
2 cups chopped walnuts, toasted
½ pound bacon strips, cooked and crumbled
¼ teaspoon vanilla extract

FILLING
3 large egg yolks
1½ cups packed brown sugar
⅓ cup all-purpose flour
Dash salt
1 cup 2% milk
⅓ cup unsalted butter, cubed
1 teaspoon vanilla extract
Sweetened whipped cream

1. For crust, in a large bowl, mix the flour, sugar and salt; cut in butter until crumbly. Gradually add ice water, tossing with a fork until the dough holds together when pressed. Shape dough into a disk; wrap in plastic wrap. Refrigerate dough 1 hour or overnight.

2. For toffee, grease a 15x10x1-in. pan with ½ teaspoon butter. In a large heavy saucepan, combine sugar, salt and remaining butter. Cook over medium heat until a candy thermometer reads 300° (hard-crack stage), stirring constantly. Remove from heat. Stir in walnuts, bacon and vanilla. Immediately pour into prepared pan. Let stand until set, about 45 minutes. Coarsely chop enough toffee to measure 4 cups; set aside. Break the remaining toffee into pieces; refrigerate to serve with pie or save for another use.

3. On a lightly floured surface, roll pastry dough to a ⅛-in.-thick circle; transfer to a 9-in. deep-dish pie plate. Trim pastry to ½ in. beyond rim of plate; flute edge. Refrigerate 30 minutes. Preheat oven to 425°.

4. Line pastry with a double thickness of foil. Fill with pie weights, dried beans or uncooked rice. Bake on a lower oven rack 20-25 minutes. Remove foil and weights; bake 3-6 minutes longer or until bottom is golden brown. Cool on a wire rack.

5. For filling, place egg yolks in a small bowl; let stand at room temperature 30 minutes. In a large heavy saucepan, mix brown sugar, flour and salt. Whisk in milk. Cook and stir over medium heat until thickened and bubbly. Reduce heat to low; cook and stir 4 minutes. Remove from heat.

6. Gradually whisk a small amount of hot mixture into egg yolks; return all to pan, whisking constantly. Bring to a gentle boil; cook and stir 2 minutes. Immediately transfer to a clean bowl; stir in butter and vanilla until smooth.

7. Place 3 cups of the chopped toffee into crust; pour filling over toffee. Top with remaining 1 cup chopped toffee. Refrigerate, covered, at least 2 hours before serving. Serve with whipped cream and remaining toffee pieces.

NOTE *To toast nuts, bake in a shallow pan in a 350° oven for 5-10 minutes or cook in a skillet over low heat until lightly browned, stirring occasionally.*

Lattice-Topped Pear Slab Pie

A lattice top serves as a charming frame for this special holiday dessert filled with fresh pears and candied fruit. Add a dollop of whipped cream if you like.
—**JOHNNA JOHNSON** SCOTTSDALE, AZ

PREP: 30 MIN. + CHILLING • **BAKE:** 40 MIN. + COOLING • **MAKES:** 2 DOZEN

1 cup butter, softened
1 package (8 ounces) cream cheese, softened
2 tablespoons sugar
½ teaspoon salt
2¼ cups all-purpose flour

FILLING
¾ cup sugar
3 tablespoons all-purpose flour
2 teaspoons grated lemon peel
8 cups thinly sliced peeled fresh pears (about 7 medium)
1 cup chopped mixed candied fruit
1 tablespoon 2% milk
3 tablespoons coarse sugar

1. In a small bowl, beat butter, cream cheese, sugar and salt until blended. Gradually beat in flour. Divide dough in two portions so that one portion is slightly larger than the other. Shape each into a rectangle; wrap in plastic wrap. Refrigerate 1 hour or overnight.

2. Preheat oven to 350°. For filling, in a large bowl, combine the sugar, flour and lemon peel. Add the pears and candied fruit; toss to coat.

3. On a lightly floured surface, roll out larger portion of dough into an 18x13-in. rectangle.

Transfer to a greased 15x10x1-in. baking pan. Press onto the bottom and up the sides of pan; add filling.

4. Roll out remaining dough to a ⅛-in.-thick rectangle; cut into ½-in.-wide strips. Arrange over filling in a lattice pattern. Trim and seal strips to edge of bottom pastry. Brush pastry with milk; sprinkle with coarse sugar.

5. Bake 40-45 minutes or until crust is golden brown and filling is bubbly. Cool on a wire rack.

FINISHING TOUCHES FOR PIES

To top off a double-crust or lattice pie before baking, use a pastry brush to lightly and evenly apply one of the following washes to the top crust, avoiding the edges.

- For a shine and light browning, brush with a large egg white lightly beaten with 1 teaspoon of water.
- For a glossy, golden appearance, brush with a large egg yolk beaten with 1 teaspoon of water.
- For a slight shine, brush with half-and-half cream or heavy whipping cream.
- For a crisp brown crust, brush with water.
- For a little sparkle, sprinkle with sugar or decorator sugar after applying one of the washes.
- To give shine to a baked double-crust pie, warm 1 tablespoon of light corn syrup. Gently brush over the warm crust.

easter gatherings

Spring fever starts when the snow melts and the flowers begin to bloom. One of the best ways to celebrate the changing season is with a light and lively meal. Whether you're preparing an Easter feast or simply spending an afternoon in a sunny spot with a friend or two, this section is full of recipes that promise to satisfy your craving for garden-fresh favorites.

T ake your taste buds on a trip this Easter with a menu that combines the flavors of Asia and the tropics. Since this holiday is a time of growth and new life, it's the perfect occasion to celebrate with multicultural cuisine.

This chapter is full of the classics your family loves, spiced up with a few exotic twists. You'll feel proud carrying mouthwatering Citrus-Spice Glazed Ham to the table and passing around a basket of Pina Colada Biscuits.

So for your next get-together, treat your guests to a meal like no other. From the Crab Louie Lettuce Wrap appetizers to the Coconut Pound Cake with Lime Glaze dessert, this unique feast will satisfy with a world of delicious surprises.

Edamame Corn Carrot Salad (p. 134)
Pina Colada Biscuits (p. 129)
Citrus-Spice Glazed Ham (p. 132)

EASTER **FUSION**

Crab Louie Lettuce Wraps

Party guests can mingle and enjoy these tasty portable lettuce wraps without having to juggle plates and forks.
—**MICHAEL WATZ** NORMAL, IL

START TO FINISH: 30 MIN.
MAKES: 12 SERVINGS

- 1 cup (8 ounces) sour cream
- ½ cup sweet chili sauce
- 2 tablespoons minced fresh gingerroot
- 1 tablespoon lime juice
- ¼ teaspoon ground cumin
- 1 can (6 ounces) lump crabmeat, drained and squeezed dry
- 12 Bibb or Boston lettuce leaves
- 2 medium mangoes, peeled and thinly sliced
- 2 medium ripe avocados, peeled and thinly sliced
- 4 green onions, thinly sliced
- 1 medium carrot, shredded
- ¼ cup fresh cilantro leaves
- ¼ cup fresh mint leaves, chopped if desired
- 2 tablespoons toasted sesame seeds

1. In a small bowl, mix the first five ingredients.
2. To serve, place about 1 tablespoon crabmeat in each lettuce leaf. Top with remaining ingredients. Drizzle with some of the sauce. Serve with remaining sauce.

Sparkling Pineapple Grape Juice

I love this versatile non-alcoholic drink. Not only is it fun to serve for Easter, it goes well with cake at wedding or baby showers. It's not too sweet, so there's no sugar overload. Sometimes I mix up a batch to enjoy for no reason at all.
—**DANA MOORE** ALVATON, KY

START TO FINISH: 5 MIN. • **MAKES:** 14 SERVINGS (¾ CUP EACH)

- 1 liter ginger ale, chilled
- 4 cups white grape juice, chilled
- 4 cans (6 ounces each) unsweetened pineapple juice, chilled

In a large pitcher, combine ginger ale, grape juice and pineapple juice. Serve immediately.

Pina Colada Biscuits

This recipe is quick to make and tastes great. You'll think you're on a tropical vacation!
—**CAROLYN PIETTE** JOHNSTON, RI

START TO FINISH: 30 MIN. • **MAKES:** 1 DOZEN

2½ cups biscuit/baking mix
2 tablespoons sugar
¼ cup cold butter, cubed
¼ cup 2% milk
1 large egg
½ teaspoon vanilla extract
½ cup unsweetened pineapple tidbits, well drained
½ cup flaked coconut
¼ cup chopped macadamia nuts

1. Preheat oven to 450°. In a large bowl, whisk biscuit mix and sugar. Cut in butter until mixture resembles coarse crumbs. In another bowl, whisk milk, egg and vanilla; stir into crumb mixture just until moistened. Stir in remaining ingredients.
2. Turn onto a lightly floured surface; knead gently 8-10 times.

Pat or roll dough to ½-in. thickness; cut with a floured 2½-in. biscuit cutter. Place 1 in. apart on an ungreased baking sheet. Bake 7-9 minutes or until golden brown. Serve warm.

Peas with Sesame Dressing

This is a delicious way to eat your veggies. My 6-year-old daughter loves this recipe—and she even helps to make it. It's a favorite at our dinner table.
—**SHANNON AVRA** LITTLE ROCK, AR

START TO FINISH: 20 MIN. • **MAKES:** 8 SERVINGS

1 pound fresh sugar snap peas, trimmed
3 cups fresh or frozen peas, thawed
DRESSING
2 tablespoons rice vinegar
1 tablespoon brown sugar
1 tablespoon sesame oil
1 tablespoon reduced-sodium soy sauce
1 teaspoon salt
½ teaspoon pepper

1. In a 6-qt. stockpot, bring 8 cups water to a boil. Add sugar snap peas; cook, uncovered, 1-2 minutes or just until crisp-tender. Add remaining peas during the last 30 seconds of cooking. Drain and immediately drop into ice water. Drain and pat dry.
2. Transfer peas to a large bowl. In a small bowl, whisk the dressing ingredients until blended. Pour over peas; toss to coat. Using a slotted spoon, serve peas at room temperature.

SUGAR SNAP PEAS

To prepare peas for cooking, rinse with cold water. Remove strings if desired. Cut off stem ends. Do not shell. If using raw, blanch before using.

Crab Rangoon Canapes

I love crab rangoon, but try to avoid fried food. This has all the flavors of the classic dish, only with fewer calories. It's a great summer appetizer. You can usually find wonton strips at the store with the croutons and other salad toppings.

—CHERYL WOODSON LIBERTY, MO

START TO FINISH: 30 MIN. • **MAKES:** 16 APPETIZERS

- 2 **medium cucumbers**
- 6 **ounces reduced-fat cream cheese**
- ½ **cup lump crabmeat, drained**
- 1 **tablespoon finely chopped green onion**
- ¼ **teaspoon salt**
- ¼ **teaspoon garlic powder**
- ⅛ **teaspoon paprika**
- ½ **cup wonton strips**

1. Cut each cucumber into eight thick slices. Scoop out centers, leaving bottoms intact.

2. In a small bowl, combine cream cheese, crab, green onion, salt and garlic powder. Spoon 1 tablespoon into each cucumber slice. Sprinkle with paprika; top with wonton strips.

Mixed Greens with Orange-Ginger Vinaigrette

Zingy vinaigrette starts with orange juice, ginger and a flick of cayenne. Just whisk, toss with greens and top the salad your way.

—JOY ZACHARIA CLEARWATER, FL

START TO FINISH: 20 MIN. • **MAKES:** 8 SERVINGS

- ¼ **cup orange juice**
- ¼ **cup canola oil**
- 2 **tablespoons white vinegar**
- 2 **tablespoons honey**
- 2 **teaspoons grated fresh gingerroot**
- ½ **teaspoon salt**
- ¼ **teaspoon cayenne pepper**

SALAD
- 12 **cups torn mixed salad greens**
- 2 **medium navel oranges, peeled and sliced crosswise**
- 1 **cup thinly sliced red onion**

In a small bowl, whisk the first seven ingredients until blended. In a large bowl, toss greens with ¼ cup vinaigrette; transfer to a serving dish. Top with oranges and onion. Serve immediately with remaining vinaigrette.

Tropical Ginger Rice

PICTURED AT LEFT

Fragrant and fruity, this ginger-scented rice goes with Asian, Indian and other fusion dishes.

—CHARLENE CHAMBERS
ORMOND BEACH, FL

START TO FINISH: 25 MIN.
MAKES: 8 SERVINGS

- 2 cups uncooked long grain rice
- 1 tablespoon minced fresh gingerroot
- 4 cups chicken broth
- ⅔ cup dried tropical fruit
- ⅔ cup chopped pecans, toasted

In a large saucepan, combine rice, ginger and broth; bring to a boil. Reduce heat; simmer, covered, 18-22 minutes or until liquid is absorbed and rice is tender. Stir in dried fruit and pecans.

INSTANT RICE VS. LONG GRAIN RICE

Instant rice (which is partially boiled before packaging) and long grain rice require different amounts of liquid to cook, so you can't substitute one for the other in recipes that call for raw rice. You can, however, use any kind of cooked rice in recipes that call for prepared rice.

Citrus-Spice Glazed Ham

My dad gave me this recipe. It's a fun twist on traditional ham.
—AMANDA LAMBERT BETHEL, OH

PREP: 10 MIN. • **BAKE:** 2¾ HOURS • **MAKES:** 12 SERVINGS

1 **fully cooked bone-in ham (7 to 9 pounds)**
GLAZE
½ **cup orange juice, divided**
1 **teaspoon Chinese five-spice powder**
⅓ **cup packed brown sugar**
1 **tablespoon honey**
4 **teaspoons cornstarch**
2 **medium oranges, peeled and sectioned**
1 **can (20 ounces) unsweetened pineapple tidbits, drained**

1. Preheat oven to 325°. Place ham on a rack in a shallow roasting pan. Cover and bake 2½ to 3 hours or until a thermometer reads 130°.

2. Meanwhile, in a small saucepan, combine ¼ cup orange juice and Chinese five-spice; bring to a boil. Reduce heat; simmer, uncovered, 1-2 minutes or until thickened. Stir in brown sugar and honey. In a small bowl, mix cornstarch and remaining orange juice until smooth; stir into brown sugar mixture. Return to a boil, stirring constantly; cook and stir 1-2 minutes or until thickened.

3. Remove ham from oven. Brush with half of the glaze. Bake ham, uncovered, 15-20 minutes longer or until a thermometer reads 140°. Just before serving, stir fruit into remaining glaze; heat through. Serve with ham.

Jasmine Ice Cream with Plum Sauce

Velvety smooth, this ice cream has a delicate floral note reminiscent of jasmine blossoms. The plum sauce adds subtle tartness and rich color to the dessert.
—LILY JULOW LAWRENCEVILLE, GA

PREP: 30 MIN. + FREEZING • **MAKES:** 1 QUART (1 CUP SAUCE)

1 **tablespoon loose-leaf jasmine tea**
¼ **cup boiling water**
1 **can (15 ounces) plums, pitted**
2 **tablespoons minced fresh basil**
½ **teaspoon vanilla extract**
4 **cups vanilla ice cream, softened**
Fresh basil leaves, optional

1. Place tea in a 1-cup glass measuring cup. Add boiling water; steep 4-6 minutes according to taste. Strain tea, discarding tea leaves. Cool to room temperature.

2. Drain plums, reserving ¼ cup syrup. Place plums, basil, vanilla and reserved syrup in a food processor; process until smooth. Press plum mixture through a fine-mesh strainer into a small bowl; discard pulp. Refrigerate, covered, until serving.

3. Place ice cream in a large bowl; stir in tea until blended. Cover and freeze 4 hours or until firm. Serve with sauce. If desired, top with basil leaves.

Mango Avocado Spring Rolls

As a fan of mangoes and avocados, I love these wraps. You can substitute tortillas for rice paper wrappers, and lettuce or spinach for sprouts.
—**GENA STOUT** RAVENDEN, AR

START TO FINISH: 20 MIN.
MAKES: 8 SPRING ROLLS

- 4 **ounces reduced-fat cream cheese**
- 2 **tablespoons lime juice**
- 1 **teaspoon Sriracha Asian hot chili sauce or ½ teaspoon hot pepper sauce**
- 1 **medium sweet red pepper, finely chopped**
- ⅔ **cup cubed avocado**
- ⅓ **cup minced fresh cilantro**
- 3 **green onions, thinly sliced**
- 8 **round rice paper wrappers (8 inches)**
- 1½ **cups thinly sliced peeled mangoes**
- 2 **cups alfalfa sprouts**

1. In a small bowl, combine cream cheese, lime juice and chili sauce. Stir in pepper, avocado, cilantro and onions.

2. Fill a wide shallow dish with water. Dip a rice paper wrapper into water just until pliable, about 45 seconds (do not soften completely); allow excess water to drip off.

3. Place wrapper on a flat surface. Layer cream cheese mixture, mango and alfalfa sprouts across bottom third of wrapper. Fold in both ends of wrapper; fold bottom side over filling, then roll up tightly. Place on a serving plate, seam side down. Repeat with remaining ingredients.

Coconut Pound Cake with Lime Glaze

This pound cake is the best! Oven temps will vary, so if the cake is not done after 1 hour and 20 minutes, continue baking in 5-minute intervals. Use fresh, not bottled, lime juice for the glaze.

—JO McFARLAND STERLING, VA

PREP: 30 MIN. • **BAKE:** 1¼ HOURS MIN. + COOLING • **MAKES:** 16 SERVINGS

1½ cups butter, softened
1 package (8 ounces) cream cheese, softened
3 cups sugar
6 large eggs, room temperature
2 teaspoons coconut extract
1 teaspoon vanilla extract
⅛ teaspoon almond extract
3 cups all-purpose flour
½ teaspoon baking powder
½ teaspoon salt
2 cups flaked coconut

GLAZE
½ cup sugar
¼ cup lime juice
1 teaspoon grated lime peel
1 teaspoon coconut extract
Toasted flaked coconut, optional

1. Preheat oven to 350°. Grease and flour a 10-in. fluted tube pan.
2. In a large bowl, cream butter, cream cheese and sugar until light and fluffy. Add eggs, one at a time, beating well after each addition. Beat in extracts. In another bowl, whisk flour, baking powder and salt; gradually beat into creamed mixture just until combined. Fold in coconut.
3. Transfer batter to prepared pan. Bake 75-85 minutes or until a toothpick inserted in center comes out clean. Cool in pan 20 minutes before removing to a wire rack to cool completely.
4. In a small saucepan, combine glaze ingredients. Cook and stir over medium heat 2-3 minutes or until sugar is dissolved. Brush over cake. If desired, sprinkle with coconut.

Edamame Corn Carrot Salad

Here's a colorful protein-filled salad suitable for vegetarians and vegans. It's ideal for a spring potluck; everyone will love it!

—MAIAH MILLER MONTEREY, CA

PREP: 25 MIN + CHILLING • **MAKES:** 8 SERVINGS

2½ cups frozen shelled edamame
3 cups julienned carrots
1½ cups frozen corn, thawed
4 green onions, chopped
2 tablespoons minced fresh cilantro

VINAIGRETTE
3 tablespoons rice vinegar
3 tablespoons lemon juice
4 teaspoons canola oil
2 garlic cloves, minced
½ teaspoon salt
½ teaspoon pepper

1. Place edamame in a small saucepan; add water to cover. Bring to a boil; cook 4-5 minutes or until tender. Drain; cool slightly.
2. In a large bowl, combine carrots, corn, green onions, cilantro and edamame. In a small bowl, whisk the vinaigrette ingredients until blended. Pour vinaigrette over salad; toss to coat. Refrigerate at least 2 hours before serving.

With a net full of fresh fish and vegetables, your next meal will be a real keeper. Whether Cod with Raspberry Sauce, Avocado Crab Boats or Cedar Plank Scallops, these sumptuous seafood dishes are packed with pleasing springtime flavors.

Got crab, shrimp, tuna or tilapia? You have the makings for a main course that will turn just about anyone into a seafood lover. And if you're looking for a little something different for Easter, salmon makes both a wonderful meal and an elegant centerpiece.

Thai Lime Shrimp & Noodles (p. 140)

SPRING **SEAFOOD**

Avocado Crab Boats

These boats are great with tortilla chips, beans or rice. You also can cover them, pack them on ice, and take them to a picnic or potluck. Straight from the oven or cold, they're always delicious.

—**FRANCES BENTHIN** SCIO, OR

START TO FINISH: 20 MIN.
MAKES: 4 SERVINGS

- 5 medium ripe avocados, peeled and halved
- ½ cup mayonnaise
- 2 tablespoons lemon juice
- 2 cans (6 ounces each) lump crabmeat, drained
- ¼ cup chopped fresh cilantro, divided
- 2 tablespoons minced chives
- 1 serrano pepper, seeded and minced
- 1 tablespoon capers, drained
- ¼ teaspoon pepper
- 1 cup (4 ounces) shredded pepper jack cheese
- ½ teaspoon paprika
  Lemon wedges

1. Preheat broiler. Place two avocado halves in a large bowl; mash lightly with a fork. Add mayonnaise and lemon juice; mix until well blended. Stir in crab, 3 tablespoons cilantro, chives, serrano pepper, capers and pepper. Spoon into avocado halves.

2. Transfer to a 15x10x1-in. baking pan. Sprinkle with cheese and paprika. Broil 4-5 in. from heat 3-5 minutes or until cheese is melted. Sprinkle with remaining cilantro; serve with lemon wedges.

NOTE *Wear disposable gloves when cutting hot peppers; the oils can burn skin. Avoid touching your face.*

Fish Tacos with Chipotle Aioli

I came up with this recipe after having fish tacos at a seafood restaurant. Instead of frying the fish, I grill it and add a couple of fresh items to give this light healthy meal new flair.
—**ANTHONY DOLBY** HOWLAND, OH

PREP: 45 MIN. • **GRILL:** 15 MIN. • **MAKES:** 8 SERVINGS

- 1 can (15 ounces) black beans, rinsed and drained
- ½ cup sliced red onion
- 1 tablespoon balsamic vinegar
- 1 tablespoon canola oil
- ¼ teaspoon salt
- ⅛ teaspoon pepper

AIOLI

- 1 cup (8 ounces) sour cream
- 2 tablespoons mayonnaise
- 1 tablespoon lime juice
- ½ teaspoon ground chipotle pepper
- ½ teaspoon ground cumin
- ¼ teaspoon Louisiana-style hot sauce

TACOS

- 1½ pounds mahi mahi
- 1 tablespoon canola oil

- 1 envelope taco seasoning
- 8 flour tortillas (8 inches)
- 2 cups coleslaw mix
- 1 cup (4 ounces) shredded Mexican cheese blend
- 2 jalapeno peppers, seeded and sliced
  Lime slices

1. In a small bowl, toss the first six ingredients. In another bowl, mix aioli ingredients; refrigerate until assembly.

2. Brush fish with oil; sprinkle with taco seasoning. Moisten a paper towel with cooking oil; using long-handled tongs, rub on grill rack to coat lightly. Grill fish, covered, over medium-high heat or broil 4 in. from heat 6-8 minutes on each side or until fish just begins to flake easily with a fork. Remove fish from grill, cover loosely with foil to keep warm.

3. Place tortillas on grill. Grill, 5-10 seconds or until lightly browned, turning occasionally.

4. To assemble, flake fish into pieces. Spread half of the aioli over tortillas. Top with fish, black bean mixture, coleslaw, cheese and jalapeno. Serve with lime and remaining aioli.

NOTE *Wear disposable gloves when cutting hot peppers; the oils can burn skin. Avoid touching your face.*

Spicy Crunchy Tuna Wraps

These quick-to-fix wraps are ideal for lunch or dinner. They're versatile, too—you can replace the tuna with chicken, turkey or ham. Adapt them to whatever you have on hand for a fun alternative to sandwiches.
—**AMY SMELTZER** BARTON, MD

START TO FINISH: 15 MIN. • **MAKES:** 4 SERVINGS

- 4 pouches (2.6 ounces each) sweet and spicy chunk light tuna
- 1½ cups coleslaw mix
- ⅓ cup chopped salted peanuts
- 1 tablespoon rice vinegar
- ¼ teaspoon crushed red pepper flakes
- ⅛ teaspoon pepper

- 12 Bibb or Boston lettuce leaves (about 1 medium)
  Reduced-sodium soy sauce

In a small bowl, combine the first six ingredients; toss lightly to combine. Serve in lettuce leaves with soy sauce.

THROW A TASTY WRAP PARTY

The next time you have friends over, set out platters of various types of lettuce—romaine, escarole, Bibb—and different fillings. Guests will have a blast making their own lettuce wraps.

Cod with Raspberry Sauce
PICTURED AT RIGHT

My sister-in-law shared this recipe with me. I'm not usually crazy about fish, but the fresh raspberry sauce makes this cod simply scrumptious.
—ANGELA LEINENBACH MECHANICSVILLE, VA

START TO FINISH: 30 MIN. • **MAKES:** 4 SERVINGS (½ CUP SAUCE)

1½ pints fresh raspberries
¼ cup water
2 tablespoons brown sugar
1 tablespoon balsamic vinegar
1 teaspoon salt, divided
⅛ teaspoon plus ½ teaspoon coarsely ground pepper, divided
¼ cup butter, softened
4 cod fillets (6 ounces each)
2 tablespoons canola oil
Fresh minced mint leaves, optional

1. Preheat oven to 375°. Reserve ½ cup raspberries. In a small saucepan, combine water, brown sugar, vinegar and remaining raspberries; bring to a boil. Reduce heat; simmer, covered, 4-6 minutes or until sugar is dissolved and raspberries have broken down, stirring occasionally. Press raspberry mixture through a fine-mesh strainer into a bowl; discard seeds. Stir in ½ teaspoon salt and ⅛ teaspoon pepper; return to pan. Bring to a boil. Reduce heat; simmer, uncovered, 2-3 minutes or until liquid is reduced to ½ cup.

2. In a small bowl, stir butter until smooth. Stir in remaining salt and pepper. Spread butter mixture over fillets.

3. In a large ovenproof skillet, heat oil over medium heat. Add fillets; cook 1-2 minutes on each side. Bake 6-8 minutes or until fish just begins to flake easily with a fork. Serve with sauce. Top with reserved raspberries and, if desired, mint.

Thai Lime Shrimp & Noodles

The flavors just pop in this quick dinner! You can add more or less lime peel and chili paste according to personal taste. My family likes spicy foods, but I kept the heat moderate in this version.
—TERI RASEY CADILLAC, MI

START TO FINISH: 25 MIN. • **MAKES:** 6 SERVINGS

1 cup minced fresh basil
3 tablespoons lime juice
4 teaspoons Thai red chili paste
1 garlic clove, minced
1 teaspoon minced fresh gingerroot
1½ pounds uncooked shrimp (26–30 per pound), peeled and deveined
12 ounces cooked angel hair pasta
4 teaspoons olive oil, divided
1 can (14½ ounces) chicken broth
1 can (13.66 ounces) coconut milk

1 teaspoon salt
1 tablespoon cornstarch
2 tablespoons cold water
2 tablespoons grated lime peel

1. Place the first five ingredients in a blender; cover and process until blended. Remove 1 tablespoon mixture; toss with shrimp.

2. Cook pasta according to package directions. Meanwhile, in a large nonstick skillet, heat 2 teaspoons oil over medium-high heat. Add half of the shrimp mixture; stir-fry 2-4 minutes or until shrimp turn pink. Remove from pan; keep warm. Repeat with remaining oil and shrimp mixture.

3. Add broth, coconut milk, salt and remaining basil mixture to same pan. In a small bowl, mix cornstarch and water until smooth. Stir into broth mixture. Bring to a boil; cook and stir 1-2 minutes or until slightly thickened. Stir in lime peel.

4. Drain pasta; add pasta and shrimp to sauce, tossing to coat.

Cedar Plank Scallops

The fishmonger at our local farmers market inspired me to try my hand at scallops cooked on a cedar plank. After a little experimenting, I was proud to serve this dish to friends.
—**ROBERT HALPERT**
NEWBURYPORT, MA

PREP: 10 MIN. + SOAKING • **GRILL:** 15 MIN. • **MAKES:** 4 SERVINGS

- 2 cedar grilling planks
- ¼ cup dry white wine
- 2 tablespoons olive oil
- 2 teaspoons minced fresh basil
- 1 teaspoon minced fresh thyme
- 1 teaspoon lime juice
- 12 sea scallops (about 1½ pounds)

1. Soak planks in water at least 1 hour. In a large bowl, whisk wine, oil, basil, thyme and lime juice. Add scallops; gently toss to coat. Let stand 15 minutes.

2. Place planks on grill rack over direct medium heat. Cover and heat 4-5 minutes or until light to medium smoke comes from the plank and the wood begins to crackle. (This indicates the plank is ready.) Turn plank over and place on indirect heat. Drain scallops, discarding marinade. Place scallops on plank. Grill, covered, over indirect medium heat 10-12 minutes or until firm and opaque.

TIPS FOR USING GRILLING PLANKS

You can buy packages of grill-ready cedar, maple, cherry or apple wood planks at grocery, hardware and kitchen stores. Or buy untreated 1-by-6s or 1-by-8s at a lumberyard and cut them into sections. (Never cook with wood that has been chemically treated.) Immerse the plank in water and let it soak for 3-4 hours or overnight. (You may have to weigh it down with a soup can.) This helps to make the aromatic smolder and slows the burning process during grilling. For even more flavor, add white wine, beer, apple cider or fresh herbs to the soaking water. To use, dry off the plank and grill as the recipe directs. Remove the cooked food from the plank. Let the plank cool on the grill grate before removing.

Mighty Mango Shrimp

Served hot or cold, this shrimp has a nice kick of spice, balanced by the sweetness of mango.
—**THOMAS FAGLON** SOMERSET, NJ

PREP: 10 MIN. + MARINATING • **GRILL:** 10 MIN. • **MAKES:** 4 SERVINGS

1¼ cups mango nectar
2 tablespoons lime juice
4 teaspoons minced chipotle peppers in adobo sauce
1½ teaspoons grated lime peel
1¼ teaspoons ground cumin
16 uncooked jumbo shrimp, peeled and deveined

1. In a large bowl, whisk the first five ingredients until blended. Reserve ½ cup for basting. Add shrimp to remaining marinade; gently toss to coat. Let stand 15 minutes.
2. Drain shrimp, discarding marinade. On four metal or soaked wooden skewers, thread shrimp. Moisten a paper towel with cooking oil; using long-handled tongs, rub on grill rack to coat lightly.

3. Grill shrimp, covered, over medium heat or broil 4 in. from heat 3-4 minutes on each side or until shrimp turn pink, basting occasionally with reserved marinade.

Grilled Lemon-Parmesan Tilapia

We say goodbye to winter by breaking out the grill. And nothing says "spring" like the taste of fresh fish. This recipe also works well with catfish, sea bass or any other firm fish.
—**WENDY G. BALL** BATTLE CREEK, MI

START TO FINISH: 25 MIN. • **MAKES:** 6 SERVINGS

¾ cup shredded Parmesan cheese
¼ cup butter, softened
¼ cup mayonnaise
2 teaspoons grated lemon peel
2 tablespoons lemon juice
½ teaspoon dill weed
¼ teaspoon dried basil
¼ teaspoon pepper
⅛ teaspoon onion powder
⅛ teaspoon celery salt
6 tilapia fillets (6 ounces each)
    Lemon wedges

1. In a small bowl, mix the first 10 ingredients until blended.
2. Moisten a paper towel with cooking oil; using long-handled tongs, rub on grill rack to coat lightly. Place fish on grill rack. Grill, covered, over medium heat 4 minutes. Turn; spread cheese mixture over fillets. Grill, covered, 3-4 minutes longer or until fish just begins to flake easily with a fork. Serve with lemon wedges.

PARMESAN POINTER

When a recipe calls for shredded Parmesan cheese, use the cheese found in bags in the grocery store dairy section. You can substitute either shredded or grated Parmesan in equal proportions in your favorite recipes.

Salmon with Cucumber Dill Sauce

Here's a simple dinner you can enjoy any day of the week. The dill sauce adds a refreshing tang to the sturdy fish. Serve the dish with a green salad and steamed seasonal vegetables such as asparagus.
—NOELLE MYERS GRAND FORKS, ND

START TO FINISH: 25 MIN. • **MAKES:** 4 SERVINGS

4 salmon fillets (1¼ inch thick and 4 ounces each)
1 medium onion, cut into wedges
2 lemon slices
2 garlic cloves, minced
½ teaspoon salt
1 bay leaf

SAUCE
1 cup sour cream ranch dip
1 medium cucumber, peeled, seeded and chopped
1 tablespoon 2% milk
2 teaspoons snipped fresh dill
2 teaspoons grated onion
2 teaspoons Dijon mustard

1. Place salmon in a large skillet with high sides, skin side down. Add onion, lemon slices, garlic, salt, bay leaf and enough water to cover salmon. Bring just to a boil. Adjust heat to maintain a gentle simmer. Cook, uncovered, 5-7 minutes or until fish just begins to flake easily with a fork.

2. Meanwhile, in a small bowl, mix sauce ingredients until blended. Serve with salmon.

Steamed Tilapia in Wine Sauce

I developed this recipe while working at a local winery. It's fast and easy to prepare and became an instant classic at my house. I use a lively dry pear wine in the sauce and recommend avoiding those that are sweet or semi-sweet.
—TENNEILLE BREWER FAYETTE, NY

START TO FINISH: 20 MIN. • **MAKES:** 4 SERVINGS

4 tilapia fillets (6 ounces each)
1 teaspoon salt, divided
¼ teaspoon plus ⅛ teaspoon pepper, divided
1 pound fresh sugar snap peas, trimmed
2 tablespoons minced chives
4 tablespoons butter
½ cup dry white wine
Hot cooked rice

1. Sprinkle fillets with ¾ teaspoon salt and ¼ teaspoon pepper. Place each fillet on a piece of heavy-duty foil (about 18x12-in. rectangle). Top with peas, chives and butter. Drizzle with wine; sprinkle with the remaining salt and pepper. Fold foil around fish and peas, sealing tightly.

2. Grill, covered, over medium heat 10-15 minutes or until fish flakes easily with a fork. Open foil carefully to allow steam to escape. Spoon juices over fish and peas. Serve with rice.

Salmon Vegetable Salad with Pesto Vinaigrette

A bounty of vegetables keeps this salad light on calories, while salmon makes it hearty enough for a meal. It's become a springtime staple at our house.
—FRANCES PIETSCH FLOWER MOUND, TX

PREP: 30 MIN. • **BAKE:** 15 MIN.
MAKES: 6 SERVINGS

- 1 **pound red potatoes (about 4 medium), cubed**
- 1 **pound fresh asparagus, trimmed and cut into 1-inch pieces**
- 1 **teaspoon kosher salt, divided**
- ½ **teaspoon freshly ground pepper, divided**
- 4 **salmon fillets (6 ounces each)**
- 1 **cup grape tomatoes, halved**
- ¼ **cup balsamic vinegar**
- ¼ **cup prepared pesto**
- 6 **cups spring mix salad greens**
- 2 **green onions, sliced**

1. Preheat oven to 400°. Place potatoes in a large saucepan; add water to cover. Bring to a boil. Reduce heat; cook, uncovered, 10-12 minutes or until tender, adding asparagus during the last 4 minutes of cooking. Drain; rinse with cold water. Sprinkle with ½ teaspoon salt and ¼ teaspoon pepper.

2. Meanwhile, place salmon in a greased 15x10x1-in. baking pan; sprinkle with remaining salt and pepper. Bake 14-16 minutes or until fish just begins to flake easily with a fork. Break salmon into chunks; cool slightly.

3. In a large bowl, combine potato mixture, salmon and tomatoes. In a small bowl, whisk vinegar and pesto until blended. In a large serving bowl, combine salad greens, green onions and half of the dressing; toss to coat. Top with potato mixture. Serve immediately with remaining dressing.

When the snow melts and flowers bloom, a bounty of fruits and vegetables crop up, too—ready to invigorate your palate. But with your garden growing fast, how can you make use of all that lovely produce so the homegrown goodness lasts?

The answer is simple! Can and preserve your harvest to create delectable jams, jellies, spreads, relishes and more. These recipes are more than just the perfect topping for your breakfast, lunch or dinner—they are a taste of summer that will brighten meals for months to come.

Refrigerator Dill Pickles (p. 153)
Sweet Onion & Red Bell Pepper Topping (p. 150)
Peppered Squash Relish (p. 149)

CANNING & PRESERVING

Tools of the Trade

Gather these essentials for using the boiling water bath processing method.

LIST OF SUPPLIES

- Large stockpot
- Ladle
- Jar funnel
- Magnetic lid lifter
- Bubble remover &
  headspace tool
- Jar wrench
- Tongs
- Jar lifter
- Canning jars, lids & bands

1. LARGE STOCKPOT:
Choose one that holds at least 12 quarts and is tall enough to allow the jars to be fully submerged during processing.

2. LADLE:
Safely pour hot mixtures into canning jars.

3. JAR FUNNEL:
Easily fill jars without spilling.

4. MAGNETIC LID LIFTER:
Lift sterilized lids out of hot water with magnetic end.

5. BUBBLE REMOVER & HEADSPACE TOOL:
Slide along the inside walls of filled jars to release any air bubbles and measure headspace.

6. JAR WRENCH:
Turn those stubborn or sticky jar lids effortlessly.

7. TONGS (WITH COATED HANDLES):
Safely lift foods during canning or cooking.

8. JAR LIFTER:
Pluck hot jars from the boiling processing water.

9. GLASS CANNING JARS, LIDS & BANDS: Fill glass jars with your creation, then seal in the freshness with one-time-use lids and reusable bands.

Peppered Squash Relish

I cook for a local middle school and have been making this relish for more than 25 years. Whenever I take it to a dinner or picnic, it goes fast. Sometimes I put it into gift baskets with other homemade goodies.
—**ROSE COLE** SALEM, WV

PREP: 15 MIN. + CHILLING • **COOK:** 20 MIN. + COOLING • **MAKES:** 4 QUARTS

- 3 **pounds yellow summer squash, finely chopped**
- 3 **pounds zucchini, finely chopped**
- 6 **large onions, finely chopped**
- 3 **medium green peppers, finely chopped**
- 3 **medium sweet red peppers, finely chopped**
- ¼ **cup salt**
- 2 **cups sugar**
- 2 **cups packed brown sugar**
- 2 **cups white vinegar**
- 4 **teaspoons celery seed**
- 1 **teaspoon ground turmeric**
- 1 **teaspoon ground mustard**

1. In a large bowl, combine the first six ingredients. Refrigerate, covered, overnight.
2. Drain vegetable mixture. Rinse in cold water and drain again. Place vegetables in a Dutch oven. Add sugars, vinegar, celery seed, turmeric and mustard. Bring to a boil. Reduce heat; simmer, uncovered, 15-20 minutes or until liquid is clear.
3. Remove from heat; cool. Spoon into containers. Refrigerate, covered, up to 3 weeks.

Orange Rhubarb Spread

This tangy spread is easy to make and tastes especially good on hot, buttered cinnamon toast. The recipe makes enough to have on hand well beyond the growing season.
—**BETTY NYENHUIS** OOSTBURG, WI

PREP: 5 MIN. • **COOK:** 20 MIN. + STANDING • **MAKES:** 5 HALF-PINTS

- 4 **cups diced fresh or frozen rhubarb**
- 2 **cups water**
- 1 **can (6 ounces) frozen orange juice concentrate, thawed**
- 1 **package (1¾ ounces) powdered fruit pectin**
- 4 **cups sugar**

1. In a large saucepan, bring rhubarb and water to a boil. Reduce heat; simmer, uncovered, 7-8 minutes or until rhubarb is tender. Drain and reserve cooking liquid. Cool rhubarb and liquid to room temperature.
2. Place rhubarb in a blender; cover and process until pureed. Transfer to a 4-cup measuring cup; add enough reserved cooking liquid to measure 2⅓ cups. Return to saucepan.
3. Add orange juice concentrate and pectin; bring to a full rolling boil, stirring constantly. Stir in sugar. Return to a full rolling boil; boil and stir 1 minute. Remove from heat; skim off foam.
4. Pour into jars or freezer containers; cool to room temperature, about 1 hour. Cover and let stand overnight or until set, but not longer than 24 hours. Refrigerate or freeze. Refrigerate for up to 3 weeks or freeze for up to 12 months.

Pickled Green Beans

This recipe produces zippy little pickles. I like that it preserves my green beans for months...if they last that long. I crank up the heat a bit with cayenne pepper.

—MARISA MCCLELLAN
PHILADELPHIA, PA

PREP: 20 MIN. • **PROCESS:** 10 MIN.
MAKES: 4 PINTS

- 1¾ **pounds fresh green beans, trimmed**
- 1 **teaspoon cayenne pepper**
- 4 **garlic cloves, peeled**
- 4 **teaspoons dill seed or 4 fresh dill heads**
- 2½ **cups water**
- 2½ **cups white vinegar**
- ¼ **cup canning salt**

1. Pack beans into four hot 1-pint jars to within ½ in. of the top. Add cayenne, garlic and dill seed to jars.
2. In a large saucepan, bring water, vinegar and salt to a boil.
3. Carefully ladle hot liquid over beans, leaving ½-in. headspace. Remove air bubbles and adjust headspace, if necessary, by adding hot mixture. Wipe rims. Center lids on jars; screw on bands until fingertip tight.
4. Place jars into canner with simmering water, ensuring that they are completely covered with water. Bring to a boil; process for 10 minutes. Remove jars and cool.

NOTE *The processing time listed is for altitudes of up to 1,000 feet. For altitudes up to 3,000 feet, add 5 minutes; 6,000 feet, add 10 minutes; 8,000 feet, add 15 minutes; 10,000 feet, add 20 minutes.*

Sweet Onion & Red Bell Pepper Topping

As soon as the spring Vidalia onions hit the market, this is one of the first recipes I make. I use it on hot dogs, bruschetta, cream cheese and crackers. It is so versatile.

—PAT HOCKETT OCALA, FL

PREP: 15 MIN. • **COOK:** 4 HOURS • **MAKES:** 4 CUPS

- 4 **large sweet onions, thinly sliced (about 8 cups)**
- 4 **large sweet red peppers, thinly sliced (about 6 cups)**
- ½ **cup cider vinegar**
- ¼ **cup packed brown sugar**
- 2 **tablespoons canola oil**
- 2 **tablespoons honey**
- 2 **teaspoons celery seed**
- ¾ **teaspoon crushed red pepper flakes**
- ½ **teaspoon salt**

In a 5- or 6-qt. slow cooker, combine all ingredients. Cook, covered, on low 4-5 hours or until vegetables are tender. Serve with a slotted spoon.

Spinach Pesto

Serve this vibrant pesto on pasta, pizza, sandwiches and more. You can leave out the fresh oregano, if you like.
—SUSAN WESTERFIELD ALBUQUERQUE, NM

START TO FINISH: 15 MIN. • **MAKES:** 2 CUPS

- 2 cups fresh baby spinach
- 2 cups loosely packed basil leaves
- 1 cup grated Romano cheese
- 2 tablespoons fresh oregano
- 2 teaspoons minced garlic
- ½ teaspoon salt
- ½ cup chopped walnuts, toasted
- 1 tablespoon lemon juice
- 2 teaspoons grated lemon peel
- 1 cup olive oil
  Hot cooked pasta

1. Place the first six ingredients in a food processor; cover and pulse until chopped. Add the walnuts, lemon juice and peel; cover and process until blended. While processing, gradually add oil in a steady stream.

2. Serve desired amount of pesto with pasta. Transfer remaining sauce to ice cube trays. Cover and freeze for up to 1 month.
TO USE FROZEN PESTO *Thaw in the refrigerator for 3 hours. Serve with pasta.*

Citrus Blueberry Marmalade

I have four young children, so berry picking is the ideal family activity for us. It also inspired me to start preserving this season. I made use of the berries we picked in this easy recipe, using basic ingredients and no added pectin.
—SARAH HAENGEL BOWIE, MD

PREP: 1 HOUR • **PROCESS:** 10 MIN. • **MAKES:** 5 HALF-PINTS

- 4 cups sugar
- 2 cups water
- 1 medium orange, quartered, thinly sliced and seeds removed
- 1 medium lemon, quartered, thinly sliced and seeds removed
- 1 medium lime, quartered, thinly sliced and seeds removed
- 5 cups fresh blueberries

1. In a Dutch oven, combine sugar, water, orange, lemon and lime slices; bring to a boil. Reduce heat; simmer, uncovered, 15-20 minutes or until fruit is tender.
2. Add blueberries; increase heat to medium-high. Cook and stir 25-30 minutes or until slightly thickened.
3. Remove from heat; skim off foam. Ladle hot mixture into five hot half-pint jars, leaving ¼-in. headspace. Remove air bubbles and adjust headspace, if needed,

by adding hot mixture. Wipe rims. Center lids on jars; screw on bands until fingertip tight.
4. Place jars in canner with simmering water, ensuring that they are completely submerged. Bring to a boil; process for 10 minutes. Remove jars and cool.
NOTE *The processing time listed is for altitudes of 1,000 feet or less. Add 1 minute to the processing time for each 1,000 feet of additional altitude.*

Strawberry Freezer Jam

PICTURED AT RIGHT

A dear friend gave this recipe to me when we lived in Germany. It's good on ice cream, too!

—MARY JEAN ELLIS INDIANAPOLIS, IN

PREP: 40 MIN. + FREEZING • **MAKES:** 4½ PINTS

- 2 **quarts fresh strawberries**
- 5½ **cups sugar**
- 1 **cup light corn syrup**
- ¼ **cup lemon juice**
- ¾ **cup water**
- 1 **package (1¾ ounces) powdered fruit pectin**

1. Wash and mash berries, measuring out enough mashed berries to make 4 cups; place in a large bowl. Stir in sugar, corn syrup and lemon juice. Let stand 10 minutes.

2. In a Dutch oven, combine strawberry mixture and water. Stir in pectin. Bring to a full rolling boil over high heat, stirring constantly. Boil 1 minute, stirring constantly. Remove from heat; skim off foam.

3. Pour into jars or freezer containers, leaving ½-in. headspace. Cover and let stand overnight or until set, but not longer than 24 hours. Refrigerate for up to 3 weeks or freeze for up to 12 months.

Mint Jelly

Here's a classic condiment to go with roasted lamb. With its bright green color, the jelly is a pretty addition to the holiday buffet table.

—NAOMI GIDDIS TWO BUTTES, CO

PREP: 15 MIN. + STANDING • **PROCESS:** 10 MIN. • **MAKES:** 11 HALF-PINTS

- 4½ **cups water**
- 3 **cups packed fresh mint, crushed**
- 7 **cups sugar**
- ¼ **cup lemon juice**
- 2 **to 4 drops green food coloring**
- 2 **pouches (3 ounces each) liquid pectin**

1. In a large saucepan, bring water and mint to a boil. Remove from heat; cover and let stand 15 minutes. Strain, reserving 3⅓ cups liquid (discard remaining liquid).

2. In a Dutch oven, combine sugar, lemon juice, food coloring and reserved liquid. Bring to a boil; cook and stir 1 minute. Add pectin; return to a boil. Cook and stir 1 minute. Remove from heat; let stand 5 minutes.

3. Skim off foam. Ladle hot liquid into hot half-pint jars, leaving ¼-in. headspace. Wipe rims. Center lids on jars; screw on bands until fingertip tight. Place jars in canner with simmering water ensuring that they are completely submerged. Bring to a boil; process 10 minutes. Remove jars and cool.

NOTE *The processing time listed is for altitudes of up to 1,000 feet. Add 1 minute to the processing time for each 1,000 feet of additional altitude.*

Refrigerator Dill Pickles

Easy and economical, these irresistible pickles are tangy, zesty and crispy. No one will believe you made them yourself!
—**JAKE HAEN** OCALA, FL

PREP: 40 MIN. + CHILLING • **MAKES:** ABOUT 100 PICKLE SPEARS

- 6 to 8 pounds pickling cucumbers
- 40 fresh dill sprigs
- 2 large onions, thinly sliced
- 5 garlic cloves, sliced
- 1 quart water
- 1 quart white vinegar
- ¾ cup sugar
- ½ cup canning salt

1. Cut each cucumber lengthwise into four spears. In a large bowl, combine the cucumbers, dill, onions and garlic; set aside. In a Dutch oven, combine the remaining ingredients. Bring to a boil; cook and stir just until salt is dissolved. Pour over cucumber mixture; cool.

2. Cover tightly and refrigerate for at least 24 hours. Store in the refrigerator for up to 2 months.

Basil Jelly

We grow lots of basil for our local farmers market, and this is a unique way to use it. The jelly is very good with cream cheese as an appetizer. I also like to combine a jar with one cup of barbecue sauce and simmer mini meatballs or cocktail wieners in the mixture.

—SUE GRONHOLZ BEAVER DAM, WI

PREP: 25 MIN. • **PROCESS:** 15 MIN. • **MAKES:** 6 HALF-PINTS

- 4 cups water
- 2 cups firmly packed fresh basil leaves, finely chopped
- 1 package (1¾ ounces) powdered fruit pectin
- 3 drops green food coloring, optional
- 5 cups sugar

1. In a large saucepan, bring water and basil to a boil. Remove from heat; cover and let stand 10 minutes. Strain and discard basil.

Return 3⅔ cups liquid to the pan. Stir in pectin and, if desired, food coloring. Return to a rolling boil over high heat. Stir in sugar. Boil 1 minute, stirring constantly. Remove from heat; skim off foam.

2. Ladle hot liquid into hot half-pint jars, leaving ¼-in. headspace. Wipe rims. Center lids on jars; screw on bands until fingertip tight.

3. Place jars into canner with simmering water, ensuring that they are completely covered with water. Bring to a boil; process for 15 minutes. Remove jars and cool.

NOTE *The processing time listed is for altitudes of up to 1,000 feet. Add 1 minute to the processing time for each 1,000 feet of additional altitude.*

STERILIZED VS. HOT JARS

There's a reason some canning recipes call for hot sterilized jars while others call simply for hot jars. If the mixture will be processed for 10-plus minutes up to 1,000 feet above sea level, jars just need to be hot. If processing time is shorter, jars must be sterilized in boiling water for 10 minutes (add 1 minute for each 1,000 feet of additional altitude).

Homemade Lemon Curd

PICTURED AT RIGHT

Lemon curd is a scrumptious spread for scones, biscuits or other baked goods. You can find it in larger grocery stores with the jams and jellies or the baking supplies—but it's more fun to make it from scratch.

—*TASTE OF HOME* TEST KITCHEN

PREP: 20 MIN. + CHILLING • **MAKES:** 1⅔ CUPS

- 3 large eggs
- 1 cup sugar
- ½ cup lemon juice (about 2 lemons)
- ¼ cup butter, cubed
- 1 tablespoon grated lemon peel

In a small heavy saucepan over medium heat, whisk eggs, sugar and lemon juice until blended.

Add butter and lemon peel; cook, whisking constantly, until mixture is thickened and coats the back of a metal spoon. Transfer to a small bowl; cool 10 minutes. Refrigerate, covered, until cold.

LIME CURD *Substitute lime juice and peel for lemon juice and peel. Proceed as directed.*

Spring Canning Jars

You put up jams, jellies, pickles and preserves with a lot of love. So why not dress up the jars containing the fruits of your labor? These labels and jar toppers are a snap to make and will turn your canned goods into attractive gifts for family and friends.

MATERIALS

Canning jars and lids
Card stock
Fabric scraps
Buttons
Striped twine
Scallop-edge circle punch
 (1 in. or desired size)
Hole punch
Pinking shears

DIRECTIONS

1. Print homemade labels onto card stock. Or visit *countrywomanmagazine.com/ project/free-printable-canning-labels* to download printable labels.

2. Use a circle punch to cut labels from card stock. Use a hole punch to punch a hole at the top of the label.

3. With pinking shears, cut a scalloped circle of fabric about 3 in. wider in diameter than the canning jar lid.

4. Cover the lid with fabric and twist the band in place over it. Trim fabric if needed.

5. Thread twine through one hole of a button and the hole in the label. Wrap twine around the lid band and up through the opposite hole of the button. Tie in place.

special celebrations

Are you looking for a simple and tasty meal to enjoy al fresco on a warm summer evening? Need some hearty snacks to pass around at the Super Bowl party? Whether you're carving Halloween pumpkins with the kids or hosting an afternoon tea with your favorite gal pals, turn here for recipes to help you celebrate any season or occasion.

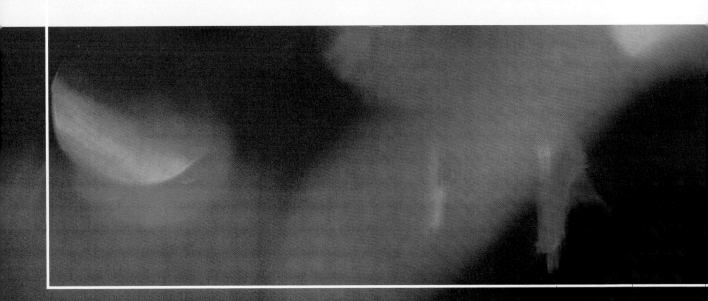

It doesn't matter which team you cheer for in the Super Bowl, everyone's a winner when this lineup of "fan food" takes the culinary field. Turn here for mouthwatering versions of stick-to-your-ribs favorites: Nachos flavored with beer and hearty brats, and Southwestern-style buffalo wings that will have everyone reaching for seconds. You'll also find bold upgrades of sliders, potato skins, mac and cheese and other classics.

If your sweet tooth calls at halftime, reach for Frosted Turtle Brownies or Snickerdoodle Blondie Bars. They're great for game-day snacking or any get-together where you need to score a touchdown at the buffet.

Beer and Brats Nachos (p. 166)
Spicy Almonds (p. 165)
Touchdown Brat Sliders (p. 161)
Spicy Sweet Potato Chips &
Cilantro Dip (p. 166)

SUPER BOWL **PARTY**

Buffalo Macaroni and Cheese Bites

This pub-style appetizer turns comforting mac and cheese and Louisiana hot sauce into perfect munchies. Crispy and cheesy at the same time, these bites are a great meat-free option, too.

—ANN DONNAY MILTON, MA

PREP: 45 MIN. + CHILLING
BAKE: 15 MIN.
MAKES: 2 DOZEN

- 1 package (7¼ ounces) macaroni and cheese dinner mix
- 6 cups water
- 2 tablespoons 2% milk
- 1 tablespoon butter
- ¼ cup Louisiana-style hot sauce
- 1 cup all-purpose flour
- 1 large egg, beaten
- 1 can (6 ounces) French-fried onions, crushed
  Blue cheese salad dressing

1. Set the cheese packet from dinner mix aside. In a large saucepan, bring water to a boil. Add macaroni; cook for 8-10 minutes or until tender. Drain. Stir in the contents of the cheese packet, milk and butter.
2. Press 2 tablespoonfuls into greased miniature muffin cups. Cover and refrigerate for 3 hours or overnight.
3. Place the hot sauce, flour, egg and onions in separate shallow bowls. Remove macaroni bites from cups. Dip in the hot sauce and flour, then coat with egg and onions. Place 2 in. apart on a lightly greased baking sheet.
4. Bake at 400° for 12-15 minutes or until golden brown. Serve with dressing.

Crispy Taco Wings

Your family will love these addictive snacks. Serve the chicken wings with ranch salad dressing, and stand back and watch everyone dig in!

—BLANCHE GIBSON GORDON, WI

PREP: 15 MIN. • **BAKE:** 30 MIN. • **MAKES:** 2 DOZEN

- ½ cup all-purpose flour
- 1 envelope taco seasoning
- ½ cup butter, melted
- 1¾ cups crushed corn chips
- 2½ pounds chicken wingettes and drummettes

1. Preheat oven to 350°. In a shallow bowl, mix flour and taco seasoning. Place melted butter and corn chips in separate shallow bowls. Dip wings in flour mixture to coat both sides; shake off excess. Dip in butter, then in crumb mixture, patting to help coating adhere.
2. Transfer wings to a greased 15x10x1-in. baking pan. Bake, uncovered, 30-40 minutes or until juices run clear.

Touchdown Brat Sliders

My husband is crazy about these sliders, featuring the three B's—bratwurst, bacon and beer! Topped with seasoned potato chips, they're an ideal halftime attraction.
—KIRSTEN SHABAZ LAKEVILLE, MN

START TO FINISH: 30 MIN. • **MAKES:** 16 SLIDERS

5 thick-sliced bacon strips, chopped
1 pound uncooked bratwurst links, casings removed
1 large onion, finely chopped
2 garlic cloves, minced
1 package (8 ounces) cream cheese, cubed
1 cup dark beer or nonalcoholic beer
1 tablespoon Dijon mustard
¼ teaspoon pepper

16 dinner rolls, split and toasted
2 cups cheddar and sour cream potato chips, crushed

1. In a large skillet, cook bacon over medium heat until crisp. Remove to paper towels with a slotted spoon; drain, reserving drippings. Cook bratwurst and onion in drippings over medium heat until meat is no longer pink. Add garlic; cook 1 minute longer. Drain.

2. Stir in the cream cheese, beer, mustard and pepper. Bring to a boil. Reduce heat; simmer, uncovered, for 8-10 minutes or until thickened, stirring occasionally. Stir in bacon. Spoon ¼ cup onto each roll; sprinkle with chips. Replace tops.

Game Day Miniature Peppers

My mom's recipe for stuffed peppers inspired this smaller version that's just right for munching. I make them healthier by using ground turkey and brown rice, but you can stuff them with pork, beans, goat cheese...let your imagination go wild!
—ROSE MUCCIO METHUEN, MA

PREP: 55 MIN. • **BAKE:** 20 MIN. • **MAKES:** 2 DOZEN

8 each miniature sweet red, orange and yellow peppers
4 ounces ground turkey
½ cup finely chopped fresh mushrooms
¼ cup chopped sweet onion
1 garlic clove, minced
1 can (15 ounces) tomato sauce, divided
¼ cup cooked brown rice
1 tablespoon grated Parmesan cheese
1 tablespoon shredded part-skim mozzarella cheese
½ teaspoon dried basil

¼ teaspoon salt
¼ teaspoon cayenne pepper
¼ teaspoon pepper

1. Cut and reserve tops off peppers; remove seeds. Cut thin slices from pepper bottoms to level; set aside peppers.
2. In a large skillet, cook the turkey, mushrooms, onion and garlic over medium heat until meat is no longer pink. Remove from the heat; let stand for 5 minutes.

3. Stir in ¼ cup tomato sauce, rice, cheeses and seasonings; spoon into peppers. Place upright in a greased 11x7-in. baking dish.
4. Spoon remaining tomato sauce over peppers; replace pepper tops. Cover and bake at 400° for 18-22 minutes or until heated through and peppers are crisp-tender.

Pork Taquitos

Even the most devoted football fan will leave the TV to grab a few of these meaty taquitos. They freeze well, too, so you can make a big batch and enjoy them the week after the big game.
—TASTE OF HOME TEST KITCHEN

PREP: 40 MIN. • **BAKE:** 10 MIN. • **MAKES:** 1 DOZEN

- 1 **medium onion, finely chopped**
- 1 **tablespoon canola oil**
- 2 **garlic cloves, minced**
- 2 **teaspoons ground cumin**
- 1 **teaspoon dried oregano**
- 1 **teaspoon chili powder**
- ¼ **teaspoon cayenne pepper**
- 2 **cups shredded cooked pork**
- 1 **cup (4 ounces) shredded Mexican cheese blend**
- ¼ **cup minced fresh cilantro**
- ¼ **cup salsa verde**
- 1 **tablespoon lime juice**
- 12 **corn tortillas (6 inches), warmed**
- **Toppings: sour cream, guacamole and additional salsa verde**

1. In a large skillet, saute onion in oil until tender. Add the garlic, cumin, oregano, chili powder and cayenne; cook 1 minute longer. Add the pork, cheese, cilantro, salsa and lime juice. Cook and stir until the cheese is melted.
2. Place 2 tablespoons filling over lower third of each tortilla. Roll up tightly. Secure with toothpicks. Place taquitos on a greased baking sheet. Bake at 400° for 8 minutes.
3. Cool completely on a wire rack. Discard toothpicks. Place taquitos on a waxed paper-lined 15x10-in. baking sheet; freeze until firm. Transfer to a resealable plastic freezer bag. May be frozen for up to 3 months.
TO USE FROZEN TAQUITOS
Arrange desired number of taquitos in a single layer on a greased baking sheet. Bake at 400° for 12-15 minutes or until golden brown. Serve with toppings.

Snickerdoodle Blondie Bars

My boys' football team voted me "Most Valuable Baker" when I whipped up a batch of these chewy, cinnamon-highlighted blondies for a post-game treat.
—VALONDA SEWARD COARSEGOLD, CA

PREP: 15 MIN. • **BAKE:** 35 MIN. + COOLING • **MAKES:** ABOUT 1½ DOZEN

- 1 **cup butter, softened**
- 2 **cups packed brown sugar**
- 2 **large eggs**
- 3 **teaspoons vanilla extract**
- 2⅔ **cups all-purpose flour**
- 2 **teaspoons baking powder**
- 1 **teaspoon ground cinnamon**
- ¼ **teaspoon ground nutmeg**
- ½ **teaspoon salt**

TOPPING
- 1½ **teaspoons sugar**
- ½ **teaspoon ground cinnamon**

1. Preheat oven to 350°. In a large bowl, cream butter and brown sugar until fluffy. Beat in eggs and vanilla. In another bowl, whisk flour, baking powder, spices and salt; gradually beat into creamed mixture. Spread into a greased 9-in.-square baking pan.
2. Mix topping ingredients; sprinkle over top. Bake 35-40 minutes or until set and golden brown. Cool in pan on a wire rack. Cut into bars.

Meaty Sloppy Joe Pockets

It's easy to turn sloppy joes into hearty hot pocket snacks. I make the filling ahead and use refrigerated biscuits. I time them so they're done baking just before kickoff.
—**SHELLY FLYE** ALBION, ME

PREP: 45 MIN. + COOLING
BAKE: 20 MIN. • **MAKES:** 8 SERVINGS

- 1 **pound lean ground beef (90% lean)**
- ¼ **cup finely chopped onion**
- ¼ **cup finely chopped celery**
- ¼ **cup shredded carrot**
- 1 **can (8 ounces) tomato sauce**
- ¼ **cup ketchup**
- 2 **tablespoons brown sugar**
- 1 **tablespoon red wine vinegar**
- 1 **tablespoon Worcestershire sauce**
- 1 **tablespoon tomato paste**
- 1 **tube (16.3 ounces) large refrigerated buttermilk biscuits**
- ½ **cup shredded cheddar cheese, optional**

1. In a large skillet, cook beef, onion, celery and carrot over medium heat 6-8 minutes or until beef is no longer pink and vegetables are tender, breaking up beef into crumbles; drain.

2. Stir in the tomato sauce, ketchup, brown sugar, vinegar, Worcestershire sauce and tomato paste. Bring to a boil. Reduce heat; simmer, uncovered, 10-15 minutes or until thickened, stirring occasionally. Cool completely.

3. Preheat oven to 350°. On a lightly floured surface, pat or roll each biscuit into a 6-in. circle. Spoon a scant ⅓ cup beef mixture over half of each circle to within ½ in. of edge. If desired, sprinkle with cheddar cheese. Fold dough over the filling; press edge with a fork to seal.

4. Place on an ungreased baking sheet. Cut three slits in top of each. Bake 18-20 minutes or until golden brown.

Frosted Turtle Brownies

Homemade brownies are a sweet addition to the appetizer table on game day. Your guests might forget the score, but I guarantee they'll remember these treats!

—SHERRY MILLER COLUMBIA HEIGHTS, MN

PREP: 20 MIN.
BAKE: 25 MIN. + CHILLING
MAKES: 2 DOZEN

- 1 **cup butter, softened**
- 2 **cups sugar**
- 2 **teaspoons vanilla extract**
- 4 **large eggs**
- 1 **cup baking cocoa**
- 1 **cup all-purpose flour**
- ½ **teaspoon baking powder**
- ¼ **teaspoon salt**

TOPPING
- 3 **cups confectioners' sugar**
- ¾ **cup baking cocoa**
- ½ **cup butter, melted**
- ⅓ **cup 2% milk**
- ¾ **teaspoon vanilla extract**
- 1 **cup chopped pecans, toasted**
- 12 **caramels**
- 1 **tablespoon heavy whipping cream**

1. In a large bowl, cream butter and sugar until light and fluffy. Add vanilla. Add eggs, one at a time, beating well after each addition. Combine the cocoa, flour, baking powder and salt; gradually add to butter mixture.

2. Spread into a greased 13x9-in. baking pan. Bake at 350° for 23-28 minutes or until a toothpick inserted near the center comes out clean (do not overbake). Cool on a wire rack.

3. In a large bowl, beat the confectioners' sugar, cocoa, butter, milk and vanilla until fluffy. Frost brownies. Sprinkle with pecans. Refrigerate for at least 1 hour.

4. In a microwave, melt caramels with cream; stir until smooth. Drizzle over brownies.

Spicy Almonds

These delicious spiced nuts make a nutritious snack for camping and hiking trips, and they are a must for nervous munching when your team is battling on the gridiron.
—GINA MYERS SPOKANE, WA

START TO FINISH: 25 MIN. • **MAKES:** 2½ CUPS

1 tablespoon sugar
1½ teaspoons kosher salt
1 teaspoon paprika
½ teaspoon ground cinnamon
½ teaspoon ground cumin
½ teaspoon ground coriander
¼ teaspoon cayenne pepper
2½ cups unblanched almonds
1 tablespoon canola oil

1. In a small bowl, combine the first seven ingredients. In another small bowl, combine almonds and oil. Sprinkle with spice mixture; toss to coat.
2. Transfer almonds to a foil-lined 15x10x1-in. baking pan coated with cooking spray. Bake at 325° for 15-20 minutes or until lightly browned, stirring twice. Cool completely. Store in an airtight container.

Fajita Potato Skins

Nothing satisfies a hungry crowd like these potato skins stuffed with spicy fajita-style beef. Think football... think basketball...think Friday night appetizer party!
—SAMANTHA LANG ROCHESTER, MI

PREP: 25 MIN. • **BAKE:** 10 MIN. • **MAKES:** 12 SERVINGS

6 medium baking potatoes
1 beef top sirloin steak (1 pound), cut into thin slices
1 tablespoon canola oil
½ cup taco sauce
1 envelope fajita seasoning mix
2 cups (8 ounces) shredded Colby-Monterey Jack cheese
½ cup sour cream
2 green onions, sliced

1. Scrub and pierce potatoes; place on a microwave-safe plate. Microwave, uncovered, on high for 8-10 minutes or until tender, turning once.
2. Meanwhile, in a large skillet, brown beef in oil. Add taco sauce and seasoning mix. Bring to a boil. Reduce heat; simmer, uncovered, for 3-5 minutes or until meat is tender, stirring occasionally.
3. Cut each potato in half lengthwise. Scoop out pulp, leaving a ¼-in. shell (discard pulp or save for another use). Place on greased baking sheets. Spoon beef mixture onto potato shells; sprinkle with cheese.
4. Bake at 350° for 8-10 minutes or until heated through and cheese is melted. Top with sour cream and onions.

BEEFED-UP KITCHEN TIP

It can be a challenge to cut fresh steak into thin, uniform slices. So pop it in the freezer for a few minutes. Once it is partially frozen, the beef is a snap to slice. Continue with the recipe as directed.

Beer and Brats Nachos

I turn game day into a Midwestern celebration with crunchy nachos smothered in cheddar sauce spiked with beer. Topped with slices of bratwurst, these are guaranteed to score a touchdown!
—**KELLY BOE** WHITELAND, IN

START TO FINISH: 30 MIN. • **MAKES:** 12 SERVINGS

1 package (14 ounces) fully cooked smoked bratwurst links, sliced
2¼ cups frozen pepper and onion stir-fry blend
3 cups (12 ounces) shredded cheddar cheese
2½ teaspoons all-purpose flour
1 cup chopped onion
1 tablespoon olive oil
1 garlic clove, minced
¾ cup beer or beef broth
12 cups tortilla chips

1. In a large skillet, saute bratwurst for 1 minute. Add stir-fry blend; cook 3-5 minutes longer or until vegetables are tender. Set aside and keep warm.
2. In a large bowl, combine cheese and flour. In a large saucepan, saute onion in oil until tender. Add garlic; cook 1 minute longer. Stir in beer; heat over medium heat until bubbles form around sides of pan.
3. Reduce heat to medium-low; add a handful of cheese mixture.

Stir constantly, using a figure-eight motion, until almost completely melted. Continue adding cheese, one handful at a time, allowing cheese to almost completely melt between additions.
4. Arrange tortilla chips on a large serving platter. Spoon cheese mixture over chips. Top with bratwurst mixture. Serve immediately.

Spicy Sweet Potato Chips & Cilantro Dip
PICTURED AT RIGHT

This irresistible combo could become your new signature snack food. Park these spicy baked chips next to a bowl of the cool, creamy dip and let the gang have at it. What a great twist on traditional chips and dip!
—**LIBBY WALP** CHICAGO, IL

PREP: 20 MIN. • **BAKE:** 25 MIN./BATCH • **MAKES:** 12 SERVINGS (1½ CUPS DIP)

2 to 3 large sweet potatoes (1¾ pounds), peeled and cut into ⅛-inch slices
2 tablespoons canola oil
1 teaspoon chili powder
½ teaspoon garlic powder
½ teaspoon taco seasoning
¼ teaspoon salt
¼ teaspoon ground cumin
¼ teaspoon pepper
⅛ teaspoon cayenne pepper

DIP
¾ cup mayonnaise
½ cup sour cream
2 ounces cream cheese, softened
4½ teaspoons minced fresh cilantro
1½ teaspoons lemon juice
½ teaspoon celery salt
⅛ teaspoon pepper

1. Place sweet potatoes in a large bowl. In a small bowl, mix oil and seasonings; drizzle over potatoes and toss to coat.
2. Arrange the potatoes in a single layer in two ungreased 15x10x1-in. baking pans. Bake at 400° for 25-30 minutes or until golden brown, turning once. Repeat with remaining potatoes.
3. In a small bowl, beat dip ingredients until blended. Serve with chips.

Chalkboard Table Runner

Keep a play by play account of your Super Bowl buffet with this creative runner. Use it to label foods or simply sketch out a few moves for the defense team. However you use it, this is one table topper you'll turn to time and again!

MATERIALS
- 72x18-in. chalkboard table runner or chalk fabric
- Chalk
- Scissors or rotary cutter

DIRECTIONS

1. Roll out chalk fabric on a work surface. Using scissors or rotary cutter, trim to desired size.

2. Lay runner on serving or buffet table. Use chalk to label recipes or sketch as desired.

Celebrated on the third Monday in February, Presidents Day honors those who have occupied our nation's highest office. The focus is often on George Washington and Abraham Lincoln, whose birthdays fall in February, but celebrations can embrace other presidents, too.

A Presidents Day party is an opportunity to delve into their lives, to uncover interesting tidbits that reveal the men behind the historical figures. For instance, did you know that Washington's first job was as a land surveyor? That Thomas Jefferson played the cello? And that Lincoln's favorite writer was William Shakespeare?

So gather the kids—and some grown-up history buffs—to share a look at the fascinating facts of some of our country's leaders, and to sample dishes that are truly presidential.

Cherry Nut Cake (p. 175)

PRESIDENTS **DAY**

★ HARRY S. TRUMAN ★

Ultimate Steak de Burgo

When asked why Midwesterners prepare their beef well-done, President Truman responded that "only coyotes and predatory animals eat raw beef." Regardless of how you cook your steak, you'll love this traditional beef entree seasoned with butter, herbs and garlic. Serve it with French onion soup and a green salad to round out the meal.

—HOLLIS MONROE AMES, IA

START TO FINISH: 30 MIN. • **MAKES:** 4 SERVINGS

- **1** garlic clove, minced
- **¾** teaspoon salt, divided
- **4** beef tenderloin steaks (1-inch thick and 4 ounces each)
- **¼** teaspoon pepper
- **1** tablespoon butter
- **½** cup butter, cubed
- **½** cup half-and-half cream
- **2** tablespoons sweet white wine
- **½** teaspoon minced fresh oregano or ⅛ teaspoon dried oregano
- **½** teaspoon minced fresh basil or ⅛ teaspoon dried basil

1. Place garlic on a cutting board; sprinkle with ¼ teaspoon salt. Mash garlic with flat side of the knife blade, forming a smooth paste. Sprinkle steaks with pepper and remaining salt.

2. In a large skillet, heat 1 tablespoon butter over medium heat. Add steaks; cook 4-6 minutes on each side or until meat reaches desired doneness (for medium-rare, a thermometer should read 145°; medium, 160°; well-done, 170°). Remove from pan; keep warm.

3. In same skillet, melt ½ cup butter over medium heat. Whisk in garlic paste, cream and wine; heat through. Serve over steaks; sprinkle with herbs.

Rustic Fish Chowder

JFK's affinity for fish chowder was likely inspired by his love of sailing off the coast of New England. In my version, I use fresh halibut my brother-in-law, a commercial fisherman, catches in Kodiak, Alaska. Top servings with grated Parmesan or minced green onions.

—DIANA LASSEN EUGENE, OR

PREP: 15 MIN. • **COOK:** 30 MIN. • **MAKES:** 8 SERVINGS (3 QUARTS)

- ¼ cup butter, cubed
- 1 small onion, finely chopped
- 1 garlic clove, minced
- 3 pounds potatoes (about 6 medium), cut into ½-inch cubes
- 1½ cups fresh or frozen corn
- 5 cups chicken broth
- 1½ teaspoons salt
- ¾ teaspoon celery salt
- ¾ teaspoon pepper
- ½ teaspoon dried thyme
- 1 pound cod or halibut fillets, cut into ¾-inch pieces
- 1 cup heavy whipping cream

1. In a 6-qt. stockpot, heat butter over medium heat. Add onion; cook and stir 3-4 minutes or until tender. Add garlic; cook 1 minute longer. Add potatoes, corn, broth, salt, celery salt, pepper and thyme; bring to a boil. Reduce heat; simmer, covered, 10-15 minutes or until potatoes are tender. Mash potatoes slightly.

2. Stir in cod and cream; bring to a boil. Reduce heat; simmer, covered, 6-8 minutes or until fish just begins to flake easily with a fork.

Black-Eyed Peas with Collard Greens

Time to gather round the table, y'all! Texan Lyndon B. Johnson loved his Southern food. This dish has special meaning on New Year's Day, when Southerners eat greens for future wealth and black-eyed peas for prosperity.

—ATHENA RUSSELL FLORENCE, SC

START TO FINISH: 25 MIN. • **MAKES:** 6 SERVINGS

- 2 tablespoons olive oil
- 1 garlic clove, minced
- 8 cups chopped collard greens
- ½ teaspoon salt
- ¼ teaspoon cayenne pepper
- 2 cans (15½ ounces each) black-eyed peas, rinsed and drained
- 4 plum tomatoes, seeded and chopped
- ¼ cup lemon juice
- 2 tablespoons grated Parmesan cheese

In a Dutch oven, heat oil over medium heat. Add garlic; cook and stir 1 minute. Add collard greens, salt and cayenne; cook and stir 6-8 minutes or until greens are tender. Add peas, tomatoes and lemon juice; heat through. Sprinkle servings with cheese.

POT LIKKER

Pot likker, also known as collard liquor, is the savory liquid left in the pot after cooking collards—considered a real treat among connoisseurs of Southern fare. It's used as a base in soups and stews, poured over grits, or soaked up directly off the plate with corn bread or rolls.

☆ JIMMY CARTER ☆
Chewy Salted Peanut Bars
PICTURED AT RIGHT

My rich bars are studded with the all-American peanut. I like to think famed peanut farmer Jimmy Carter would approve.
—ANN MARIE HEINZ STURGEON BAY, WI

PREP: 10 MIN. • **BAKE:** 20 MIN. + COOLING • **MAKES:** 2 DOZEN

- 1½ cups all-purpose flour
- ¾ cup packed brown sugar
- ½ cup cold butter, cubed
- 2 cups lightly salted dry roasted peanuts
- 1 cup butterscotch chips
- ½ cup light corn syrup
- 2 tablespoons butter

1. Preheat oven to 350°. Line a 13x9-in. baking pan with foil, letting ends extend up sides; grease foil. In a small bowl, mix flour and brown sugar; cut in butter until crumbly. Press into prepared pan. Bake 8-10 minutes or until lightly browned. Sprinkle peanuts over crust.

2. In a small saucepan, melt butterscotch chips, corn syrup and butter over medium heat; stir until smooth. Drizzle over peanuts. Bake 6-8 minutes longer or until bubbly. Cool completely in pan on a wire rack. Lifting with foil, remove from pan. Cut into bars.

☆ RONALD REAGAN ☆
Jelly Bean Cookies
PICTURED AT RIGHT

The 40th president's affection for jelly beans began when Ronald Reagan ran for governor of California in 1966. During the campaign, he ate licorice jelly beans in an attempt to give up smoking. It's a family tradition for my grandmother and I to make these colorful cookies every year for the holidays.
—CHEYENNE FINK PLEASANTVILLE, PA

PREP: 15 MIN. • **BAKE:** 10 MIN./BATCH • **MAKES:** ABOUT 2½ DOZEN

- ½ cup shortening
- ¾ cup sugar
- 1 large egg
- 2 tablespoons 2% milk
- 1 teaspoon vanilla extract
- 1½ cups all-purpose flour
- 1¼ teaspoons baking powder
- ½ teaspoon salt
- ¾ cup small jelly beans

1. Preheat oven to 350°. In a large bowl, cream shortening and sugar until blended. Beat in egg, milk and vanilla. In another bowl, whisk flour, baking powder and salt; gradually beat into creamed mixture. Stir in jelly beans.

2. Drop dough by tablespoonfuls 1½ in. apart onto greased baking sheets. Bake 8-10 minutes or until edges are light golden brown. Cool on pans 2 minutes. Remove to wire racks to cool.

Cottage Cheese Pancakes

A breakfast of cottage cheese with ketchup and pepper might seem scandalous to some, but to President Nixon it was standard morning fare. The cottage cheese in these flapjacks adds nice texture and an old-fashioned flavor reminiscent of blintzes. If you want to top them with something red, I suggest strawberry syrup.
—**THERESA JOHNS**
FORT WAYNE, IN

START TO FINISH: 20 MIN.
MAKES: 8 PANCAKES

- 4 **large eggs, lightly beaten**
- 1 **cup 2% cottage cheese**
- 6 **tablespoons butter, melted**
- ½ **cup all-purpose flour**

1. In a small bowl, whisk eggs, cottage cheese and butter until blended. Add flour; stir just until moistened.
2. Lightly grease a griddle; heat over medium heat. Pour batter by ¼ cupfuls onto griddle. Cook until bottoms are golden brown. Turn; cook until second side is golden brown.

★ ABRAHAM LINCOLN ★
Lemon-Filled Gingerbread Muffins

Honest Abe rarely spoke about food in his speeches. But in one of his famous debates with Stephen Douglas, Lincoln told a story from his childhood about sharing gingerbread men with a friend. The tale charmed his audience—these gingerbread muffins will charm you, too.
—SUZETTE JURY KEENE, CA

PREP: 25 MIN. • **BAKE:** 15 MIN. • **MAKES:** 1½ DOZEN

½ cup butter, softened
⅔ cup sugar
2 large eggs
½ cup molasses
2 cups all-purpose flour
1½ teaspoons ground ginger
1 teaspoon baking soda
½ teaspoon salt
½ teaspoon ground allspice
1 cup water
FILLING
4 ounces cream cheese, softened
¼ cup confectioners' sugar
1 tablespoon lemon juice
2 teaspoons grated lemon peel

1. Preheat oven to 375°. In a large bowl, cream butter and sugar until light and fluffy. Add eggs, one at a time, beating well after each addition. Beat in molasses. In another bowl, whisk flour, ginger, baking soda, salt and allspice; add to creamed mixture alternately with water, beating after each addition just until combined. (Batter may appear curdled.)

2. Fill paper-lined muffin cups one-fourth full. In a small bowl, beat filling ingredients until blended. Drop filling by rounded teaspoonfuls into center of each muffin; cover with remaining batter.

3. Bake 14-18 minutes or until a toothpick inserted in the muffin portion comes out clean. Cool 5 minutes before removing from pans to wire racks. Serve warm.

★ FRANKLIN D. ROOSEVELT ★
Bacon & Cheese Sandwiches

FDR, who saw the nation through the Great Depression and World War II, also knew a thing or two about grilled cheese. This mean melt, with its two kinds of cheese, bacon and Dijon mustard, would have pleased the 32nd president.
—SHARON DELANEY-CHRONIS SOUTH MILWAUKEE, WI

START TO FINISH: 25 MIN. • **MAKES:** 4 SERVINGS

¼ cup mayonnaise
2 teaspoons Dijon mustard
8 slices sourdough bread
8 slices Swiss cheese (¾ ounce each)
8 slices cheddar cheese (¾ ounce each)
8 slices tomato
4 slices sweet onion
8 cooked bacon strips
2 tablespoons butter, softened

1. In a small bowl, mix the mayonnaise and mustard; spread over four bread slices. Layer with cheeses, tomato, onion and bacon. Top with remaining bread. Butter outsides of sandwiches.

2. On a griddle, toast sandwiches over medium heat 2-3 minutes on each side or until golden brown and cheese is melted.

Cherry Nut Cake

The story of George Washington cutting down his father's cherry is generally understood to be a myth. But it is true that the nation's first president liked cherries. If you're looking for something special to pay homage to this Founding Father, try my grandmother's divine cake. It's worthy of a patriotic celebration.

—DIANA JENNINGS LEBANON, MO

PREP: 30 MIN.
BAKE: 25 MIN. + COOLING
MAKES: 12 SERVINGS

- 6 **large egg whites**
- ½ **cup butter, softened**
- ½ **cup shortening**
- 1½ **cups sugar**
- 1 **cup half-and-half cream**
- ¼ **cup maraschino cherry juice**
- 3 **cups cake flour**
- 2½ **teaspoons baking powder**
- 1 **teaspoon salt**
- 40 **maraschino cherries, chopped**
- ½ **cup chopped walnuts**

TOPPING

- 1 **cup heavy whipping cream**
- 2 **tablespoons confectioners' sugar**
- 1 **teaspoon vanilla extract**
    Maraschino cherries with stems, drained and patted dry

1. Place egg whites in a large bowl; let stand at room temperature 30 minutes. Preheat oven to 350°. Line bottoms of two greased 9-in. round baking pans with parchment paper; grease paper.

2. In a large bowl, cream butter, shortening and sugar until light and fluffy. In a small bowl, mix cream and cherry juice. In another bowl, whisk flour, baking powder and salt; add to creamed mixture alternately with cream mixture, beating well after each addition. Fold in cherries and walnuts. With clean beaters, beat egg whites on medium speed until stiff glossy peaks form. Fold into batter.

3. Transfer batter to prepared pans. Bake 25-30 minutes or until a toothpick inserted in center comes out clean. Cool in pans 10 minutes before removing to wire racks; remove paper. Cool completely.

4. In a large bowl, beat cream until it begins to thicken. Add confectioners' sugar and vanilla; beat until stiff peaks form. Place one cake layer on a serving plate; spread top with half of the whipped cream. Top with remaining cake layer; spread with remaining whipped cream. Decorate with cherries.

If the words "tea party" bring to mind raised pinkies, crumpets and oh-so-proper ladies...think again, friend. A tea party has become a fashionable way to entertain or to celebrate everything from birthdays and weddings to new babies.

Tea's a treat hot or cold. So offer a pot of warming Lemon Thyme Green Tea or a chilled pitcher of Rhubarb Mint or Peach Citrus Iced Teas for sipping. It's not all about the beverage, however—it's the accompanying food that people remember.

Delicately cut Roast Beef Finger Sandwiches and a walnut-studded strawberry spinach salad are part of a simple, elegant menu. Mini Lemon Cheesecake Tarts and a showstopping Strawberry Mascarpone Cake are the perfect finish to an afternoon steeped in hospitality.

A MODERN **TEA PARTY**

Strawberry Spinach Salad with Candied Walnuts

This classic salad goes with just about anything you're serving. The juicy berries add a pop of color to the greens, and the sweet, crunchy nuts are good enough to eat all on their own.

—SUSAN HOWELL ROYAL OAK, MI

START TO FINISH: 20 MIN.
MAKES: 10 SERVINGS (1 CUP EACH)

½ cup sugar
¼ cup water
½ teaspoon ground cinnamon
½ teaspoon chili powder
¼ teaspoon curry powder
2 cups walnut halves

SALAD
1 package (9 ounces) fresh baby spinach
2 cups sliced fresh strawberries (about 1 pound)
1 medium cucumber, halved and sliced

VINAIGRETTE
¼ cup olive oil
2 tablespoons balsamic vinegar
2 tablespoons seedless raspberry jam
1 teaspoon lemon juice
¼ teaspoon salt
⅛ teaspoon pepper
⅓ cup grated Parmesan cheese

1. In a small heavy saucepan, combine the first five ingredients; stir gently to moisten all the sugar. Cook over medium-low heat, gently swirling pan occasionally, until sugar is dissolved. Cover; bring to a boil over medium heat. Cook 1 minute. Uncover pan; continue to boil and gently swirl pan until syrup turns a deep amber color, about 2-3 minutes. Immediately remove from heat and carefully stir in walnuts until evenly coated. Spread onto foil to cool completely. Break into pieces.

2. In a large bowl, combine spinach, strawberries and cucumber. In a small bowl, whisk the first six vinaigrette ingredients. Drizzle over salad; toss to coat. Sprinkle with cheese and candied walnuts. Serve immediately.

Lemon Thyme Green Tea

Fresh sprigs of lemon thyme make this citrusy tea so refreshing that it's like sipping summer from a cup. In our family we like to drink it on the porch, while enjoying the warm weather.
—**MELISSA BIRDSONG** WALESKA, GA

START TO FINISH: 20 MIN. • **MAKES:** 8 SERVINGS

2 **quarts water**
8 **individual green tea bags**
12 **fresh lemon thyme sprigs or 8 fresh thyme sprigs plus ½ teaspoon grated lemon peel**
¼ **cup honey**
3 **tablespoons lemon juice**
  Sugar, optional

In a large saucepan, bring water to a boil; remove from heat. Add tea bags and lemon thyme sprigs; steep, covered, 3 minutes. Discard tea bags; steep, covered, 3 minutes longer. Strain tea. Add honey and lemon juice; stir until honey is dissolved. Stir in sugar if desired. Serve immediately.

Turkey Tea Sandwiches with Basil Mayonnaise

The basil mayonnaise is the secret to these tasty little sandwiches. Keep any extra in the fridge to spread on other meat sandwiches, stir into egg salad or spread on a pizza crust before topping it with other ingredients.
—**LARA PENNELL** MAULDIN, SC

START TO FINISH: 15 MIN. • **MAKES:** 20 TEA SANDWICHES

½ **cup mayonnaise**
⅓ **cup loosely packed basil leaves**
10 **slices white bread, crusts removed**
10 **ounces thinly sliced deli turkey**
5 **slices provolone cheese**

Place mayonnaise and basil in a food processor; process until basil is finely chopped, scraping down sides as needed. Spread mayonnaise mixture over each bread slice. Layer five bread slices with turkey and cheese; top with remaining bread. Cut each sandwich into four triangles.

BASIL BASICS

Basil is available as fresh green or purple leaves, or dried and crushed. It has a sweet flavor with hints of mint, pepper and cloves.

Mini Lemon Cheesecake Tarts

Dainty and light, these tartlets feature two of my favorites—lemon and cheesecake—
in one yummy morsel. They look lovely topped with fresh raspberries,
but sliced strawberries are just as pretty and delicious.

—GWYN BRANDT HIBBING, MN

PREP: 35 MIN. + CHILLING • **BAKE:** 20 MIN. + COOLING • **MAKES:** 2 DOZEN

8 **ounces cream cheese, softened, divided**
½ **cup plus 2 teaspoons butter, softened, divided**
¼ **teaspoon grated lemon peel**
1 **cup all-purpose flour**
½ **cup plus ⅓ cup sugar, divided**
1 **teaspoon plus 2 tablespoons lemon juice, divided**
½ **teaspoon vanilla extract**
1 **large egg, lightly beaten**
4 **teaspoons cornstarch**
⅓ **cup water**
2 **drops yellow food coloring**
  Fresh raspberries

1. In a small bowl, beat 3 ounces cream cheese, ½ cup butter and lemon peel until blended. Gradually add flour, mix well. Refrigerate, covered, 1 hour or until firm.

2. Preheat oven to 325°. Shape dough into 1-in. balls; press onto the bottom and up sides of 24 ungreased mini muffin cups.

3. For filling, in a small bowl, beat ½ cup sugar and remaining cream cheese until smooth. Beat in 1 teaspoon lemon juice and vanilla. Add egg; beat on low speed just until blended. Fill cups half full with cream cheese mixture. Bake 18-22 minutes or until set. Carefully run a knife around tarts to loosen from pan. Cool in pans on wire racks.

4. Meanwhile, in a small saucepan, combine cornstarch and remaining sugar; whisk in water. Bring to boil, stirring constantly; cook and stir 1-2 minutes or until thickened. Remove from heat; gently stir in food coloring and remaining lemon juice and butter. Cool to room temperature.

5. Remove cooled tarts from pans. Spoon on topping; top with raspberries. Store in an airtight container in the refrigerator.

Peach Citrus Iced Tea

My husband and I are peach tea fans, but couldn't find a decaffeinated version.
After experimenting, I came up with this lightly carbonated recipe that
nicely blends fruit and tea flavors. All ages are sure to enjoy it.

—JANICE HARRISON NASHVILLE, TN

PREP: 20 MIN. + CHILLING • **MAKES:** 8 SERVINGS (ABOUT 1 CUP EACH)

7 **cups water**
6 **individual regular or decaffeinated tea bags**
2 **cans (12 ounces each) sparkling peach citrus soda, chilled**
  Ice cubes
  Sugar, optional

1. In a large saucepan, bring water to a boil; remove from heat. Add tea bags; steep, covered, 3-5 minutes according to taste. Discard tea bags. Transfer to a pitcher; refrigerate until cool.

2. Just before serving, stir in soda. Serve over ice; stir in sugar if desired.

Nutty Tea Sandwiches

I created this recipe to serve at my tearoom, and my customers gave it rave reviews. The sandwiches are sweet and nutty and look beautiful on a platter lined with a bed of romaine lettuce.

—APRIL SIMMONS
FORT LARAMIE, WY

START TO FINISH: 15 MIN.
MAKES: 8 TEA SANDWICHES

- 1 **package (8 ounces) reduced-fat cream cheese**
- 2 **tablespoons brown sugar**
- 2 **tablespoons finely chopped celery**
- 1 **tablespoon finely chopped pecans**
- ¼ **teaspoon almond extract**
- 8 **slices oat bread, crusts removed**

In a small bowl, beat cream cheese until smooth. Stir in brown sugar, celery, pecans and extract. Spread cream cheese mixture over each of 4 bread slices; top with remaining bread. Cut each sandwich into 2 triangles.

Slice & Bake Coconut Shortbread Cookies

PICTURED ABOVE

Light and buttery, these delicate shortbread cookies are melt-in-your-mouth good. The coconut flavor makes them extra special.

—ROBERTA OTTO DULUTH, MN

PREP: 15 MIN. + CHILLING • **BAKE:** 20 MIN./BATCH • **MAKES:** 4 DOZEN

- 1 **cup butter, softened**
- ¾ **cup sugar**
- 1 **teaspoon vanilla extract**
- 1¾ **cups all-purpose flour**
- 1 **cup flaked coconut**

1. In a large bowl, cream butter and sugar until light and fluffy. Beat in vanilla. Gradually beat flour into creamed mixture. Stir in coconut.

2. Using a sheet of waxed paper, shape dough into a 12x3x1-in. rectangle. Wrap in waxed paper; refrigerate 3 hours or overnight.

3. Preheat oven to 300°. Unwrap and cut dough crosswise into ¼-in. slices. Place 1 in. apart on ungreased baking sheets. Bake 18-20 minutes or until edges are light golden. Cool on pans 5 minutes. Remove to wire racks to cool.

Rhubarb Mint Tea

A bumper crop of rhubarb and mint from my garden inspired me to create this thirst-quenching pick-me-up. Raspberries deepen the tea's vibrant red color, making these drinks a pretty addition to your table.

—LAURIE BOCK LYNDEN, WA

PREP: 15 MIN. • **COOK:** 45 MIN. + CHILLING
MAKES: 12 SERVINGS (1 CUP EACH)

- 4 **cups chopped fresh rhubarb**
- 2 **cups fresh raspberries**
- 2 **packages (¾ ounce each) fresh mint leaves**
- 3 **quarts water**
- 4 **individual black tea bags**
- 2 **cups sugar**
- 12 **mint sprigs**

In a 6-qt. stockpot, combine rhubarb, raspberries, mint and water; bring to a boil. Reduce heat; simmer, uncovered, 30 minutes. Remove from heat. Add tea bags; steep, covered, 3-5 minutes according to taste. Using a fine mesh strainer, strain tea, discarding tea bags and pulp. Stir in sugar until dissolved; cool slightly. Transfer to a pitcher; refrigerate until cooled completely. Serve over ice with mint sprigs.

Double Chocolate Scones

Chocolate lovers will adore these moist, decadent scones that won me a blue ribbon in a baking competition. They're perfect for a tea or brunch, and the mix of cocoa and chocolate chips makes them sweet enough for dessert.

—STEPHANIE SORBIE GLENDALE, AZ

PREP: 15 MIN. • **BAKE:** 20 MIN. • **MAKES:** 8 SCONES

- 1¾ **cups all-purpose flour**
- ½ **cup baking cocoa**
- ⅓ **cup sugar**
- 1½ **teaspoons baking powder**
- ½ **teaspoon salt**
- 4 **ounces cream cheese, cubed**
- ¼ **cup cold butter, cubed**
- 2 **large eggs**
- ¾ **cup heavy whipping cream**
- 2 **teaspoons vanilla extract**
- ⅔ **cup semisweet chocolate chips**

1. Preheat oven to 375°. In a large bowl, whisk the first five ingredients. Cut in cream cheese and butter until mixture resembles coarse crumbs. In another bowl, whisk one egg, cream and vanilla; stir into crumb mixture just until moistened. Stir in chocolate chips.

2. Turn onto a floured surface; knead gently 10 times. Pat dough into a 6-in. circle. Cut into eight wedges. Place wedges on a greased baking sheet. In a small bowl, whisk remaining egg; brush over scones. Bake 18-20 minutes or until a toothpick inserted in center comes out clean. Serve scones warm.

SCONE SECRETS

When making scones, pat the dough into a circle and cut it into wedges. If you pull the wedges apart, the scones will have a crisp crust. If you cut through the circle without separating the wedges, the scones will be soft. Flour the knife or biscuit cutter after each cut to prevent sticking.

Pineapple-Orange Spiced Tea

The sweet aroma of this tea wafting from a slow cooker warms the dreariest day.
My daughter served it for a holiday open house, and coffee drinkers were
instantly converted. I bring it to the office to spice up our break room beverage selections.
—**CAROLE J. DRENNAN** ABILENE, TX

PREP: 15 MIN. • **COOK:** 2 HOURS • **MAKES:** 12 SERVINGS (1 CUP EACH)

2 quarts boiling water
16 individual tea bags
2 cinnamon sticks (3 inches)
1 piece fresh gingerroot
   (½ inch), peeled and thinly
   sliced
4 whole cloves
1 cup sugar
1 can (12 ounces) frozen orange
   juice concentrate, thawed

1 can (12 ounces) frozen
   pineapple juice concentrate,
   thawed
1 cup pomegranate or cranberry
   juice
½ cup lemon juice

1. In a 5- or 6-qt. slow cooker,
combine boiling water and tea
bags. Cover and let stand 5
minutes.

2. Meanwhile, place cinnamon
sticks, ginger and cloves on a
double thickness of cheesecloth.
Gather corners of cloth to enclose
seasonings; tie securely with
string. Discard tea bags. Stir in
remaining ingredients; add spice
bag. Cook, covered, on low 2-3
hours or until heated through.
Discard the spice bag. Stir tea
before serving.

Roast Beef Finger Sandwiches

These simple sandwiches are ideal for a bridal shower, brunch
or high tea, when the menu is a bit more substantial.
The mustard adds a nice kick without being overly spicy.
—**ANNDREA BAILEY** HUNTINGTON BEACH, CA

START TO FINISH: 15 MIN. • **MAKES:** 1½ DOZEN

½ cup butter, softened
½ cup chopped pitted Greek
   olives
¼ cup spicy brown mustard
¼ teaspoon pepper
6 slices whole wheat bread,
   crusts removed
6 ounces thinly sliced deli roast
   beef
6 slices white bread, crusts
   removed

Place butter, olives, mustard and
pepper in a food processor; pulse
until chopped. Spread butter
mixture over wheat bread; top
with roast beef and white bread.
Cut each sandwich crosswise into
thirds.

Strawberry Mascarpone Cake

Don't let the number of steps in this recipe fool you—it's easy to assemble. The cake bakes up high and fluffy, and the berries add a fresh fruity flavor. Cream cheese is a good substitute if you don't have mascarpone cheese handy.

—CAROL WITCZAK TINLEY PARK, IL

PREP: 1 HOUR + CHILLING
BAKE: 30 MIN. + COOLING
MAKES: 12 SERVINGS

- 6 **cups fresh strawberries, halved (2 pounds)**
- 2 **tablespoons sugar**
- 1 **teaspoon grated orange peel**
- 1 **tablespoon orange juice**
- ½ **teaspoon almond extract**

CAKE

- 6 **large eggs, separated**
- 2 **cups cake flour**
- 2 **teaspoons baking powder**
- ¼ **teaspoon salt**
- 1½ **cups sugar, divided**
- ½ **cup canola oil**
- ¼ **cup water**
- 1 **tablespoon grated orange peel**
- ½ **teaspoon almond extract**

WHIPPED CREAM

- 2 **cups heavy whipping cream**
- ⅓ **cup confectioners' sugar**
- 2 **teaspoons vanilla extract**

FILLING

- 1 **cup mascarpone cheese**
- ½ **cup heavy whipping cream**

1. In a large bowl, combine the first five ingredients. Refrigerate, covered, at least 30 minutes.

2. Place egg whites in a large bowl; let stand at room temperature 30 minutes. Meanwhile, preheat oven to 350°. Grease bottoms of two 8-in. round baking pans; line with parchment paper. Sift flour, baking powder and salt together twice; place dry ingredients in another large bowl.

3. In a small bowl, whisk egg yolks, 1¼ cups sugar, oil, water, orange peel and almond extract until blended. Add to flour mixture; beat until well blended.

4. With clean beaters, beat egg whites on medium until soft peaks form. Gradually add remaining sugar, 1 tablespoon at a time, beating on high after each addition until sugar is dissolved. Continue beating until soft glossy peaks form. Fold a fourth of the egg whites into batter, then fold in remaining whites.

5. Gently transfer batter to prepared pans. Bake on lowest oven rack 30-35 minutes or until tops spring back when lightly touched. Cool cakes in pans 10 minutes before removing to wire racks; remove parchment paper. Cool completely.

6. Meanwhile, for whipped cream, in a large bowl, beat cream until it begins to thicken. Add confectioners' sugar and vanilla; beat until soft peaks form. Refrigerate, covered, at least 1 hour. For filling, in a small bowl, beat mascarpone cheese and cream until stiff peaks form. Refrigerate until assembling.

7. Drain strawberries, reserving juice mixture. Using a serrated knife, trim tops of cakes if domed. Place one cake layer on a serving plate. Brush with half of reserved juice mixture; spread with ¾ cup filling. Arrange strawberries over top, creating an even layer; spread with remaining filling. Brush remaining cake layer with remaining juice mixture; place layer over filling, brushed side down.

8. Gently stir whipped cream; spread over the top and sides of cake. Just before serving, arrange strawberries over cake.

ummer is prime time for a backyard bash—be it a barbecue on a busy weeknight or a fun-filled Fourth of July cookout.

When it comes to a red-hot menu, declare your independence from prep work with help from the no-fuss dishes in this chapter. Not counting items such as water, salt, pepper and oil, these tasty barbecue basics only require five ingredients!

The gang will be hungry for all-American classics like juicy flank steaks with a Southwestern kick and colorful kabobs pairing charbroiled chicken and zucchini. Toss in change-of-pace Minty-Watermelon Cucumber Salad and Blue Cheese & Bacon Stuffed Peppers and you have the makings for a bang-up celebration.

Don't forget to have a batch of Chocolaty S'mores Bars on hand while watching the fireworks. Ooh... aah–are they good!

Blue Cheese & Bacon Stuffed Peppers (p. 189)
Salami & Provolone Pasta Salad (p. 189)
Southwest Steak (p. 192)
Marinated Chicken & Zucchini Kabobs (p. 192)

5-INGREDIENT **COOKOUT**

Bacon-Tomato Salad

We love this wonderful salad that tastes like a piled-high BLT without the time or effort. Plus, you can make it hours ahead and keep it in the fridge till serving time.

—DENISE THURMAN COLUMBIA, MO

START TO FINISH: 15 MIN. • **MAKES:** 6 SERVINGS

- 1 **package (9 ounces) iceberg lettuce blend**
- 2 **cups grape tomatoes, halved**
- ¾ **cup coleslaw salad dressing**
- ¾ **cup shredded cheddar cheese**
- 12 **bacon strips, cooked and crumbled**

In a large bowl, combine lettuce blend and tomatoes. Drizzle with dressing; sprinkle with cheese and bacon.

CHEDDAR MAKES IT ALL BETTER

When you'd like a bolder flavor, select packages of shredded sharp cheddar cheese. If you are shredding the cheese yourself, however, choose from medium, sharp and extra sharp.

Blue Cheese & Bacon Stuffed Peppers

Grilling is a huge summer highlight for my family, which is one reason we're such fans of this idea. Whenever I put out a plate of these colorful appetizers, people come flocking.
—TARA CRUZ KERSEY, CO

START TO FINISH: 20 MIN. • **MAKES:** 1 DOZEN

- 3 medium sweet yellow, orange or red peppers
- 4 ounces cream cheese, softened
- ½ cup crumbled blue cheese
- 3 bacon strips, cooked and crumbled
- 1 green onion, thinly sliced

1. Cut peppers into quarters. Remove and discard stems and seeds. In a small bowl, mix cream cheese, blue cheese, bacon and green onion until blended.

2. Grill peppers, covered, over medium-high heat or broil 4 in. from heat 2-3 minutes on each side or until slightly charred.

3. Remove peppers from grill; fill each with about 1 tablespoon cheese mixture. Grill 2-3 minutes longer or until cheese is melted.

Salami & Provolone Pasta Salad

Everyone needs a recipe for a perfect pasta salad! This one is so easy, I even prepare it on busy weeknights. It's just the thing when I need to round out a hot summer meal.
—JILL DONLEY WARSAW, IN

PREP: 25 MIN. + CHILLING • **MAKES:** 8 SERVINGS

- 3 cups uncooked cellentani pasta or elbow macaroni
- 1 medium sweet red pepper, chopped
- 4 ounces provolone cheese, cubed (about 1 cup)
- 4 ounces hard salami, cubed (about 1 cup)
- ⅓ cup prepared Italian salad dressing

Additional Italian salad dressing and minced fresh basil, optional

1. Cook pasta according to package directions. Meanwhile, in a large bowl, combine pepper, cheese and salami.

2. Drain pasta and rinse in cold water. Add to pepper mixture.

Drizzle with ⅓ cup dressing and toss to coat. Refrigerate, covered, at least 1 hour. If desired, stir in additional dressing to moisten and sprinkle with basil before serving.

Minty-Watermelon Cucumber Salad

Capturing the fantastic flavors of summer, this refreshing, beautiful salad will be the talk of any picnic or potluck.
—**ROBLYNN HUNNISETT** GUELPH, ON

START TO FINISH: 20 MIN. • **MAKES:** 16 SERVINGS (¾ CUP EACH)

- 8 **cups cubed seedless watermelon**
- 2 **English cucumbers, halved lengthwise and sliced**
- 6 **green onions, chopped**
- ¼ **cup minced fresh mint**
- ¼ **cup balsamic vinegar**
- ¼ **cup olive oil**
- ½ **teaspoon salt**
- ½ **teaspoon pepper**

In a large bowl, combine watermelon, cucumbers, green onions and mint. In a small bowl, whisk remaining ingredients. Pour over salad and toss to coat. Serve immediately or refrigerate, covered, up to 2 hours before serving.

No-Fuss Avocado Onion Salad

My mother could take a simple salad and turn it into something incredible. This one is a particular favorite of mine. It's a great change from green, pasta or veggie salads.
—**MARINA CASTLE** CANYON COUNTRY, CA

START TO FINISH: 15 MIN. • **MAKES:** 12 SERVINGS

- 3 **medium ripe avocados, peeled and thinly sliced**
- 1 **large sweet onion, halved and thinly sliced**
- ⅓ **cup olive oil**
- ¼ **cup stone-ground mustard**
- 2 **tablespoons lemon juice**
- 1 **tablespoon honey**

Arrange avocado and onion slices on a large platter. In a small bowl, whisk remaining ingredients; drizzle over salad. Serve immediately.

Chocolaty S'mores Bars

One night, my husband had some friends over to play poker and he requested these s'mores bars. The players polished off the pan and asked for more! I shared the recipe, and now his friends make them at home, too.
—**REBECCA SHIPP** BEEBE, AR

PREP: 15 MIN. + COOLING
MAKES: 1½ DOZEN

- ¼ cup butter, cubed
- 1 package (10 ounces) large marshmallows
- 1 package (12 ounces) Golden Grahams cereal
- ⅓ cup milk chocolate chips, melted

1. In a large saucepan, melt butter over low heat. Add marshmallows; cook and stir until blended. Remove from heat. Stir in cereal until coated.

2. Using a buttered spatula, press evenly into a greased 13x9-in. pan. Drizzle with melted chocolate chips. Cool completely. Cut into bars. Store in an airtight container.

Southwest Steak

Lime juice tenderizes this mouthwatering steak while garlic, chili powder and red pepper flakes add punch. My husband and I came up with the recipe when we wanted something lighter to make on the grill.
—**CAROLINE SHIVELY** NEW YORK, NY

PREP: 15 MIN. + MARINATING • **GRILL:** 15 MIN. • **MAKES:** 8 SERVINGS

¼ cup lime juice
6 garlic cloves, minced
4 teaspoons chili powder
4 teaspoons canola oil
1 teaspoon salt
1 teaspoon crushed red pepper flakes
1 teaspoon pepper
2 beef flank steaks (1 pound each)

1. In a small bowl, mix the first seven ingredients; spread over both sides of steaks. Place in a large resealable plastic bag; refrigerate 6 hours or overnight, turning occasionally.

2. Moisten a paper towel with cooking oil; using long-handled tongs, rub on grill rack to coat lightly. Grill steaks, covered, over medium heat or broil 4 in. from heat 6-9 minutes on each side or until meat reaches desired doneness (for medium-rare, a thermometer should read 145°; medium, 160°; well-done, 170°).

3. Let steaks stand 5 minutes. Thinly slice across the grain.

Marinated Chicken & Zucchini Kabobs

These succulent kabobs are a family favorite. Feel free to substitute turkey tenderloins and other veggies such as summer squash or sweet bell peppers.
—**TAMMY SLADE** STANSBURY PARK, UT

PREP: 25 MIN. + MARINATING • **GRILL:** 10 MIN. • **MAKES:** 8 SERVINGS

¾ cup lemon-lime soda
½ cup reduced-sodium soy sauce
½ cup canola oil, divided
2 pounds boneless skinless chicken breasts or turkey breast tenderloins, cut into 1-inch cubes
3 medium zucchini, cut into 1-inch pieces
2 medium red onions, cut into 1-inch pieces
½ teaspoon salt
¼ teaspoon pepper

1. In a large resealable plastic bag, combine soda, soy sauce and ¼ cup oil. Add chicken; seal bag and turn to coat. Refrigerate 8 hours or overnight.

2. Drain chicken, discarding marinade. On eight metal or soaked wooden skewers, alternately thread chicken and vegetables. Brush vegetables with remaining oil; sprinkle with salt and pepper.

3. Moisten a paper towel with cooking oil; using long-handled tongs, rub on grill rack to coat lightly. Grill kabobs, covered, over medium heat 8-10 minutes or until chicken is no longer pink and vegetables are tender, turning occasionally.

Friends who knead are friends indeed. And after a stressful week, a bread-making party with friends may be the ideal therapy you crave.

Try a variety of recipes, including something savory, such as Tomato Spinach Bread, and a sweet bread, such as Cinnamon Bagels with Crunchy Topping, which are surprisingly easy to make.

Prepare a couple of loaves in advance for sampling, perhaps with a few flavored olive oils for dipping. And be sure to have guests bring their own loaf pans so they can take their mixed doughs home to let rise and bake later.

Tomato Spinach Bread (p. 200)

ARTISAN **BREADS**

Khachapuri

While in Russia, where we adopted our two children, my husband and I discovered these marvelous cheese pies. The traditional pastries can be served with a salad for a cozy supper or shaped into hors d'oeuvres.

—RACHEL SAUDER TREMONT, IL

PREP: 30 MIN. + RISING
BAKE: 30 MIN.
MAKES: 6 SERVINGS

3½ teaspoons active dry yeast
¾ cup warm milk (110° to 115°)
6 tablespoons butter, melted
2 tablespoons honey
2 to 2½ cups all-purpose flour
1 teaspoon salt
¼ teaspoon ground coriander

FILLING
1 large egg, lightly beaten
12 ounces brick cheese, shredded

1. In a large bowl, dissolve yeast in warm milk. Stir in butter and honey. In another bowl, combine 1¾ cups flour, salt and coriander; gradually add to yeast mixture, beating until smooth. Stir in enough remaining flour to form a soft dough.

2. Turn onto a lightly floured surface; knead until smooth and elastic, about 6-8 minutes. Place in a greased bowl, turning once to grease top. Cover and let rise in a warm place until doubled, about 1 hour.

3. Punch dough down. Let rise until doubled, about 30 minutes. Turn onto a lightly floured surface; divide into six balls. Roll each into a 6½-in. circle.

4. In a small bowl, combine egg and cheese. Mound about ½ cup cheese mixture in the center of each circle. Fold dough over filling, gathering and twisting into a knot to seal. Place on an ungreased baking sheet. Let stand for 10 minutes. Bake at 375° for 30-35 minutes or until lightly browned. Serve immediately.

Soft Beer Pretzels

What goes together better than beer and pretzels? Not much that I can think of. That's why I put them together into one delicious recipe. I'm always looking for new ways to combine fun flavors, and this pretzel recipe does just that.

—ALYSSA WILHITE WHITEHOUSE, TX

PREP: 1 HOUR + RISING • **BAKE:** 10 MIN. • **MAKES:** 8 PRETZELS

- 1 bottle (12 ounces) amber beer or nonalcoholic beer
- 1 package (¼ ounce) active dry yeast
- 2 tablespoons unsalted butter, melted
- 2 tablespoons sugar
- 1½ teaspoons salt
- 4 to 4½ cups all-purpose flour
- 10 cups water
- ⅔ cup baking soda

TOPPING
- 1 large egg yolk
- 1 tablespoon water
  Coarse salt

1. In a small saucepan, heat beer to 110°-115°; remove from heat. Stir in yeast until dissolved. In a large bowl, combine the butter, sugar, 1½ teaspoons salt, yeast mixture and 3 cups flour; beat on medium speed until smooth. Stir in enough remaining flour to form a soft dough (the dough will be sticky).

2. Turn dough onto a floured surface; knead until smooth and elastic, about 6-8 minutes. Place in a greased bowl, turning once to grease the top. Cover with plastic wrap and let rise in a warm place until doubled, about 1 hour.

3. Preheat oven to 425°. Punch dough down. Turn onto a lightly floured surface; divide and shape into eight balls. Roll each into a 24-in. rope. Curve ends of each rope to form a circle; twist ends once and lay over opposite side of circle, pinching ends to seal.

4. In a Dutch oven, bring the water and baking soda to a boil. Carefully drop pretzels, two at a time, into boiling water. Cook 30 seconds. Remove with a slotted spoon; drain well on paper towels.

5. Place 2 in. apart on greased baking sheets. In a small bowl, whisk egg yolk and water; brush over pretzels. Sprinkle with coarse salt. Bake 10-12 minutes or until golden brown. Remove from pans to a wire rack to cool.

FREEZE OPTION *Freeze cooled pretzels in resealable plastic freezer bags. To use, thaw at room temperature or, if desired, microwave each pretzel on high 20-30 seconds or until heated through.*

HOW TO SHAPE PRETZELS

To make traditional pretzels:

Divide and shape dough into eight balls; roll each into a 24-in. rope. Curve ends of rope to form a circle; twist ends once and lay over opposite side of circle, pinching ends to seal. Boil, top and bake as directed. Yield: 8 pretzels.

To make pretzel bites:

Divide and shape dough into eight balls; roll each into a 12-in. rope. Cut each rope into 1-in. pieces. Boil and top as directed; bake at 400° for 6-8 minutes or until golden brown. Yield: 8 dozen bites.

Black Raspberry Bubble Ring

I first made this pretty raspberry bread years ago for a 4-H project. It helped me win Grand Champion for my county and took me to the Ohio State Fair. It takes some time to prepare, but I pull out this recipe whenever I want a sweet bread that will really impress.

—KILA FRANK REEDSVILLE, OH

PREP: 35 MIN. + RISING • **BAKE:** 25 MIN. • **MAKES:** 1 LOAF (16 WEDGES)

1 package (¼ ounce) active dry yeast
¼ cup warm water (110° to 115°)
1 cup warm milk (110° to 115°)
¼ cup plus 2 tablespoons sugar, divided
½ cup butter, melted, divided
1 large egg
1 teaspoon salt
4 cups all-purpose flour
1 jar (10 ounces) seedless black raspberry preserves

SYRUP
⅓ cup corn syrup
2 tablespoons butter, melted
½ teaspoon vanilla extract

1. In a large bowl, dissolve yeast in warm water. Add the milk, ¼ cup sugar, ¼ cup butter, egg, salt and 3½ cups flour. Beat until smooth. Stir in enough remaining flour to form a soft dough.

2. Turn onto a floured surface; knead until smooth and elastic, about 6-8 minutes. Place in a greased bowl, turning once to grease top. Cover and let rise in a warm place until doubled, about 1¼ hours.

3. Punch dough down. Turn onto a lightly floured surface; divide into 32 pieces. Flatten each into a 3-in. disk. Place about 1 teaspoon preserves on the center of each piece; bring the edges together and seal.

4. Place 16 dough balls in a greased 10-in. fluted tube pan. Brush with half of the remaining butter; sprinkle with 1 tablespoon sugar. Top with remaining balls, butter and sugar. Cover and let rise until doubled, about 35 minutes.

5. Bake at 350° for 25-30 minutes or until golden brown. Combine syrup ingredients; pour over warm bread. Cool for 5 minutes before inverting onto a serving plate.

Sage Fontina Focaccia

This rustic loaf has plenty of sage flavor and makes a tasty addition to any feast.

—BETH DAUENHAUER PUEBLO, CO

PREP: 30 MIN. + RISING • **BAKE:** 10 MIN. • **MAKES:** 1 LOAF (8 WEDGES)

1¼ teaspoons active dry yeast
½ cup warm water (110° to 115°)
½ teaspoon honey
¾ to 1 cup all-purpose flour
¼ cup whole wheat flour
1 tablespoon olive oil
2 teaspoons minced fresh sage
¼ teaspoon salt

TOPPING
1½ teaspoons olive oil, divided
8 fresh sage leaves
½ cup shredded fontina cheese

1. In a large bowl, dissolve yeast in warm water. Stir in honey; let stand for 5 minutes. Add ¾ cup all-purpose flour, whole wheat flour, oil, minced sage and salt. Beat on medium speed for 3 minutes or until smooth. Stir in enough remaining flour to form a soft dough (dough will be sticky).

2. Turn onto a lightly floured surface; knead until smooth and elastic, about 6-8 minutes. Place in a large bowl coated with cooking spray, turning once to coat the top. Cover and let rise in a warm place until doubled, about 1 hour.

3. Punch dough down. Cover and let rest for 5 minutes. Shape into an 8-in. circle; place on a baking sheet coated with cooking spray. Cover and let rise until doubled, about 30 minutes. Using the end of the handle of a wooden spoon, make ¼-in. indentations in loaf.

4. For topping, brush dough with 1 teaspoon oil. Top with sage leaves; brush leaves with remaining oil. Sprinkle with cheese. Bake at 400° for 8-10 minutes or until golden brown. Remove to a wire rack. Serve warm.

Tomato Spinach Bread

I've been making these savory swirled loaves for many years. The rustic colors really add to the festive feel of any Christmas meal.

—AVANELL HEWITT NORTH RICHLAND HILLS, TX

PREP: 1 HOUR 20 MIN. + CHILLING
BAKE: 35 MIN. + COOLING
MAKES: 2 LOAVES (10 SLICES EACH)

1 package (¼ ounce) active dry yeast
1¼ cups warm water (110° to 115°)
4 teaspoons butter, melted
1 teaspoon salt
3¼ to 3¾ cups bread flour

SPINACH DOUGH

¼ cup cold water
1 package (10 ounces) frozen chopped spinach, thawed and squeezed dry
1 package (¼ ounce) active dry yeast
¾ cup warm water (110° to 115°)
4 teaspoons butter, melted
1 teaspoon salt
3¼ to 3½ cups bread flour

TOMATO DOUGH

1 package (¼ ounce) active dry yeast
1 cup warm water (110° to 115°)
4 teaspoons butter, melted
1 teaspoon salt
1 can (6 ounces) tomato paste
3¼ to 3¾ cups bread flour
1 large egg white
1 teaspoon cold water

1. For plain dough, in a large bowl, dissolve yeast in warm water. Add butter, salt and 2 cups flour; beat until smooth. Add enough remaining flour to form a firm dough.

2. Turn onto a lightly floured surface; knead until smooth and elastic, about 6-8 minutes. Place in a greased bowl, turning once to grease top. Cover and refrigerate overnight.

3. For spinach dough, puree cold water and spinach in a food processor. In a large bowl, dissolve yeast in warm water. Add butter, salt, 2 cups flour and spinach mixture; beat until smooth. Add enough remaining flour to form a firm dough.

4. Turn onto a lightly floured surface. With lightly floured hands, knead until smooth and elastic, about 6-8 minutes. Place in a greased bowl, turning once to grease top. Cover and refrigerate overnight.

5. For tomato dough, in a large bowl, dissolve yeast in warm water. Add butter, salt, tomato paste and 2 cups flour; beat until smooth. Add enough remaining flour to form a firm dough.

6. Turn onto a lightly floured surface. With lightly floured hands, knead until smooth and elastic, about 6-8 minutes. Place in a greased bowl, turning once to grease top. Cover and refrigerate overnight.

7. Punch down each dough and divide each in half; cover. On a lightly floured surface, roll out one portion of each dough into a 10x8-in. rectangle. Place a rectangle of spinach dough on plain dough; top with tomato dough. Roll into a 12x10-in. rectangle. Roll up jelly-roll style, starting with a long side; pinch seams to seal and tuck ends under.

8. Place seam side down on a greased baking sheet. Repeat with remaining dough. Cover and let rise in a warm place until doubled, about 30 minutes.

9. With a sharp knife, make three shallow diagonal slashes across the top of each loaf. Beat egg white and cold water; brush over loaves. Bake at 350° for 35-45 minutes or until golden brown. Remove to wire racks to cool.

Cinnamon Bagels with Crunchy Topping

Once you get the hang of it, you won't believe how simple it is to make these bakery-quality bagels right in your very own kitchen!
—KRISTEN STREEPEY GENEVA, IL

PREP: 40 MIN. + RISING • **BAKE:** 15 MIN. + COOLING • **MAKES:** 1 DOZEN

- 2 teaspoons active dry yeast
- 1½ cups warm water (110° to 115°)
- 4 tablespoons brown sugar, divided
- 3 teaspoons ground cinnamon
- 1½ teaspoons salt
- 2¾ to 3¼ cups all-purpose flour

TOPPING
- ¼ cup sugar
- ¼ cup packed brown sugar
- 3 teaspoons ground cinnamon

1. In a bowl, dissolve yeast in warm water. Add 3 tablespoons brown sugar, cinnamon and salt; mix well. Stir in enough flour to form a soft dough.

2. Turn onto a lightly floured surface; knead until smooth and elastic, about 6-8 minutes. Place in a bowl coated with cooking spray, turning once to coat the top. Cover and let rise in a warm place until doubled, about 1 hour.

3. Punch dough down. Shape into 12 balls. Push thumb through centers to form a 1½-in. hole. Stretch and shape dough to form an even ring. Place on a floured surface. Cover and let rest for 10 minutes.

4. Fill a Dutch oven two-thirds full with water and remaining brown sugar; bring to a boil. Drop bagels, two at a time, into boiling water. Cook for 45 seconds; turn and cook 45 seconds longer. Remove with a slotted spoon; drain well on paper towels.

5. In a small bowl, mix topping ingredients; sprinkle over bagels. Place 2 in. apart on baking sheets coated with cooking spray. Bake at 400° for 15-20 minutes or until golden brown. Remove to wire racks to cool.

Roasted Red Pepper Bread

These savory loaves are moist, tender and loaded with flavor from grated Parmesan cheese and roasted sweet red peppers. They're great at dinner or as an appetizer.
—CHERYL PERRY HERTFORD, NC

PREP: 45 MIN. + RISING • **BAKE:** 20 MIN. + COOLING • **MAKES:** 2 LOAVES (12 SLICES EACH)

- 1½ cups roasted sweet red peppers, drained
- 1 package (¼ ounce) active dry yeast
- 2 tablespoons warm water (110° to 115°)
- 1¼ cups grated Parmesan cheese, divided
- ⅓ cup warm 2% milk (110° to 115°)
- 2 tablespoons butter, softened
- 1¼ teaspoons salt
- 3¼ to 3¾ cups all-purpose flour
- 1 large egg
- 1 tablespoon water
- 1½ teaspoons coarsely ground pepper

1. Place red peppers in a food processor; cover and process until pureed. In a large bowl, dissolve yeast in warm water. Add the red peppers, 1 cup cheese, milk, butter, salt and 1½ cups flour. Beat until smooth. Stir in enough remaining flour to form a firm dough.

2. Turn onto a floured surface; knead until smooth and elastic, about 6-8 minutes. Place in a greased bowl, turning once to grease the top. Cover and let rise in a warm place until doubled, about 1 hour.

3. Punch dough down. Turn onto a lightly floured surface; divide dough into six pieces. Shape each into a 18-in. rope. Place three ropes on a greased baking sheet and braid; pinch ends to seal and tuck under. Repeat with remaining dough. Cover and let rise until doubled, about 1 hour.

4. In a small bowl, combine egg and water; brush over braids. Sprinkle with pepper and remaining cheese. Bake at 350° for 18-22 minutes or until golden brown.

Sourdough Starter

Sourdough breads have a unique tangy flavor, which is achieved from the use of a yeast starter. Use a portion of the starter to make bread as soon as the starter is ready, and replenish the rest of the starter to use another time.

—DELILA GEORGE JUNCTION CITY, OR

PREP: 10 MIN. + STANDING • **MAKES:** ABOUT 3 CUPS

2 cups all-purpose flour
1 package (¼ ounce) active dry yeast
2 cups warm water (110° to 115°)

1. In a covered 4-qt. glass, ceramic or plastic container, mix flour and yeast. Gradually stir in warm water until smooth. Cover loosely with a kitchen towel; let stand in a warm place 2-4 days or until mixture is bubbly, sour smelling and a clear liquid has formed on top. (Starter may darken, but if starter turns another color or develops an offensive odor or mold, discard and start over.)

2. Cover tightly and refrigerate starter until ready to use. To keep starter alive, use and replenish, or nourish starter, once every 1-2 weeks.

TO USE AND REPLENISH STARTER *Stir to blend in any liquid on top. Remove amount of starter needed; bring to room temperature before using. For each ½ cup starter removed, add ½ cup flour and ½ cup warm water to the remaining starter and stir until smooth. Cover loosely and let stand in a warm place 1-2 days or until light and bubbly. Stir; cover loosely and refrigerate.*

TO NOURISH STARTER *Remove half of the starter. Stir in equal parts of flour and warm water; cover loosely and let stand in a warm place 1-2 days or until light and bubbly. Stir; cover loosely and refrigerate.*

Cranberry Sourdough Muffins with Streusel Topping

Sourdough, tart dried fruit and crunchy hazelnuts take these muffins to a new level. We serve them warm or at room temperature.

—PATRICIA QUINN OMAHA, NE

PREP: 30 MIN. • **BAKE:** 20 MIN. • **MAKES:** 1 DOZEN

1 cup Sourdough Starter
½ cup packed brown sugar
⅓ cup plus 1½ cups all-purpose flour, divided
½ teaspoon ground cinnamon
¼ cup cold butter, cubed
¼ cup chopped hazelnuts
½ cup sugar
1 teaspoon baking powder
½ teaspoon baking soda
½ teaspoon salt
1 large egg
½ cup butter, melted
1½ teaspoons grated orange peel
1 cup fresh or frozen cranberries, thawed
¼ cup chopped dried apricots

1. Let Sourdough Starter come to room temperature before using.

2. Preheat oven to 400°. In a small bowl, mix brown sugar, ⅓ cup flour and cinnamon; cut in cold butter until crumbly. Stir in hazelnuts.

3. In a large bowl, whisk sugar, baking powder, baking soda, salt and remaining flour. In another bowl, whisk egg, melted butter and orange peel until blended; stir in Sourdough Starter. Add to flour mixture; stir just until moistened. Fold in cranberries and apricots.

4. Fill paper-lined muffin cups three-fourths full. Sprinkle with hazelnut mixture.

5. Bake 16-20 minutes or until a toothpick inserted in center comes out clean. Cool 5 minutes before removing from pan to a wire rack. Serve warm.

Sage & Gruyere Sourdough Bread

A sourdough starter gives loaves extra flavor and helps the rising process. This bread, with sage and Gruyere cheese, comes out so well that I'm thrilled to share it.

—DEBRA KRAMER BOCA RATON, FL

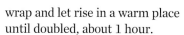

PREP: 35 MIN. + RISING • **BAKE:** 25 MIN. • **MAKES:** 1 LOAF (16 SLICES)

½ cup Sourdough Starter
1⅛ teaspoons active dry yeast
⅓ cup warm water (110° to 115°)
½ cup canned pumpkin
½ cup shredded Gruyere cheese, divided
4 teaspoons butter, softened
1 tablespoon sugar
1 tablespoon minced fresh sage
1 teaspoon salt
2¼ to 2¾ cups all-purpose flour
1 large egg, lightly beaten

1. Let Sourdough Starter come to room temperature before using.

2. In a small bowl, dissolve yeast in warm water. In a large bowl, combine Sourdough Starter, pumpkin, ¼ cup cheese, butter, sugar, sage, salt, yeast mixture and 1 cup flour; beat on medium speed until smooth. Stir in enough remaining flour to form a stiff dough (dough will be slightly sticky).

3. Turn dough onto a floured surface; knead until smooth and elastic, about 6-8 minutes. Place in a greased bowl, turning once to grease the top. Cover with plastic wrap and let rise in a warm place until doubled, about 1 hour.

4. Punch down dough. Turn onto a lightly floured surface; shape into a round loaf. Place on a greased baking sheet. Cover with a kitchen towel; let rise in a warm place until doubled, about 30 minutes. Preheat oven to 375°.

5. Brush egg over loaf; sprinkle with remaining cheese. Bake 25-30 minutes or until golden brown. Remove from pan to a wire rack to cool.

SECRETS TO A SOURDOUGH STARTER

- Starters contain acid that can react with metal, so only prepare sourdough starters in nonmetallic bowls. Be sure to use a large bowl since the starter will significantly increase in volume and may overflow a small bowl.
- If you don't use the starter immediately, stir it and transfer it to a clean glass, ceramic or plastic container. Cover loosely and store in the refrigerator. Always bring the starter to room temperature before using. This will take 2 to 12 hours. The longer it stands at room temperature, the more tangy it will be.
- To use, stir the starter and remove the desired amount. Bring to room temperature if refrigerated, and use in the recipe as directed. Replenish the starter with equal amounts of flour and water to restore the volume; stir. (For example, if ½ cup starter was removed for a recipe, combine ½ cup all-purpose flour and ½ cup warm water. Stir into starter.) Let the replenished starter stand in a warm place (80° to 90°) for 12 to 24 hours or until light and bubbly. Stir starter; cover loosely and refrigerate.
- If you don't use any starter within 2 weeks, you will need to nourish it to keep it active. To nourish, remove half of the starter and share with a friend or discard. Transfer remaining starter to a large nonmetallic bowl. Add equal parts of all-purpose flour and warm water. Let stand in a warm place (80° to 90°) for 12 to 24 hours or until light and bubbly. Stir starter and transfer to a clean storage container; cover loosely and refrigerate.
- Discard a starter if it develops an offensive odor, changes color or becomes slimy or stringy. Sterilize the storage container before using it for a new batch of starter.

The June solstice marks the official start of summer and the longest day of the year in the northern hemisphere. Why not salute the celestial event with a leisurely party outdoors?

Kick off with a frosty round of Peachy Keen Wine Cocktails, followed by savory Avocado Endive Cups with Salsa. Honor the solstice tradition of fire with Barbecue-Glazed Sweet Onion Burgers, Lemony Vegetable Kabobs with Butter Sauce, Grilled Chipotle Salmon Tacos and Grilled Pizza with Greens & Tomatoes. Cool down with Triple Berry Shortcake for dessert.

After sunset, keep the mood bright with strings of Upcycled Mason Jar Luminarias (p. 213). There are few things better for the soul than a laugh with friends on a warm summer's eve, candles glowing softly in the night.

Avocado Endive Cups with Salsa (p. 211)
Grilled Lime-Balsamic Sweet Potatoes (p. 212)
Grilled Chipotle Salmon Tacos (p. 207)

SUMMER **SOLSTICE PARTY**

Grilled Pizza with Greens & Tomatoes

This smoky grilled pizza scores big with me for two reasons. It encourages my husband and son to eat greens, and it showcases fresh produce.
—**SARAH GRAY** ERIE, CO

PREP: 15 MIN. + RISING
GRILL: 10 MIN
MAKES: 2 PIZZAS (4 SLICES EACH)

1½ cups all-purpose flour
1½ cups whole wheat flour
2 teaspoons kosher salt
1 teaspoon active dry yeast
3 tablespoons olive oil, divided
1¼ to 1½ cups warm water (120° to 130°)

TOPPING

2 tablespoons olive oil
10 cups beet greens, coarsely chopped
4 garlic cloves, minced
2 tablespoons balsamic vinegar
¾ cup prepared pesto
¾ cup shredded Italian cheese blend
½ cup crumbled feta cheese
2 medium heirloom tomatoes, thinly sliced
¼ cup fresh basil leaves, chopped

1. Place flours, salt and yeast in a food processor; pulse until blended. While processing, add 2 tablespoons oil and enough water in a steady stream until dough forms a ball. Turn dough onto a floured surface; knead until smooth and elastic, about 6-8 minutes.

2. Place in a greased bowl, turning once to grease the top. Cover with plastic wrap and let rise in a warm place until almost doubled, about 1½ hours.

3. Punch down dough. On a lightly floured surface, divide dough into two portions. Press or roll each portion into a 10-in. circle; place each on a piece of greased foil (about 12 in. square). Brush tops with remaining oil; cover with plastic wrap and let rest 10 minutes.

4. For topping, in a 6-qt. stockpot, heat oil over medium-high heat. Add beet greens; cook and stir 3-5 minutes or until tender. Add garlic; cook 30 seconds longer. Remove from heat; stir in vinegar.

5. Moisten a paper towel with cooking oil; using long-handled tongs, rub on grill rack to coat lightly. Carefully invert pizza crusts onto grill rack; remove foil. Grill, covered, over medium heat 3-5 minutes or until bottoms are lightly browned. Turn; grill 1-2 minutes or until second side begins to brown.

6. Remove from grill. Spread with pesto; top with beet greens, cheeses and tomatoes. Return pizzas to grill. Cook, covered, over medium heat 2-4 minutes or until cheese is melted. Sprinkle with basil.

Grilled Chipotle Salmon Tacos

When fresh fish is available, I pull out my salmon taco recipe and fire up the grill. Try it with whitefish or mahi mahi, too.
—**BRENDA WASHNOCK** NEGAUNEE, MI

PREP: 20 MIN. + MARINATING • **GRILL:** 10 MIN. • **MAKES:** 12 SERVINGS

- ¼ cup olive oil
- ¼ cup lemon juice
- 2 tablespoons lime juice
- 3 chipotle peppers plus 2 teaspoons adobo sauce
- 3 tablespoons reduced-sodium soy sauce
- 2 garlic cloves, minced
- ½ teaspoon dried oregano
- 3 pounds salmon fillets (about 1 inch thick)

SLAW
- ½ cup cider vinegar
- ¼ cup olive oil
- 3 tablespoons sugar
- ½ teaspoon salt
- ¼ teaspoon pepper
- 2 cups shredded red cabbage
- 2 cups shredded green cabbage
- ½ medium red onion, thinly sliced
- ¼ cup fresh cilantro leaves, chopped

ASSEMBLY
- 12 corn tortillas (6 inches), warmed

1. Place oil, citrus juices, chipotle peppers, adobo sauce, soy sauce, garlic and oregano in a blender; cover and process until blended. Pour half of the marinade into a 13x9-in. dish. Add salmon, skin side down. Turn fillets to coat both sides; refrigerate, covered, 30 minutes. Reserve remaining marinade for basting fish.

2. For slaw, in a large bowl, whisk vinegar, oil, sugar, salt and pepper until blended. Add cabbages, onion and cilantro; toss to coat. Refrigerate until serving.

3. Moisten a paper towel with cooking oil; using long-handled tongs, rub on grill rack to coat well. Remove salmon from marinade; discard any remaining marinade in dish.

4. Place salmon on grill rack, skin side down. Grill, covered, over medium heat 5 minutes. Spoon some of the reserved marinade over fish. Grill 4-6 minutes longer or until fish just begins to flake easily with a fork, basting occasionally with remaining marinade.

5. Break fish into bite-size pieces, removing skin if desired. Serve in tortillas with slaw.

Peachy Keen Wine Cocktail

A bushel of peaches gave me a reason to create a wine cocktail. I meant to serve it with our meal, but we "taste-tested" it while grilling.
—**KATIE FERRIER GAGE** HOUSTON, TX

PREP: 15 MIN. • **COOK:** 15 MIN. + COOLING • **MAKES:** 6 SERVINGS

- 2 cups sugar
- 1 cup water
- 1 large piece fresh gingerroot (about 3 inches), peeled and coarsely chopped

COCKTAIL
- ¼ cup orange liqueur
- 2 medium ripe peaches, peeled and halved
- 1 bottle (750 milliliters) white wine, chilled
- Ice cubes
- 1 to 1½ cups chilled ginger ale
- Fresh mint leaves and peach slices, optional

1. In a large saucepan, combine sugar, water and ginger; bring to a boil. Reduce heat; simmer 10 minutes. Cool completely. Pour syrup through a strainer into a covered container; discard ginger.

2. Place liqueur and ¼ cup ginger syrup in a blender. (Cover and refrigerate remaining syrup for another use.) Add peaches; cover and process until smooth.

3. Transfer mixture to a 2-qt. pitcher; stir in wine. Serve over ice, topping with ginger ale. If desired, serve with mint and peach slices.

Barbecue-Glazed Sweet Onion Burgers

Our family loves burgers made with roasted sweet onions and barbecue seasoning. Top these grilled beauties with extras like lettuce, cheese and a good pickle.
—**PAULA MARCHESI** LENHARTSVILLE, PA

PREP: 1 HOUR • **GRILL:** 10 MIN. • **MAKES:** 8 SERVINGS

- 1 **large sweet onion, cut into ½-inch pieces**
- 2 **tablespoons plus ⅔ cup canola oil, divided**
- 1½ **teaspoons salt, divided**
- ½ **teaspoon pepper**
- 8 **tablespoons barbecue seasoning, divided**
- ¼ **cup packed brown sugar**
- 2 **pounds ground beef**
- 8 **hamburger buns, split**
  Optional toppings: lettuce leaves and sliced cheddar cheese and dill pickles

1. Preheat oven to 350°. Toss onion with 2 tablespoons oil and ½ teaspoon each salt and pepper; spread in a single layer in a 15x10x1-in. baking pan. Roast 25-30 minutes or until golden brown, stirring once. Transfer to a large bowl; stir in 2 tablespoons barbecue seasoning. Cool completely.

2. In a small bowl, mix brown sugar and the remaining oil, salt and barbecue seasoning until blended. Remove half of the mixture to another bowl; reserve for brushing burgers while cooking.

3. Add beef to onion mixture; mix lightly but thoroughly. Shape into eight ½-in.-thick patties. Spread both sides of patties with remaining paste mixture.

4. Moisten a paper towel with cooking oil; using long-handled tongs, rub on grill rack to coat lightly. Grill burgers, covered, over medium heat or broil 4 in. from heat 4-6 minutes on each side or until a thermometer reads 160°; brush with reserved paste mixture during the last 3 minutes of cooking. Serve on buns with toppings if desired.

Lemony Vegetable Kabobs with Butter Sauce

My children love to eat food they've helped prepare. Get your kids involved by letting them skewer the colorful veggies for grilling.
—**MARI PIORO** SHELBY TOWNSHIP, MI

PREP: 1 HOUR + MARINATING • **GRILL:** 10 MIN. • **MAKES:** 10 SERVINGS

- 3 **medium ears sweet corn, cut into ½-inch slices**
- 2 **large red onions, cut into wedges**
- 2 **medium zucchini, cut into ¾-inch slices**
- 2 **medium sweet red peppers, cut into 1-inch pieces**
- 1 **pound large fresh mushrooms**
- 1½ **cups cherry tomatoes**
- ½ **cup olive oil**
- ¼ **cup lemon juice**
- 2 **garlic cloves, minced**
- 2 **teaspoons white wine vinegar**
- 1 **teaspoon salt**
- ¼ **teaspoon pepper**

SAUCE
- ¾ **cup butter**
- ½ **teaspoon grated lemon peel**
- ¼ **cup lemon juice**
- 1 **teaspoon dried parsley flakes**
- ½ **teaspoon salt**

1. In a large saucepan, bring 6 cups water to a boil. Add corn; cook, uncovered, 3 minutes. Drain and immediately drop into ice water. Drain and pat dry.

2. Divide corn and remaining vegetables between two large resealable plastic bags. In a small bowl, whisk oil, lemon juice, garlic, vinegar, salt and pepper until blended. Pour half of the marinade into each bag; seal bags and turn to coat. Refrigerate 8 hours or overnight.

3. On 10 metal skewers, alternately thread vegetables. In a small saucepan, melt butter; stir in remaining ingredients.

4. Brush kabobs with some of the sauce. Grill, covered, over medium heat 10-12 minutes or until peppers and onions are crisp-tender, turning and basting occasionally with remaining sauce.

Honeydew Prosciutto Salad

For parties, I turn melon and prosciutto into an easy salad with a honey mustard dressing. To add zip, stir in fresh basil and mint.

—JULIE MERRIMAN SEATTLE, WA

START TO FINISH: 30 MIN.
MAKES: 12 SERVINGS

- ⅓ cup olive oil
- ½ teaspoon grated lime peel
- 2 tablespoons lime juice
- 2 tablespoons white wine vinegar
- 2 tablespoons honey
- 1 teaspoon Dijon mustard
- ¼ teaspoon salt
- ¾ cup fresh cilantro leaves

SALAD

- 8 cups fresh arugula or baby spinach (about 5 ounces)
- ½ medium red onion, thinly sliced
- ¼ cup thinly sliced fresh mint leaves
- ¼ cup thinly sliced fresh basil leaves
- 8 cups diced honeydew
- 1 package (8 ounces) fresh mozzarella cheese pearls
- ¼ pound thinly sliced prosciutto, cut into wide strips

Place the first eight ingredients in a blender; cover and process until smooth. Place arugula, onion and herbs in a large bowl. Drizzle with ⅓ cup vinaigrette and toss lightly to coat. Top with honeydew, mozzarella cheese and prosciutto. Serve with remaining vinaigrette.

CHILL OUT WITH A COOL OUTDOOR SALAD BAR

Al fresco dining is delightful...as long as you and the food keep cool. When setting out chilled salads or other cold dishes, consider placing the serving container in a larger pan filled with ice. Another option is to use a child's inflatable swimming pool with a plug. You can keep replenishing the ice, and pull the plug to drain out water. Inflatable buffet coolers are also readily available at discount stores and online.

Triple Berry Shortcake

My great-great grandmother handed down her shortcake recipe. I'm sharing it because it's way too fabulous to keep it a secret!

—SARA KINGSMORE
VADNAIS HEIGHTS, MN

PREP: 25 MIN.
BAKE: 25 MIN. + COOLING
MAKES: 15 SERVINGS

- 1 **cup butter, softened**
- 2 **cups sugar**
- 4 **large eggs**
- 2 **tablespoons vanilla extract**
- 3 **cups all-purpose flour**
- 1 **teaspoon baking powder**
- ½ **teaspoon baking soda**
- ½ **teaspoon salt**
- 1 **cup buttermilk**

TOPPING

- 1½ **cups fresh blueberries**
- 1½ **cups sliced fresh strawberries**
- 1½ **cups fresh raspberries**
- 2 **tablespoons sugar**
  Sweetened whipped cream, optional

1. Preheat oven to 350°. In a large bowl, cream butter and sugar until light and fluffy. Add eggs, one at a time, beating well after each addition. Beat in vanilla. In another bowl, whisk flour, baking powder, baking soda and salt; add to creamed mixture alternately with buttermilk, beating well after each addition.

2. Transfer batter to a greased 13x9-in. pan. Bake 25-30 minutes or until a toothpick inserted in center comes out clean. Cool completely in pan on a wire rack.

3. For topping, in a large bowl, combine berries; add sugar and toss gently to coat. Serve with cake; top with whipped cream, if desired.

Grilled Red Pepper Dip

We grill peppers with rosemary and garlic, then blend them with sun-dried tomatoes for a creamy spread to pass with pita chips.
—DONNA ALWINE BLOOMINGTON, IN

PREP: 20 MIN. + COOLING • **GRILL:** 5 MIN. • **MAKES:** 4¾ CUPS

- 2 **large sweet red peppers, halved and seeded**
- 1 **tablespoon olive oil**
- 1 **teaspoon garlic powder**
- 1 **teaspoon minced fresh rosemary**
- 2 **packages (8 ounces each) cream cheese, softened**
- ⅔ **cup finely chopped oil-packed sun-dried tomatoes**
- 2 **garlic cloves, minced**
- 1 **teaspoon onion salt**
- 2 **cups (8 ounces) crumbled feta cheese**
  Pita chips

1. Toss peppers with oil, garlic powder and rosemary to coat. Grill peppers, covered, over medium-high heat or broil 4 in. from heat 2-3 minutes on each side or until tender. Cool completely. Cut peppers into ¼-in. pieces.

2. In a large bowl, beat cream cheese, sun-dried tomatoes, garlic and onion salt until blended. Beat in feta cheese and red chopped peppers until blended. Serve with pita chips. Refrigerate leftovers.

Avocado Endive Cups with Salsa

I jazz up guacamole by serving it atop endive leaves. Add a brilliant red pepper salsa, and you've got a standout appetizer.
—GILDA LESTER MILLSBORO, DE

PREP: 45 MIN. • **MAKES:** 2½ DOZEN

- 1 jar (12 ounces) roasted sweet red peppers, drained and finely chopped
- 1 cup finely chopped fennel bulb
- ¼ cup sliced ripe olives, finely chopped
- 2 tablespoons olive oil
- 1 tablespoon minced fresh cilantro
- ½ teaspoon salt, divided
- ½ teaspoon pepper, divided
- 2 medium ripe avocados, peeled and pitted
- 3 tablespoons lime juice
- 2 tablespoons diced jalapeno pepper
- 1 green onion, finely chopped
- 1 garlic clove, minced
- ½ teaspoon ground cumin
- ¼ teaspoon hot pepper sauce
- 2 plum tomatoes, chopped
- 30 endive leaves
  Chopped fennel fronds

1. In a small bowl, combine red peppers, fennel, olives, oil and cilantro; stir in ¼ teaspoon each salt and pepper.

2. In another bowl, mash avocados with a fork. Stir in lime juice, jalapeno, green onion, garlic, cumin, pepper sauce and the remaining salt and pepper. Stir in tomatoes.

3. Spoon about 1 tablespoon avocado mixture onto each endive leaf; top each with about 1 tablespoon pepper mixture. Sprinkle with fennel fronds.

Watermelon Salsa with Wonton Chips

We love to feature summer produce in this salsa of avocado, watermelon and raspberries. Take it to a get-together and the bowl will come back empty.
—PAULA MARCHESI LENHARTSVILLE, PA

START TO FINISH: 30 MIN. • **MAKES:** 2½ CUPS (48 WONTON CHIPS)

- 24 wonton wrappers, halved diagonally
  Cooking spray
- 1 medium ripe avocado, peeled and finely chopped
- 1 cup finely chopped seedless watermelon
- 1 cup canned black beans, rinsed and drained
- ½ cup frozen corn, thawed
- ¼ cup chopped fresh cilantro
- 3 tablespoons white wine vinegar
- 2 tablespoons olive oil
- 1 teaspoon grated lime peel
- ½ teaspoon salt
- ⅛ teaspoon pepper
  Fresh raspberries

1. Preheat oven to 400°. Arrange wontons in a single layer on two greased baking sheets; spritz with cooking spray. Bake 4-6 minutes or until golden brown. Cool completely on wire racks.

2. In a small bowl, combine avocado, watermelon, beans, corn and cilantro. In another bowl, whisk vinegar, oil, lime peel, salt and pepper until blended. Drizzle over avocado mixture; toss lightly to coat. Top with raspberries. Serve with wonton chips.

Grilled Lime-Balsamic Sweet Potatoes

For me, tailgating is about camaraderie and food that's good to grill. One of my favorites is sweet potato wedges. Yum!
—RAQUEL PERAZZO WEST NEW YORK, NJ

PREP: 15 MIN. • **GRILL:** 10 MIN./BATCH • **MAKES:** 8 SERVINGS

5 **medium sweet potatoes (about 3 pounds)**
2 **tablespoons olive oil**
1 **teaspoon salt**
¼ **teaspoon pepper**
¼ **cup chopped fresh cilantro**
¼ **cup packed brown sugar**
¼ **cup lime juice**
3 **tablespoons white or regular balsamic glaze**

1. Peel and cut each sweet potato lengthwise into eight wedges; place in a large bowl. Toss with oil, salt and pepper.
2. Moisten a paper towel with cooking oil; using long-handled tongs, rub on grill rack to coat lightly. In batches, grill potatoes, covered, over medium heat 8-10 minutes or until tender, turning occasionally.
3. In a large bowl, mix remaining ingredients; add potatoes and toss to coat.

Bing Cherry-Amaretti Fool

When Bing cherries are in season, I make this fruity custard-style fool. The sweet cherries and whipped cream balance perfectly with the sour cream.
—MARY ANN LEE CLIFTON PARK, NY

PREP: 30 MIN. + CHILLING • **MAKES:** 8 SERVINGS

1 **envelope unflavored gelatin**
⅓ **cup cold water**
1 **cup (8 ounces) sour cream**
½ **cup sugar**
1 **tablespoon lemon juice**
½ **teaspoon almond extract**
½ **teaspoon vanilla extract**
2 **cups coarsely chopped fresh Bing or other dark sweet cherries, divided**
1 **cup heavy whipping cream**
1 **cup coarsely crushed amaretti cookies (about 16 cookies)**
Optional toppings: fresh mint leaves, halved Bing cherries and additional crushed amaretti cookies

1. In a small saucepan, sprinkle gelatin over cold water; let stand 1 minute. Heat and stir over low heat until gelatin is completely dissolved. Let stand 5 minutes.
2. Place sour cream, sugar, lemon juice, extracts, 1 cup cherries and gelatin mixture in a blender; cover and process until cherries are pureed. Transfer to a large bowl.
3. In a small bowl, beat cream until soft peaks form. Remove ½ cup whipped cream; reserve for topping. Gently fold remaining whipped cream into cherry mixture. Fold in crushed cookies and remaining chopped cherries.

Divide mixture among eight dessert dishes. Refrigerate at least 2 hours.
4. Serve with reserved whipped cream and toppings if desired.

PICK A PECK OF PERFECT CHERRIES

Choose cherries that are plump, firm, and uniformly and richly colored, with shiny skin. A green stem tells you it's fresh.

Upcycled Mason Jar Luminarias

Here is ambience in a jar: Hang decorative strings of these glass candles around the yard or put them on the table as centerpieces.

MATERIALS

Medium-to-large mason jars, without lids
Small scented pillar candles
Loose sand or aquarium gravel
Flexible tape measure
12-gauge aluminum floral wire
Wire cutters

DIRECTIONS

1. For each jar, measure the circumference of the opening. Cut a length of wire 1 in. larger.
2. Wrap cut wire around the mouth of the jar below the threads. Twist ends together and push them against jar to secure.
3. To make handle, cut an 18-in. length of wire. Insert an end about 1 in. under the circle of wire around the jar mouth and twist a few times to secure. Repeat on opposite side.

4. Pour some loose sand or aquarium gravel into the bottom of the jar and press candle firmly in place.
*NOTE: *Use only jars intended for canning, which can withstand the heat; the glass will get hot. Hang luminarias away from flammable material or sit them only on heat-proof surfaces. Or use battery-operated candles.*

D oes biting into a fresh, juicy peach make you feel warm and fuzzy inside? Then you'll fall in love with our lineup of peachy-keen recipes that make this luscious summer fruit the star ingredient.

Mornings don't have to be the pits when you rise and shine with Peach Crepes. No matter how hectic or harried the day is, everything's peaches and cream when you indulge in dreamy Spiced Peach Puffs. And if you're feeling a little feverish from the hot weather, cool down with refreshing Peach Lemonade, a drink guaranteed to make summer even sweeter.

You can even take a walk on the savory side with chicken wings, pork tenderloin and gazpacho—all tinged with the fresh, fruity flavor of the oh-so-sweet glorious peach.

JUST PEACHY

Peach Crepes

My mother-in-law passed this recipe on to me.
The special ingredient, almond extract,
gives it a distinctive, delicious flavor.
—**MICHELLE GAUER** SPICER, MN

PREP: 25 MIN. + CHILLING • **COOK:** 20 MIN. • **MAKES:** 8 SERVINGS

1 cup milk
4 large eggs
1 cup all-purpose flour
2 tablespoons sugar
2 tablespoons butter, melted
1 teaspoon vanilla extract
FILLING
¾ cup sugar
2 tablespoons cornstarch
1 cup water
8 medium peaches, peeled and
thinly sliced (about 4½ cups),
divided
2 tablespoons butter
½ teaspoon almond extract
Whipped cream and ground
nutmeg, optional

1. In a blender, combine the milk, eggs, flour, sugar, butter and vanilla. Cover and process until smooth. Cover and refrigerate for 1 hour.
2. Meanwhile, in a large saucepan, combine sugar and cornstarch. Gradually whisk in water until smooth. Stir in 2 cups peaches and butter. Cook and stir over medium-high heat until thickened and bubbly. Reduce heat; cook and stir 2 minutes longer. Remove from the heat. Stir in almond extract and remaining peaches. Cover and refrigerate.

3. Heat a lightly greased 8-in. nonstick skillet over medium heat; pour about 2 tablespoons batter into the center of skillet. Lift and tilt pan to coat bottom evenly. Cook until top appears dry; turn and cook 15-20 seconds longer. Remove to a wire rack. Repeat with remaining batter, greasing skillet as needed. When cool, stack crepes with waxed paper or paper towels in between.
4. Spoon filling over crepes; roll up. Top with whipped cream and nutmeg if desired.

Upside-Down Peach Bread

This tender loaf is sure to delight. With fresh peaches,
rich cream cheese and crunchy pecans, it's impossible to resist!
—**BECKY TACKETT** PORTER, OK

PREP: 30 MIN. • **BAKE:** 45 MIN. + COOLING • **MAKES:** 2 LOAVES (12 SLICES EACH)

1 package (16 ounces) frozen
unsweetened sliced peaches,
thawed
¼ cup butter, melted
¼ cup packed brown sugar
1½ cups chopped pecans, divided
1½ teaspoons ground cinnamon,
divided
¾ cup butter, softened
4 ounces cream cheese,
softened
2 cups sugar
2 large eggs
1 teaspoon almond extract
1 teaspoon vanilla extract
3 cups all-purpose flour

1 teaspoon baking powder
½ teaspoon baking soda
½ teaspoon salt

1. Thinly slice half of the peaches; chop remaining peaches. Set aside.
2. Pour the melted butter into two greased 9x5-in. loaf pans; sprinkle with brown sugar. Arrange peach slices cut side down in a single layer over brown sugar. Sprinkle with ½ cup of pecans and ½ teaspoon of the cinnamon; set aside.
3. In a large bowl, cream the

butter, cream cheese and sugar until light and fluffy. Add eggs and extracts; mix well.
4. Combine the flour, baking powder, baking soda, salt and remaining cinnamon; add to creamed mixture. Fold in the chopped peaches and remaining pecans.
5. Transfer batter to the two prepared pans. Bake at 350° for 45-55 minutes or until a toothpick inserted near the center comes out clean. Cool for 10 minutes before inverting onto serving plates. Serve warm.

Yogurt Ice Pops

My fun, refreshing peach pops get smooth, creamy goodness from yogurt. Any fruit can be substituted in the recipe. We've even used bananas. Yum!

—DENISE PATTERSON
BAINBRIDGE, OH

PREP: 20 MIN. + FREEZING
MAKES: 16 POPS

- 1 envelope unflavored gelatin
- 1 cup cold water
- ½ cup sugar
- 1½ cups (12 ounces) peach yogurt
- 2 cups sliced peeled fresh or frozen peaches
- 1 medium ripe banana, quartered
- 16 freezer pop molds or paper cups (3 ounces each) and wooden pop sticks

1. In a small saucepan, sprinkle gelatin over cold water; let stand for 1-2 minutes. Stir in sugar. Cook and stir over low heat until gelatin and sugar are dissolved.
2. Transfer to a blender; add the yogurt, peaches and banana. Cover and process until smooth. Pour ¼ cup peach mixture into each mold or paper cup. Top molds with holders. If using cups, top with foil and insert sticks through foil. Freeze until firm.

Spiced Peach Puffs

We always made cream puffs for special occasions when I was growing up in a family of seven. My favorite filling, then and now, is whipped cream and peaches.
—AGNES WARD STRATFORD, ON

PREP: 70 MIN. • **BAKE:** 25 MIN. + COOLING • **MAKES:** 3 DOZEN

- 1 cup water
- ½ cup butter, cubed
- 1 teaspoon ground nutmeg
- ⅛ teaspoon salt
- 1 cup all-purpose flour
- 4 large eggs
- 2 cups heavy whipping cream
- ½ cup confectioners' sugar
- 1 teaspoon vanilla extract
- 2 cups chopped peeled fresh or frozen peaches, thawed
  Additional confectioners' sugar

1. In a large saucepan, bring the water, butter, nutmeg and salt to a boil. Add flour all at once and stir until a smooth ball forms. Remove from the heat; let stand for 5 minutes. Add eggs, one at a time, beating well after each addition. Continue beating until mixture is smooth and shiny.
2. Drop by tablespoonfuls 2 in. apart onto greased baking sheets. Bake at 400° for 25-30 minutes or until golden brown. Remove to a wire rack. Immediately split puffs open; remove tops and set aside. Discard soft dough from inside. Cool puffs.
3. For filling, in a large bowl, beat cream until it begins to thicken. Add the confectioners' sugar and vanilla; beat until stiff peaks form.
4. Just before serving, fill puffs with whipped cream and peaches. Dust cream puffs with additional confectioners' sugar.

Golden Summer Peach Gazpacho

Since peaches and tomatoes are both in season during the same time of the year, I blend them into a cool, delicious soup. Leftovers keep well in the fridge—but they rarely last long enough to get there!
—**JULIE HESSION** LAS VEGAS, NV

PREP: 20 MIN. + CHILLING
MAKES: 8 SERVINGS

- 3 **cups sliced peeled fresh or frozen peaches, thawed**
- 3 **medium yellow tomatoes, chopped**
- 1 **medium sweet yellow pepper, chopped**
- 1 **medium cucumber, peeled and chopped**
- ½ **cup chopped sweet onion**
- 1 **garlic clove, minced**
- ⅓ **cup lime juice**
- 2 **tablespoons rice vinegar**
- 1 **tablespoon marinade for chicken**
- 1 **teaspoon salt**
- ¼ **teaspoon hot pepper sauce**
- 1 **to 3 teaspoons sugar, optional**
  Thin cucumber slices

1. Place the first six ingredients in a food processor; process until blended. Add lime juice, vinegar, marinade for chicken, salt and pepper sauce; process until smooth. If desired, stir in sugar.
2. Refrigerate, covered, at least 4 hours. Top servings with thin cucumber slices.
NOTE *This recipe was tested with Lea & Perrins Marinade for Chicken.*

Fruity Chocolate Tortilla Cups

My south-of-the-border treats are favorites at our house. You'll love the presentation of peaches and mixed fruit in chocolate-drizzled tortilla cups.
—**MARION KARLIN** WATERLOO, IA

START TO FINISH: 30 MIN. • **MAKES:** 8 SERVINGS

- 1 to 2 tablespoons butter, softened
- 8 flour tortillas (6 inches), warmed
- ¾ cup semisweet chocolate chips
- 1 teaspoon shortening

FILLING

- 1 pound fresh apricots, halved
- 2 tablespoons honey
- 1½ cups halved fresh strawberries
- 3 small plums, sliced
- 2 medium peaches, sliced
- ½ cup heavy whipping cream
- 2 tablespoons confectioners' sugar

1. Spread butter over one side of each tortilla. Press the tortillas, butter side down, into ungreased 8-oz. custard cups. Place on a 15x10x1-in. baking pan. Bake at 400° for 10-12 minutes or until golden brown. Remove tortilla cups from custard cups; cool on wire racks.

2. In a microwave, melt the chocolate chips and shortening; stir until smooth. Drizzle over insides of tortilla cups; refrigerate for 3-4 minutes or until set.

3. For filling, in a food processor, combine apricots and honey; process until smooth. In a large bowl, combine the strawberries, plums and peaches; add apricot mixture and gently toss to coat. Spoon ½ cup fruit mixture into each tortilla cup.

4. In a small bowl, beat cream until it begins to thicken. Add confectioners' sugar; beat until stiff peaks form. Dollop whipped cream onto fruit.

Peaches & Cream Jelly Roll

Cake rolls make a lovely presentation for a party, and they are simple to cut into even slices. My father taught me how to make them. Sometimes we get together and prepare them for family and friends.
—**MALENA COLEMAN** ROCKVILLE, IN

PREP: 20 MIN. • **BAKE:** 10 MIN. + CHILLING • **MAKES:** 12 SERVINGS

- 3 large eggs
- ¼ teaspoon vanilla extract
- ⅛ teaspoon salt
- ¾ cup sugar
- ¾ cup biscuit/baking mix
- 1 cup heavy whipping cream
- ¼ cup confectioners' sugar, divided
- 3 cups chopped peeled fresh peaches

1. Line a greased 15x10x1-in. baking pan with waxed paper and grease the paper; sprinkle with flour and set aside.

2. In a large bowl, beat eggs on high speed for 3 minutes. Beat in vanilla and salt. Gradually add sugar, beating until mixture becomes thick and lemon-colored. Fold in biscuit mix. Spread in prepared pan.

3. Bake at 375° for 8-10 minutes or until cake springs back when lightly touched. Cool the cake for 5 minutes. Invert onto a kitchen towel dusted with confectioners' sugar. Gently peel off waxed paper. Roll up cake in the towel jelly-roll style, starting with a short side. Cool completely on a wire rack.

4. For filling, in a small bowl, beat cream until it begins to thicken. Add 3 tablespoons confectioners' sugar; beat until stiff peaks form.

5. Unroll cake; spread half of whipped cream over cake to within ½ in. of edges. Top with peaches and remaining whipped cream. Roll up again. Place seam side down on a serving platter. Dust cake with the remaining confectioners' sugar. Refrigerate for 2 hours.

Peach Lemonade

Looking for a new twist on lemonade? Fresh peaches lend a fruity flavor to this warm-weather favorite.
—JOAN HALLFORD NORTH RICHLAND HILLS, TX

START TO FINISH: 20 MIN. • **MAKES:** 5 SERVINGS

4 **cups water, divided**
2 **medium peaches, chopped**
1 **cup sugar**
¾ **cup lemon juice**
1 **medium lemon, sliced**
   Mint sprigs, optional

1. In a small saucepan, bring 2 cups water, peaches and sugar to a boil. Reduce heat; cover and simmer for 5-7 minutes or until peaches are tender. Remove from the heat. Cool. Strain, discarding peach skins.

2. In a large pitcher, combine the peach mixture, lemon juice and remaining water. Add lemon slices and mint if desired. Serve over ice.

Grilled Peach BBQ Chicken Wings

I was proud to include the recipe for these moist and tender chicken wings in my cookbook, *Cooking for Isaiah: Gluten-Free & Dairy-Free Recipes for Easy, Delicious Meals.* The sweet peach barbecue glaze makes them so yummy!
—SILVANA NARDONE BROOKLYN, NY

PREP: 20 MIN. + MARINATING • **COOK:** 30 MIN. • **MAKES:** 4 SERVINGS

2 **cups barbecue sauce**
2 **cloves garlic, finely chopped, divided**
2 **peaches, peeled, pitted and chopped**
   Salt and pepper
24 **chicken wings, separated at the joint and tips discarded**
1 **cup peach jam**
¼ **cup apple cider vinegar**
2 **tablespoons hot sauce, such as Frank's RedHot, or to taste**
   Scallions, green parts only, thinly sliced, for topping

1. In a food processor, combine the barbecue sauce and half of the garlic. Add the peaches and process until finely chopped; season with about 1½ teaspoons salt and about ¼ teaspoon pepper. Reserve ½ cup of the mixture for basting.

2. In a resealable plastic bag, toss together the chicken wings and remaining peach barbecue sauce; refrigerate for about 30 minutes.

3. Meanwhile, combine the peach jam, vinegar, remaining garlic, hot sauce and ½ teaspoon salt in a small saucepan. Cook mixture over medium heat until it is slightly thickened, for about 5 minutes; let cool.

4. Drain and discard marinade. Moisten a paper towel with cooking oil; using long-handled tongs, lightly coat the grill rack. Grill chicken wings, covered, over medium heat or broil 4 in. from the heat for 12-16 minutes, turning occasionally.

5. Brush wings with reserved sauce. Grill or broil, uncovered, 8-10 minutes longer or until juices run clear, basting and turning several times. Top with scallions and serve with peach jam dipping sauce.

NOTES *Read all ingredient labels for possible gluten content prior to use. Ingredient formulas can change, and production facilities vary among brands. If you're concerned that your brand may contain gluten, contact the company. Uncooked chicken wing sections (wingettes) may be substituted for whole chicken wings.*

Peach Pork Tenderloin

This pairing turned out better than I expected. We have a no-plate-licking rule in our house, but when no one was around, I licked mine clean!
—JULIA GOSLIGA ADDISON, VT

START TO FINISH: 20 MIN.
MAKES: 4 SERVINGS

- 1 pound pork tenderloin, cut into 12 slices
- ½ teaspoon salt
- ¼ teaspoon pepper
- 2 teaspoons olive oil
- 4 medium peaches, peeled and sliced
- 1 tablespoon lemon juice
- ¼ cup peach preserves

1. Flatten each tenderloin slice to ¼-in. thickness. Sprinkle with salt and pepper. In a large nonstick skillet over medium heat, cook pork in oil until tender. Remove and keep warm.
2. Add peaches and lemon juice, stirring to loosen browned bits. Cook and stir over medium heat for 3-4 minutes or until peaches are tender. Stir in the pork and preserves; heat through.

BUYING PEACHES

Purchase peaches that have an intense fragrance and yield slightly to palm pressure. Avoid those that are hard or have soft spots. One-half pound will yield about 1 cup chopped peaches.

Fresh Peach Salsa

Scooped up on a chip or in a taco, peach salsa makes everything taste like summer. It's also great served with chicken or fish, and since it comes together in a food processor, it really takes almost no time to make.
—SHAWNA LAUFER FT MYERS, FL

START TO FINISH: 15 MIN. • **MAKES:** 4 CUPS

- 4 medium peaches, peeled and pitted
- 2 large tomatoes, cut into wedges and seeded
- ½ sweet onion, cut into wedges
- ½ cup fresh cilantro leaves
- 2 garlic cloves, peeled and sliced
- 2 cans (4 ounces each) chopped green chilies
- 4 teaspoons cider vinegar
- 1 teaspoon lime juice
- ¼ teaspoon pepper
  Baked tortilla chip scoops

In a food processor, combine the first five ingredients; pulse until coarsely chopped. Add chilies, vinegar, lime juice and pepper; pulse just until blended. Transfer to a serving bowl; chill until serving. Serve with chips.

F ew things are better than an evening spent with close friends, especially when good food is involved. For your next girls' night in, try an Asian-inspired dinner. It's almost as easy as takeout.

Start the night off with savory appetizers, Crab Sushi Dip and Steamed Beef & Ginger Pot Stickers. No need to worry about decorations when colorful entrees such as Asian Tofu Noodle Soup and Spicy Orange Chicken are on the table.

And for a whimsical touch, fold napkins into the shape of fortune cookies (p. 233). Your friends will know how lucky you feel to have them close.

Spicy Orange Chicken (p. 231)
Thai Crunchy Cucumber Salad (p. 230)
Steamed Beef & Ginger Pot Stickers (p. 229)

GIRLS' NIGHT ZEN

Strawberry Cocktail

PICTURED AT TOP RIGHT

I love to sip this refreshing blend of strawberries and basil.

—CAROLYN TURNER RENO, NV

START TO FINISH: 10 MIN. • **MAKES:** 6 SERVINGS

- 6 fresh strawberries, sliced
- 12 fresh basil leaves
- ¼ cup sugar
  Ice cubes
- ⅓ cup lemon juice
- 2¼ cups club soda, chilled
  Additional fresh basil leaves,
    optional

In a shaker, muddle strawberries, basil and sugar. Fill shaker three-fourths full with ice; add lemon juice. Cover and shake 10-15 seconds or until condensation forms on outside of shaker. Strain into six rock glasses filled with ice. Top with club soda and, if desired, additional basil leaves.

Pear-Apple Cocktail

PICTURED AT BOTTOM RIGHT

Ah, the memories we made when we went to Hawaii and concocted this drink for our first toast on the island. That makes this drink special.

—NOELLE APPEL ARLINGTON, TX

START TO FINISH: 5 MIN. • **MAKES:** 6 SERVINGS

- 6 cups unsweetened apple juice,
  chilled
- ¾ cup pear-flavored vodka,
  chilled
  Ice cubes
  Cubed fresh pineapple

In a pitcher, mix apple juice and vodka. Serve over ice. Garnish with pineapple.

Mint-Green Tea Yogurt Pops

Fans of green tea ice cream will love this refreshing frozen treat. The pops have a fresh, minty flavor that wins everyone over.
—**BARBARA LENTO** HOUSTON, PA

PREP: 40 MIN. + FREEZING
MAKES: 12 POPS

- 2 **cups water**
- ½ **cup orange blossom honey**
- ¼ **cup minced fresh mint**
- 4 **individual green tea bags**
- 1 **cup plain Greek yogurt**
- 1 **cup lime sherbet**
- 3 **drops green food coloring, optional**
- 12 **freezer pop molds or paper cups (3 ounces each) and wooden pop sticks**

1. In a large saucepan, bring water to a boil; remove from heat. Add honey, mint and tea bags; steep, covered, 30 minutes. Discard tea bags. Whisk in yogurt, sherbet and, if desired, food coloring until blended.
2. Pour into molds or paper cups. Top molds with holders. If using cups, top with foil and insert sticks through foil. Freeze until firm.

Crab Sushi Dip

If your gang loves sushi like mine does, they'll enjoy this California-style dip of crab and nori. For a Texas version, add avocado and jalapeno.
—**KRISTINA ARRIETA** POINT VENTURE, TX

START TO FINISH: 20 MIN. • **MAKES:** 2¼ CUPS

- 1 **pound imitation crabmeat**
- 2 **nori sheets**
- ⅓ **cup mayonnaise**
- 2 **green onions, thinly sliced**
- 1½ **teaspoons prepared wasabi**
- 2 **tablespoons reduced-sodium soy sauce**
- 1 **tablespoon sesame seeds**
  Additional thinly sliced green onions
  Rice crackers

1. Place crab in a food processor; pulse until finely chopped.

2. Using kitchen scissors, cut nori into small pieces. In a large bowl, mix mayonnaise, green onions and wasabi. Stir in crab and nori.

3. Shape crab mixture into a disk; place on a shallow serving plate. Pour soy sauce around disk. Sprinkle with sesame seeds and green onions. Serve with crackers.

NOTE *Look for nori sheets in the international foods section.*

Pacific Rim Fried Rice

My mother lives in Honolulu, and she created this hybrid rice recipe of Western influence (the bacon) and traditional Asian flavors. Now it's my signature dish for dinner parties.
—**AARON CHUI** ARCADIA, CA

START TO FINISH: 30 MIN. • **MAKES:** 10 SERVINGS

- 2 **teaspoons canola oil**
- 3 **large eggs, lightly beaten**
- ½ **pound bacon strips, cut into ½-inch pieces**
- 1 **large onion, chopped**
- 2 **large carrots, chopped**
- 6 **green onions, thinly sliced**
- 6 **cups cold cooked long grain rice**
- ½ **cup frozen peas**
- ¼ **cup oyster sauce**
- ½ **teaspoon pepper**
  Additonal thinly sliced green onions, optional

1. In a large nonstick skillet, heat oil over medium-high heat. Pour in eggs; cook and stir until thickened and no liquid egg remains, breaking up into small pieces. Remove from pan; wipe skillet clean if necessary.

2. In same skillet, cook bacon over medium heat until crisp. Remove to paper towels to drain. Discard drippings, reserving 2 tablespoons in pan.

3. Add onion and carrots to drippings; cook and stir over medium-high heat 6-8 minutes or until tender. Add green onions; cook 1 minute longer. Add rice, peas, oyster sauce and pepper; heat through, stirring frequently. Stir in eggs and bacon. If desired, sprinkle servings with green onions.

Asian Tofu Noodle Soup

Ginger, garlic and sherry jazz up this soup loaded with veggies and noodles.
We like to accent ours with peanuts and green onions.
—**DIANA RIOS** LYTLE, TX

START TO FINISH: 30 MIN.
MAKES: 4 SERVINGS

- 1 **tablespoon canola oil**
- 1 **tablespoon minced fresh gingerroot**
- 2 **garlic cloves, minced**
- ¼ **teaspoon crushed red pepper flakes, optional**
- ½ **pound sliced fresh mushrooms**
- 1 **carton (32 ounces) reduced-sodium chicken broth**
- ¼ **cup sherry or reduced-sodium chicken broth**
- ¼ **cup reduced-sodium soy sauce**
- 7 **ounces firm tofu, drained and cut into ½-inch cubes**
- 1 **cup fresh snow peas, julienned**
- 1 **large carrot, shredded**
- 2 **green onions, thinly sliced**
- 8 **ounces uncooked Chinese egg noodles or uncooked spaghetti**
  Finely chopped peanuts and additional green onions, optional

1. In a large saucepan, heat oil over medium heat. Add ginger, garlic and, if desired, pepper flakes; cook and stir 1 minute or until fragrant.

2. Add mushrooms, broth, sherry and soy sauce; bring to a boil. Cook, uncovered, 5 minutes. Add tofu, snow peas, carrot and green onions. Reduce heat; simmer, uncovered, 4-6 minutes longer or until vegetables are crisp-tender.

3. Meanwhile, cook noodles according to package directions; drain and divide among four bowls. Pour soup over noodles. If desired, sprinkle with peanuts and green onions.

Steamed Beef & Ginger Pot Stickers

These dumplings have a hearty filling that's easy to make and a dipping sauce that's too irresistible to pass up. I prepare them in advance and freeze them.
—**TRISHA KRUSE** EAGLE, ID

PREP: 1 HOUR • **COOK:** 5 MIN./BATCH • **MAKES:** 4 DOZEN

4 green onions, thinly sliced
2 tablespoons reduced-sodium soy sauce
2 garlic cloves, minced
1 tablespoon rice vinegar
1 tablespoon minced fresh gingerroot
¼ teaspoon coarsely ground pepper
1 pound ground beef
48 pot sticker or gyoza wrappers

DIPPING SAUCE
¼ cup reduced-sodium soy sauce
2 tablespoons rice vinegar
2 tablespoons ketchup
1 tablespoon minced fresh gingerroot
2 teaspoons sesame oil
1 garlic clove, minced

1. In a large bowl, combine the first six ingredients. Add beef; mix lightly but thoroughly. Place a scant 1 tablespoon filling in center of each wrapper. (Cover remaining wrappers with a damp paper towel until ready to use.)

2. Moisten wrapper edges with water. Fold wrapper over filling; seal edges, pleating the front side several times to form a pleated pouch. Stand pot stickers on a work surface to flatten bottoms; curve slightly to form crescent shapes, if desired.

3. In a 6-qt. stockpot, place a greased steamer basket over ¾ in. of water. In batches, place dumplings in basket. Bring water to a boil. Reduce heat to maintain a low boil; steam, covered, 4-5 minutes or until cooked through.

4. Meanwhile, in a small bowl, combine sauce ingredients. Serve with dumplings.

NOTE *Wonton wrappers may be substituted for pot sticker and gyoza wrappers. Stack two or three wonton wrappers on a work surface; cut into circles with a 3½-in. biscuit or round cookie cutter. Fill and wrap as directed. Freeze option: Place uncooked pot stickers on waxed paper-lined baking sheets; freeze until firm. Transfer to resealable plastic freezer bags; return to freezer. To use, steam frozen pot stickers as directed, increasing time to 6-7 minutes or until cooked through. Serve with sauce.*

GINGERROOT 101

Fresh gingerroot adds delicious flavor to many condiments and main dishes. Look for it in the produce section. Select root pieces with smooth skin, free of wrinkles and cracks. When stored in a heavy-duty resealable plastic bag, unpeeled gingerroot can be frozen for up to 1 year. To use, simply peel and grate.

Orange Almond Cookies

I combined two recipes to make cookies with the shape and taste of sunny oranges. The whole almonds on top add an attractive finishing touch.

—**VALERIE BELLEY** ST. LOUIS, MO

PREP: 25 MIN. • **BAKE:** 15 MIN./BATCH • **MAKES:** ABOUT 3½ DOZEN

- 1 cup shortening
- 1 cup sugar, divided
- ½ cup packed brown sugar
- 1 large egg
- 1 tablespoon grated orange peel
- ¾ teaspoon vanilla extract
- 2¼ cups all-purpose flour
- 1¼ teaspoons baking soda
- ½ cup chopped almonds, toasted
- 7 drops yellow food coloring
- 3 drops red food coloring
  Whole almonds, optional

1. Preheat oven to 350°. In a large bowl, cream shortening, ½ cup sugar and brown sugar until light and fluffy. Beat in egg, orange peel and vanilla. In another bowl, whisk flour and baking soda; gradually beat into creamed mixture. Stir in chopped almonds. Place remaining sugar in a small bowl; stir in food coloring. Shape level tablespoons of dough into balls; roll in sugar mixture. Place 1 in. apart on parchment paper-lined baking sheets. If desired, press a whole almond onto top of each cookie.

2. Bake 12-14 minutes or until bottoms are golden brown. Remove to wire racks to cool.

Thai Crunchy Cucumber Salad

This crunchy, refreshing cucumber salad was one of the first dishes I made when I set out to learn Thai cuisine.

—**FARAH CLAUSSEN** CLEARWATER, FL

PREP: 15 MIN. + CHILLING • **MAKES:** 6 SERVINGS

- 3 large cucumbers, peeled, halved, seeded and thinly sliced
- 3 medium carrots, julienned
- 1 medium red onion, halved and thinly sliced
- 1 serrano pepper, seeded and minced
- ⅓ cup sugar
- ⅓ cup lime juice
- 1 tablespoon fish sauce or reduced-sodium soy sauce
- ½ cup dry roasted peanuts, coarsely chopped

1. In a large bowl, combine cucumbers, carrots, onion and serrano pepper.

2. In a small bowl, mix sugar, lime juice and fish sauce. Pour over vegetables; toss to combine. Refrigerate, covered, 1 hour. Sprinkle with peanuts.

NOTE *Wear disposable gloves when cutting hot peppers; the oils can burn skin. Avoid touching your face.*

Spicy Orange Chicken

I created a citrusy version of General Tso's chicken. Top with sesame seeds and green onions, roasted red peppers and sugar snap peas.
—**PAULA WILLIAMS** COVINGTON, KY

PREP: 20 MIN. • **COOK:** 15 MIN.
MAKES: 6 SERVINGS

- 2 **large navel oranges**
- 2 **tablespoons cornstarch**
- ½ **cup reduced-sodium chicken broth**
- ⅓ **cup rice vinegar**
- ¼ **cup honey**
- ¼ **cup reduced-sodium soy sauce**
- 3 **tablespoons lemon juice**
- 1 **jalapeno pepper, seeded and minced**
- ⅛ **teaspoon crushed red pepper flakes**
- 1½ **pounds boneless skinless chicken breasts, cut into 1-inch cubes**
- ½ **teaspoon salt**
- ½ **teaspoon pepper**
- 2 **teaspoons canola oil, divided**
  Hot cooked rice
  Sesame seeds and thinly sliced green onions

1. Finely grate peel from one orange; place peel in a small bowl. Cut a thin slice from the top and bottom of each orange; stand oranges upright on a cutting board. With a knife, cut off peel and outer membrane from oranges. Working over a small bowl to catch juices, cut along the membrane of each segment to remove fruit; set sectioned oranges aside. Stir cornstarch, broth, vinegar, honey, soy sauce, lemon juice, jalapeno and pepper flakes into orange juice and peel.

2. Sprinkle chicken with salt and pepper. In a large skillet, heat 1 teaspoon oil over medium-high heat. Add half of the chicken; stir-fry 5-7 minutes or until no longer pink. Remove from pan. Repeat with remaining oil and chicken.

3. Stir cornstarch mixture and add to pan. Bring to a boil; cook and stir 1-2 minutes or until sauce is thickened. Stir in reserved orange sections. Serve with rice. Sprinkle servings with sesame seeds and green onions.
NOTE *Wear disposable gloves when cutting hot peppers; the oils can burn skin. Avoid touching your face.*

Fortune Cookie Folded Napkins

Set the scene for a culinary tour your gal pals will remember with napkins folded into the shape of a fortune cookie. Tuck a sentiment or a tidbit of wisdom inside for a heartfelt touch.

MATERIALS

20x20-in. square cloth napkin
White paper
Printer
Ruler
Scissors or paper cutter

DIRECTIONS

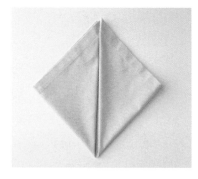

1. Lay napkin flat, wrong side up, on work surface. Fold up from bottom to make a triangle.

2. Bring the lower left point up to the top center point. Press edge.

3. Repeat step with the lower right point.

4. Carefully flip the napkin over so the folds are facing down, creating a diamond. Fold the top of the diamond down to meet the bottom point, creating an inverse triangle. Press all edges.

5. Grab the top edge at center and gently pull it towards you until the napkin sits upright.

6. Print out place settings with guests' names or fortunes. For a 20x20-in. napkin, cut paper into 5x1-in. strips. Tuck strips into napkins. Adjust paper size as needed to fit the size of the napkin.

TIP: *As you fold, press each edge with a hot iron for a sturdier shape and polished look.*

H alloween is creeping up, and you're fresh out of party ideas. Never fear! Have friends and family unleash their inner artist on a crop of pumpkins. Transforming plain gourds into dazzling jack-o'-lanterns is hungry work. So offer carvers scary-good treats such as Apple Pie Popcorn and Cinnamon Spiced Cider as they perfect their orange masterpieces. You might even provide some inspiration by making a jack-o'-lantern vase (p. 245) in advance.

Once the carving is done, reward the crew with brimming bowls of Hearty White Chicken Chili and Mini Corn Muffins with Spicy Cheddar Filling. Finish with Red Apple Butter Bars or Pumpkin Ice Cream Sandwiches.

Don't be surprised if this frightfully fun event becomes an annual tradition.

Cinnamon Spiced Cider (p. 236)
Mini Corn Muffins with Spicy Cheddar Filling (p. 237)
Hearty White Chicken Chili (p.238)

PUMPKIN CARVING **PARTY**

Cinnamon Spiced Cider

With my first sip of this brisk cider, I know autumn has arrived. It makes the kitchen smell so festive that I serve it during the holidays, too. Transfer it to a slow cooker set on low to keep it warm until the last party guest leaves.
—**TINA BUTLER** ROYSE CITY, TX

START TO FINISH: 25 MIN. • **MAKES:** 12 SERVINGS (¾ CUP EACH)

2½ quarts apple cider or juice
½ cup Red Hots
¼ teaspoon ground nutmeg
2 cinnamon sticks (3 inches)
½ teaspoon whole cloves

1. In a Dutch oven, combine cider, Red Hots and nutmeg. Place cinnamon sticks and cloves on a double thickness of cheesecloth. Gather up corners of cloth to enclose seasonings; tie securely with string. Add to Dutch oven.

2. Bring to a boil, stirring occasionally to loosen candies. Reduce heat; simmer, covered, 10-15 minutes or until flavors are blended. Discard spice bag.

Apple Pie Popcorn

This caramel corn recipe comes from my husband's family. It's our go-to treat, particularly since the apple pie spice makes it so different. It's fun to give as a present, too.
—**KEZIA (KAY) WHITTEKER** HYDE PARK, UT

PREP: 30 MIN. • **BAKE:** 1 HOUR + COOLING • **MAKES:** 4 QUARTS

12 cups popped popcorn
1 cup packed brown sugar
½ cup butter, cubed
¼ cup light corn syrup
½ teaspoon salt
1 teaspoon vanilla extract
¼ teaspoon baking soda
½ cup confectioners' sugar
2 teaspoons apple pie spice
12 ounces white baking chocolate, chopped

1. Preheat oven to 250°. Place popcorn in a greased shallow roasting pan. In a large heavy saucepan, combine brown sugar, butter, corn syrup and salt. Bring to a boil over medium heat, stirring constantly. Cook, without stirring, 5 minutes.

2. Remove from heat; stir in vanilla and baking soda (mixture will foam). Quickly pour over popcorn and mix well.

3. Bake 1 hour or until dry, stirring every 15 minutes.

Remove to waxed paper to cool completely.

4. In a small bowl, mix confectioners' sugar and pie spice. In a microwave, melt white baking chocolate; stir until smooth.

5. Transfer cooled caramel corn to a large bowl; sprinkle with the confectioners' sugar mixture and toss to coat. Drizzle with melted chocolate; toss to coat. Return to waxed paper; let stand until set.

Mini Corn Muffins with Spicy Cheddar Filling

These savory little muffins were a hit at the neighborhood card party.
They're pleasingly different from the usual chip-and-dip appetizers.
—**MARGARET BLAIR** LORIMOR, IA

PREP: 30 MIN. • **BAKE:** 25 MIN.
MAKES: 4 DOZEN

1½ **cups all-purpose flour**
1 **cup cornmeal**
2 **teaspoons sugar**
¾ **teaspoon baking powder**
½ **teaspoon salt**
1 **large egg**
¾ **cup milk**
¼ **cup canola oil**
1 **can (14¾ ounces) cream-style
   corn**

FILLING
2 **cups (8 ounces) shredded
   cheddar cheese**
1 **can (4 ounces) chopped green
   chilies**
¼ **cup diced pimientos**
1 **teaspoon chili powder**
¼ **teaspoon hot pepper sauce**

1. Preheat oven to 400°. In a large bowl, whisk the first five ingredients. In another bowl, whisk egg, milk and oil until blended. Add to flour mixture; stir just until moistened. Fold in the corn.

2. Fill greased mini-muffin cups three-fourths full. Bake 15-18 minutes or until a toothpick inserted in center comes out clean. Cool 5 minutes before removing from pans to wire racks. Reduce oven setting to 350°.

3. Meanwhile, in a large bowl, combine filling ingredients. Using a small melon baller, scoop out the center of each muffin; spoon in a rounded teaspoonful of filling into the center. Bake 10-12 minutes or until cheese is melted.

Hearty White Chicken Chili

I developed this scrumptious chicken chili after tasting something similar at a restaurant. Now my family prefers mine. Crispy tortilla strips give each serving pizazz.

—**GAIL HAILE** SCOTTSMOOR, FL

PREP: 1 HOUR 20 MIN. • **COOK:** 45 MIN. • **MAKES:** 10 SERVINGS (2½ QUARTS)

- **1 broiler/fryer chicken (3½ pounds), skin removed and cut up**
- **2 celery ribs, cut into chunks**
- **1 small onion, quartered**
- **1 teaspoon whole peppercorns**
- **¾ teaspoon salt**
- **6 cups water**

CHILI

- **8 corn tortillas (6 inches), cut into ¼-inch strips**
- **4 teaspoons canola oil, divided**
- **3 celery ribs, chopped**
- **2 medium onions, chopped**
- **2 garlic cloves, minced**
- **¼ cup all-purpose flour**
- **1 tablespoon ground cumin**
- **1 tablespoon chili powder**
- **½ teaspoon salt**
- **½ teaspoon pepper**
- **2 cans (15½ ounces each) navy beans, rinsed and drained**
- **2 medium tomatoes, chopped**
- **½ cup reduced-fat sour cream**
- **4 green onions, chopped**
- **½ cup shredded reduced-fat cheddar cheese**

1. Place the first six ingredients in a Dutch oven. Bring to a boil. Reduce heat; simmer, covered, 1 hour or until chicken is tender.

Remove chicken; cool slightly. Strain broth, discarding vegetables and peppercorns; skim fat from broth. Set broth aside.

2. Preheat oven to 400°. Remove meat from bones; cut into bite-size pieces and set aside. Discard bones.

3. In a bowl, toss tortilla strips with 1 teaspoon oil. Arrange strips on a baking sheet coated with cooking spray. Bake 8-12 minutes or until crisp, stirring once.

4. In a large saucepan, heat remaining oil over medium-high heat. Add celery, onions and garlic; cook and stir 6-8 minutes or until tender. Stir in flour and seasonings until blended. Gradually add 4 cups reserved chicken broth (save remaining broth for another use).

5. Bring to a boil; cook and stir 1-2 minutes or until slightly thickened.

6. Stir in beans, tomatoes and reserved chicken. Reduce heat; simmer, covered, 15 minutes longer. Top servings with reserved tortilla strips, sour cream, green onions and cheese.

Sweet & Savory Cream Cheese Spread

Of all the appetizers I serve, this tempting cheese spread is the most popular. It has the right combo of sweet and savory flavors our kids love. The warm topping makes it a real standout!

—LEE ANN MILLER
MILLERSBURG, OH

START TO FINISH: 20 MIN.
MAKES: 2 CUPS

- 1 **package (8 ounces) cream cheese, softened**
- 4 **teaspoons finely chopped red onion**
- ⅛ **teaspoon garlic salt**
- ¼ **cup butter, cubed**
- ¼ **cup packed brown sugar**
- 1 **teaspoon Worcestershire sauce**
- ½ **teaspoon yellow mustard**
- 1 **cup chopped pecans, toasted**
  Assorted crackers

1. In a small bowl, beat cream cheese, onion and garlic salt. Shape into a disk; transfer to a serving plate.
2. In a small saucepan combine cubed butter, brown sugar, Worcestershire sauce and mustard. Cook and stir over medium heat 4-5 minutes or until sugar is dissolved. Stir in pecans; cool slightly.
3. Spoon over cheese mixture. Serve with crackers.

Sicilian Mac & Cheese

To give our mac and cheese a Sicilian touch, we mix sausage, basil and fennel with three cheeses for an incredibly comforting casserole.
—MICHAEL COHEN
LOS ANGELES, CA

PREP: 45 MIN. • **BAKE:** 20 MIN.
MAKES: 8 SERVINGS

- 4 **Italian sausage links (4 ounces each)**
- ½ **cup water**
- 1 **package (16 ounces) elbow macaroni**
- 4 **large eggs**
- 2 **cups half-and-half cream**
- ½ **cup butter, melted**
- 2 **cups (8 ounces) shredded part-skim mozzarella cheese**
- 2 **cups grated Parmesan cheese**
- 2 **cups loosely packed basil leaves, chopped**
- 2 **tablespoons fennel seed, toasted**
- 2 **garlic cloves, minced**
- 1 **teaspoon salt**
- ½ **teaspoon pepper**
- 1 **cup shredded Romano cheese**
  Additional chopped fresh basil

1. Preheat oven to 350°. In a large skillet, brown sausages on all sides, about 5 minutes. Reduce heat to medium-low; add water. Cook, covered, 10-15 minutes or until a thermometer reads 160°. Remove from pan; cut sausage into bite-size pieces. Cook pasta according to package directions for al dente.

2. Meanwhile, in a large bowl, whisk eggs, cream and butter until blended. Stir in mozzarella cheese, Parmesan cheese, basil, fennel seed, garlic, salt, pepper and cooked sausage. Drain pasta and add to cheese mixture immediately; toss to coat.

3. Spoon mixture into eight greased 10-oz. ramekins. Sprinkle with Romano cheese. Transfer ramekins to baking sheets. Bake, uncovered, 20-25 minutes or until a thermometer reads 160°. Sprinkle with additional basil.

Campfire S'mores Snack Mix

Two crowd-pleasers, party mix and s'mores, become a sensation when you combine them.
No campfire necessary—you can make this version ahead of time.
—**MINDEE CURTIS** OMAHA, NE

START TO FINISH: 15 MIN. • **MAKES:** 3½ QUARTS

6 **cups Rice Chex**
2 **cups Golden Grahams**
1 **cup smoked almonds, coarsely chopped**
¾ **cup packed brown sugar**
½ **cup butter, cubed**
3 **tablespoons light corn syrup**
½ **teaspoon baking soda**
½ **cup miniature marshmallows**
1 **cup milk chocolate chips**
1 **tablespoon shortening**

1. In a large bowl, combine cereals and almonds. In a large microwave-safe bowl, combine brown sugar, butter and corn syrup. Microwave, uncovered, on high for 2 minutes, stirring once.

2. Whisk in baking soda until dissolved (mixture will foam). Stir in marshmallows. Cook 30-60 seconds longer or until marshmallows are melted; stir until smooth. Pour over cereal mixture; toss to coat. Spread onto a waxed paper-lined baking sheet to cool.

3. In a microwave, melt chocolate chips and shortening; stir until smooth. Drizzle over cereal mixture; refrigerate until set. Break into pieces. Store in an airtight container.

NOTE *This recipe was tested in a 1,100-watt microwave.*

Pumpkin Ice Cream Sandwiches

My grandfather loves these pumpkin-flavored treats. They remind him of a cookie
his mother made. They're fun to eat no matter what your age.
—**AMBER WAHL** ACAMPO, CA

PREP: 45 MIN. + FREEZING • **BAKE:** 10 MIN./BATCH + COOLING • **MAKES:** 2 DOZEN

3 **cups canned pumpkin**
¾ **teaspoon pumpkin pie spice**
2 **cartons (1½ quarts each) vanilla ice cream, softened if necessary**
COOKIES
½ **cup butter, softened**
½ **cup shortening**
1½ **cups sugar**
3 **large egg yolks**
3 **tablespoons pumpkin or apple butter**
1 **teaspoon vanilla extract**
1¾ **cups all-purpose flour**
1 **teaspoon cream of tartar**
1 **teaspoon baking soda**
1 **teaspoon pumpkin pie spice**
⅛ **teaspoon salt**

1. In a large bowl, mix pumpkin and pie spice until blended; stir in ice cream. Freeze, covered, until firm enough to scoop.

2. In a large bowl, cream butter, shortening and sugar until light and fluffy. Beat in egg yolks, pumpkin butter and vanilla. In another bowl, whisk flour, cream of tartar, baking soda, pie spice and salt; gradually beat into creamed mixture (dough will be soft). Refrigerate, covered, 30 minutes or until firm enough to shape.

3. Preheat oven to 325°. Shape dough into 24 (1-in.) balls; place 4 in. apart on ungreased baking sheets. Flatten to ¼-in. thickness with the bottom of a glass dipped in sugar.

4. Bake 6-8 minutes or until edges are light brown. Cool on pans 2 minutes. Remove to wire racks to cool completely.

5. To assemble, spread a scoop of ice cream on bottom of a cookie. Top with a second cookie; press gently to attach. Set on a baking sheet; freeze until firm.

6. Repeat with remaining ingredients. Wrap individually for longer storage.

NOTE *This recipe was tested with commercially prepared pumpkin butter.*

Spiced Pumpkin Doughnut Bites

You can try different flavors and coating colors in this recipe to suit any occasion. For Halloween, though, it has to be pumpkin and orange candy coating!
—JOHNNA JOHNSON SCOTTSDALE, AZ

PREP: 35 MIN. • **BAKE:** 10 MIN./BATCH + COOLING • **MAKES:** 2 DOZEN

1⅓ cups all-purpose flour
1 cup Rice Krispies
3 tablespoons plus ½ cup sugar, divided
3 teaspoons baking powder
2½ teaspoons pumpkin pie spice, divided
½ teaspoon salt
¼ cup butter-flavored shortening
⅓ cup canned pumpkin
¼ cup 2% milk
¼ cup butter
¾ cup orange candy coating disks
   Chocolate or Halloween sprinkles, optional

1. Preheat oven to 375°. In a large bowl, mix flour, Rice Krispies, 3 tablespoons sugar, baking powder, 1 teaspoon pie spice and salt; cut in shortening until mixture resembles coarse crumbs. In another bowl, whisk pumpkin and milk; stir into crumb mixture just until moistened.
2. In a microwave, melt butter. In a shallow bowl, mix the remaining sugar and pie spice. Shape level tablespoons of dough into balls. Dip in butter, then roll in sugar mixture. Place 1-in. apart on parchment paper-lined baking sheets.
3. Bake 12-14 minutes or until tops are cracked. Remove from pans to wire racks to cool completely.
4. In a microwave, melt candy coating; stir until smooth. Dip one end of each doughnut bite into melted candy coating, allow excess to drip off. If desired, decorate with sprinkles. Place on waxed paper; let stand until set.

Bloody Bug Juice

I stir up a wicked party punch in my cauldron every Halloween. It's sweet and tart with a creepy touch folks love.
—SHONNI STEVENS EDMONTON, AB

PREP: 10 MIN. + CHILLING • **MAKES:** 8 SERVINGS (1 CUP EACH)

2 packages (12 ounces each) frozen unsweetened strawberries, thawed
⅔ cup thawed lemonade concentrate
1 quart ginger ale, chilled
1 cup fresh or frozen blueberries
½ cup raisins
   Gummy worms

1. Place strawberries in a food processor; process until pureed and transfer to a large pitcher. Stir in lemonade concentrate; refrigerate until serving.
2. Just before serving, add ginger ale to strawberry mixture. Place 2 tablespoons blueberries and 1 tablespoon raisins in each of eight tall glasses; pour strawberry mixture over fruit. Decorate glasses with gummy worms. Serve immediately.

MAKE MINE A SPOOKY SLUSH

Hosting a pumpkin-carving party for the grown-ups? Spike the bug juice with some vodka or coconut-flavored rum. Add it to individual glasses before topping with the frozen strawberry mixture.

Pumpkin Bread Pudding Cupcakes

Every fall when I was young, my mom made bread pudding cupcakes. Today, I keep up her tradition with my daughter and three grandkids by baking these treats.
—**TERREL PORTER-SMITH** LOS OSOS, CA

PREP: 35 MIN. + CHILLING • **BAKE:** 25 MIN. + COOLING • **MAKES:** 2 DOZEN

- 4 **large eggs**
- 4½ **cups canned pumpkin**
- 1½ **cups 2% milk**
- 1 **cup sugar**
- 1 **cup half-and-half cream**
- 1 **teaspoon ground cinnamon**
- ½ **teaspoon salt**
- ½ **teaspoon ground nutmeg**
- 1½ **teaspoons vanilla extract, divided**
- 10 **cups cubed French bread (1-inch pieces)**
- ½ **cup butter, cubed**
- 1 **cup packed brown sugar**
- 1 **tablespoon light corn syrup**
- 1 **cup chopped pecans**

1. In a large bowl, whisk eggs, pumpkin, milk, sugar, cream, cinnamon, salt, nutmeg and ½ teaspoon vanilla until blended. Gently stir in bread. Refrigerate, covered, 1 hour.

2. Preheat oven to 350°. Fill foil-lined muffin cups with bread pudding mixture. Bake 20-25 minutes or until firm to the touch.

3. Meanwhile, in a small heavy saucepan, melt butter. Stir in brown sugar and corn syrup. Bring to a boil, stirring constantly. Cook, without stirring, 2-3 minutes longer or until slightly thickened. Remove from heat; stir in pecans and remaining vanilla.

4. Spoon 1 tablespoon sauce over each cupcake. Bake 5-6 minutes longer or until topping is set. Cool 10 minutes before removing from pans to wire racks. Serve warm. Refrigerate leftovers.

Red Apple Butter Bars

Fall means apple-picking time, and we love using the fresh fruit to bake up these bars. The streusel on top makes them even better.
—**NANCY FOUST** STONEBORO, PA

PREP: 40 MIN. • **BAKE:** 35 MIN. + COOLING • **MAKES:** 2 DOZEN

- 3 **cups all-purpose flour**
- 2 **cups quick-cooking oats**
- 2 **cups packed brown sugar**
- 1½ **teaspoons baking soda**
- ¾ **teaspoon salt**
- ¾ **teaspoon ground cinnamon**
- 1½ **cups butter, melted**
- 2 **medium apples, chopped**
- 1½ **cups apple butter**
- 1 **cup chopped walnuts**

1. Preheat oven to 350°. In a large bowl, combine the first six ingredients; stir in butter. Reserve 1⅓ cups crumb mixture for topping. Press remaining mixture onto bottom of a greased 13x9-in. baking dish. Bake 15-20 minutes or until lightly browned. Cool completely on a wire rack.

2. Sprinkle apples over crust; spread with apple butter. Stir walnuts into reserved topping; sprinkle over apple butter. Bake 35-40 minutes or until lightly browned. Cool in pan on a wire rack. Cut into bars.

NOTE *This recipe was tested with commercially prepared apple butter.*

Jack-o'-Lantern Vase

This easy autumnal centerpiece promises to bring toothy grins at your party.

MATERIALS
- **Medium-size pumpkin**
- **Clear glass vase (no taller than pumpkin)**
- **Floral foam, if desired**
- **Flowers**

DIRECTIONS

1. Cut a lid from pumpkin wide enough that the vase sits snugly in the shell. Set vase aside.

2. Remove pulp, smooth down interior walls and carve pumpkin.

3. Set vase inside pumpkin, and fill with water or floral foam.

4. Arrange flowers in vase, trimming as needed to hide rim.

GENERAL RECIPE INDEX

This lists every recipe by food category and major ingredient.

ALPHABETICAL RECIPE INDEX

A complete listing of all recipes in this book.

SHARE YOUR **MOST-LOVED RECIPES**

Do you have a special recipe that has become part of your family's
holiday tradition? Are homemade gifts and crafts included in your
celebrations? We want to hear from you. To submit a recipe or craft
for editorial consideration, visit **tasteofhome.com/submit.**

PAGE 25

PAGE 77

PAGE 167

PAGE 245